D1093668

UNDERSTANDING THE ELEMENTS OF LITERATURE

UNDERSTANDING THE ELEMENTS OF LITERATURE

ITS FORMS, TECHNIQUES AND CULTURAL CONVENTIONS

Richard Taylor

St. Martin's Press

ISBN 0–312–83216–8

Library of Congress Cataloging in Publication Data

Taylor, Richard, 1919–
   Understanding the elements of literature.

   Bibliography: p.
   Includes index.
   1. Literature.   I. Title.
PN45.T38   1981   802   81–9295
ISBN 0–312–83216–8   AACR2

For
Olu and Oba

Contents

Preface

There are any number of introductory texts for students of literature in English, but none takes into consideration the fact that every reader is not necessarily familiar with the conventions of literary expression or the cultural attitudes and values from which they spring. For many years the teaching of literature has assumed that students had already read widely, responded directly to what they had read, and that with limited guidance they could deduce from their reading the principles of both literary construction and critical analysis. Emphasis was usually placed on the historical development of literature and courses generally consisted of set texts arranged by period, genre or theme. Literary education, however, has already spread from its traditional base as an institution of the middle classes in the mainstream of European and American society which establishes and preserves that particular cultural identity. Now there is an ever greater need to supply students from other backgrounds with an outline or scheme of ideas which governs literature as well as that which operates within it.

The most obvious conventions to be considered are those which determine the way human experience is presented in literature: the selection and ordering of characters and actions, the form and nature of the literary work, the view or attitude towards the experience to be expressed, and the style of language suited to that expression. Most of these decisions are based on the unspoken values of the culture concerned; their aspirations and goals, their sense of right and wrong as well as the ideal of good taste and beauty which obtains in that society. It is possible to discuss these questions, one by one, as they pertain to literature in English and so provide an understanding of the basic elements which give form and meaning to works of literature.

Because novels, plays and poems are complete and complex entities, it is not possible to arrange the basic concepts and conventions in a strict order of increasing difficulty, and the reader will find that many interconnections and echoes will be encountered while reading through the following discussion. Redefinitions, modifications and deeper understandings of earlier points will be suggested throughout. The present work necessarily begins with general comments on the nature and cultural function of literature as well as its historical tradition before taking up the more technical elements of the three major literary forms. As many specific examples as possible are included and these have been drawn from a wide range of ethnic literatures in English.

The material in the present volume is not meant as a textbook to be studied and mastered for its own sake, but rather as a general background of basic concepts and relationships which should make the study of actual literary texts more meaningful.

Acknowledgements

I should like to thank my colleagues and students at the University of Ife where much of this material was worked out in lectures and tutorial situations over a number of years, especially Deirdre LaPin who taught me a good deal about oral literature and Peter Finley who shared the introductory lecture course with me and taught me a great many things, but unfortunately not how to speak and write with limpid simplicity. My students over a good many years in Asia, Africa, Europe and America have helped immeasurably toward the present work. Instead of accepting glib generalities they always wanted to know precisely how one came to such and such a critical statement. I am very grateful to them all. I am also grateful to my wife, Aina Pavolini, in many more ways than can be mentioned here and not least of all for her care and patience in saving this manuscript from all too many howlers. I should like to thank Erika Duncanson, as well, for her inestimable assistance in preparing the manuscript.

The author and publishers wish to thank the following who have kindly given permission for the use of copyright material: George Allen & Unwin (Publishers) Ltd and Oxford University Press, New York, for an extract from Euripedes' *The Bacchae* translated by Gilbert Murray; John Allison for his song 'Johnny Has Gone For A Soldier'; Edward Arnold Ltd for an extract from *A Passage to India* by E. M. Forster; Associated Book Publishers Ltd for an extract from *Riders to the Sea* in *The Plays and Poems of J. M. Synge* published by Eyre Methuen Ltd and an extract from *The Good Woman of Setzuan* in *Parables for the Theatre* by Bertolt Brecht, translated by Ralph Manheim and John Willett, and published by Eyre Methuen Ltd and Random House Inc; James Baldwin for an extract from *Go Tell It On The Mountain;*

Every effort has been made to trace all the copyright holders but if any have been inadvertently overlooked the publishers will be pleased to make the necessary arrangement at the first opportunity.

1 The Nature of Literature and its Historical Tradition

Literature as Presentation of Experience

Literature, like other arts, is essentially an imaginative act, that is, an act of the writer's imagination in selecting, ordering and interpreting life–experience. In the case of literature, words are the medium of expression and it makes little difference whether those words are recorded in the living memory of a people or by some mechanical means such as writing, sound recording, etc. Anything that can be said about the nature of literature holds true for both oral and written examples since they share a pre-occupation with form, style and social function. The exact details of everyday life as we know it, or as an author knew it in a particular time and place, may or may not be reflected in a literary work. However, the quality or nature of the writer's conception and understanding of that experience is expressed by the complex structure of words that he or she creates.

There is no evidence that Shakespeare, or anyone else for that matter, actually experienced the particular pattern of events that we find in *As You Like It* (1600). It is certainly highly unlikely that events should take place of their own accord in such a perfectly composed sequence or that people should normally speak with such elegance and wit. However different the surface details may be from the way things really happen in life, that play does present a dynamic pattern of forces whose workings are actually very true to life: the way people are attracted to one another and the characteristics or circumstances that frustrate their coming together.

The point is that a work of literature does not necessarily give us accurate information about the way life is actually lived (although it may do so as a secondary consideration), rather it causes us to recognise truths about human existence through the direct presentation of selected experiences. Instead of telling us about the way people act and feel, it involves us in these actions and directs our responses to them.

In George Lamming's semi-autobiographical novel, *In the Castle of My Skin* (1953), a revealing passage begins as a description of a very common and unexceptional occurance at school, the way teachers and pupils often avoid looking straight into one another's eyes.

> Sometimes a teacher might have been staring blankly down a corridor where a boy with his back turned slouched over exercise books. The boy was engrossed. He watched the exercise books or marked them with concentrated purpose. The teacher didn't notice. Something was happening in his head, and he stared blankly waiting for it to pass out. But suddenly the boy might look up, and catching the teacher's eye would feel captured. He had done nothing wrong. He had simply been seen by the teacher. He must have felt in his engrossment that he was alone. There couldn't have been anyone there to take notice of him. But suddenly his concentration collapsed, and he saw that he was seen. He did nothing wrong, but that didn't matter. He was seen by the teacher . . . Deep down he felt uneasy. He had been seen by another. He had become a part of the other's world, and therefore no longer in complete control of his own. The eye of another was a kind of cage. When it saw you the lid came down, and you were trapped. It was always happening.
>
> (Lamming, pp. 74–5)

The fictionalised example of the same phenomenon between teachers is also given, and then the feelings of a sensitive boy, first in a public square and then at a cinema waiting in the foyer until the house lights are turned down before he enters the auditorium and takes a seat. Finally there is a description of the dark privacy of the cubicles in the school lavatory.

No one could see or hear you and you mumbled your freedom away. The things you would say and do. The things you could say and do. The darkness brought a strange kind of release, and you wished secretly in your heart that darkness would descend on the whole earth so that you could get a chance to see how much energy there was stored in your little self. You could get a chance to leave the cage. You would be free.

(p. 76)

Whether or not the reader has actually had the experiences or thoughts expressed by the author, Lamming has created specific and familiar situations which we can all recognise and participate in through imagination, in order to induce us to experience the precise feelings and attitudes of the boy. Without that fictionalisation of incidents, without seeing ourselves in the actual circumstances described, we could not enter into the experience with any degree of sympathy or understanding. We could know nothing of the boy's growing awareness of himself and of his creative powers, or of the truth about his relationship to the world around him.

Surface Detail and Theme

As readers, we must acknowledge and respond to the essential truths that underlie the surface reality of literature. The particular actions, characters and settings which the author chooses constitute the subject matter of the work, the surface meaning, in fact. If asked what Wole Soyinka's poem 'The Telephone Conversation' is about, one could say that it is about a young African in England who telephones a landlady in search of a room. Recognising her hostility to Blacks, he teases her and hangs up. That is, after all, pretty much what happens in the poem. On another level, one can also say that it is a poem about race prejudice, and this latter statement is just as valid as the first.

The theme of a work — that is, the abstract idea that the subject matter exemplifies — is also part of the meaning. A theme cannot exist in a work of literature without the vehicle of subject matter, and it is in the relationship of one to the other that we see the truth the author aims at. Soyinka's poem has more to communicate than the mere facts of the action, character and setting. It also means more than a bare statement of its theme. The truth that the author is getting at is the presumption and stupidity of prejudice as well as the wit and intelligence that puts it in its place. The landlady's ill–disguised reaction and the student's cleverness with language in out–manoeuvring her over the question of race prejudice is the point.

Reading on the surface level alone is only partly satisfactory. A full understanding and appreciation of literature depends on the ability to analyse and generalise as well. First of all one must grasp the exact details of the piece, the surface level in terms of action, character, order of events and setting. Then one must begin to make deductions as to theme or themes, the larger ideas that are represented by the particular incidents of the work. A paraphrase of the plot or story, an account of what actually happens, is only the first step in the study of serious literature. The generalisations which follow must link the details of the subject matter to a specific technical element of the composition (character, action, order of events, setting, etc.) as well as to a relevant aspect of the theme which is being expressed. Such vague comments as 'realistic portrait', 'exciting events' or 'emotive and forceful language' are meaningless unless they are actual deductions from a serious discussion of the subject matter as an element of the literary composition which contributes to the expression of an underlying central idea in the work. The effectiveness of literature, a particular passage or even an isolated technique can only be explained or justified in specific relation to the theme. What effect does the given example have on a reader's response to or appreciation of that particular fictional world on the one hand and to the theme it exemplifies on the other?

The generalisations which one makes in working towards a statement of theme and its relationship to the subject matter or surface level are neither hidden nor arbitrary. In fact, they are signalled by the author at every step through the choice of incidents, the kind of characters included, the ordering of events, the nature of the setting and the character of the language. The purpose of the present discussion is to make you aware of what to look for while reading and how to evaluate the author's method in expressing his particular view of life. There are certain kinds of mental processes and generalisations which are basic to the criticism or appreciation of literature. Once these are mastered, reading becomes a more fulfilling and satisfying experience.

Function of Literature

Literature has long been held to instruct and entertain, but the instruction has never been in the form of tidy little object lessons which can be summed up in a proverb: 'Honesty is the best policy' or 'Pride goeth before a fall'. If works of literature continue to instruct through various ages, it is because living experience and not abstract information is communicated. Unfortunately, there is a widespread and popular belief that novels, plays and poems are built up around ethical precepts and that a work can be reduced to a handy catchphrase or tag by which to govern one's life. In fact, literature presents situations, interactions and oppositions. It suggests a spectrum of values, even of attitudes, but it rarely hands down formulated judgements and conclusions. The reader not only enters into the experience of the action and characters as it unfolds, but he is also left to his own conclusions and evaluation of that experience, of its truthfulness and relevance to real life.

Moral conduct, in the sense of the relative correctness of responses to given human situations, may be used as the subject of literature, especially in works which concern themselves with man in society, but this is very different from expecting that all works of literature deliver up a moral lesson. Literature instructs by opening our eyes to a wider range of experience and a deeper understanding of it. Reducing the rich texture and complexity of a literary work to a single moral statement, or even a phrase which merely states its theme, cancels out its very existence as literature.

We do not do justice to *Othello* (1605) by saying: 'Jealousy is the root of all evil', 'Don't judge others lest you yourself be judged' or 'Beware the self–interest of an informer'. The play and its significance is much more complex and worthwhile than that. To begin with, it presents a very human and understandable situation in which an unscrupulous man, bent on revenge, victimises an otherwise worthy man by arousing his over–passionate and impetuous nature at the expense of his rational self–control. The accurate observation and re–creation of human conduct, the artistic balance and construction of the fictional world, the effectiveness of the presentation and the inevitability of the outcome join together to make a great and rewarding work of art.

Fables and religious parables are the only forms of literature whose avowed intention is to teach moral lessons and which are rightly interpreted in terms of a concisely stated precept or proverb.

Authors go to infinite lengths to create a satisfying literary composition which adequately expresses their perception of life's complexities. They care at least as much about the construction and texture of a work as they do about its subject matter or meaning. Literature is not a coded message which has to be deciphered, but rather it is a pleasing and satisfying structure or composition in which both reader and writer experience pleasure in each victory over the difficulties of exact expression, in each perception of truth about the human condition. After all, the object of a football match is not merely to move the ball from one end of a playing field to the other. If that were true, the creation of an opposing team and complex rules of play would be unnecessary. The pleasure of player and spectator alike lies in the skill with which the limitations imposed are overcome by expertise and technical accomplishment. In the case of literature, and of the arts in general, such aesthetic pleasure is not just a vague and general awareness of beauty, but rather a precise recognition of design and pattern. There is, on the one hand, the larger structure and composition of events, characters and setting which should be both striking and original. On the other hand, there is the recurrence of situations, attitudes and stylistic characteristics which build up and reinforce our consciousness of a single concept or theme. At one and the same time we respond emotionally to the subject matter or surface level through our sympathy for human experience and we also respond intellectually to the design and pattern of the construction which focusses our attention on a larger and more universal truth about that experience.

Dynamics of Contrast and Opposition

One of the principal ways in which both subject matter and the design or patterning of literary construction attract our attention and focus it on a larger general truth or idea is through the dynamics of contrast and opposition. Life–giving tensions are created through the conscious antagonism of dissimilar characteristics, motives or even modes of expression. Chinua Achebe, for example, gives us an almost anthropological and idyllic account of traditional village life among the Igbo in *Things Fall Apart* (1958) and at the same time demonstrates the limitations of that society through Okonkwo's overreaching efforts to become its leader and hero. In this case conflict is generated between the hero and society (or fate). The actions and goals of the individual come into conflict with those of the society or culture and tragedy follows. In other works, characters are set in opposition to one another or torn between conflicting motives and desires.

Action and opposition, however, need not be external — that is, a question of plot incident, of someone actually doing something. It may be mental action, an interplay of ideas, for example, or even of literary techniques. Cheikh Hamadou Kane's *Ambiguous Adventure (L'aventure ambiguë,* 1961) is not so much a story about a particular young Moslem from Senegal who goes abroad to study as it is a conflict between a spiritual and communal view of the universe and the radical materialism and individualism of European thought.

Much excitement and animation can also be gained from the very way a story is told, which may result in a contrast between the fictional world created and that of everyday reality. Chronology may be distorted, events stylised and characters made unrealistic or frankly representative of ideas. Conflicting judgements or values can also be brought to bear on the same character or event, and inappropriate (contrasting) settings or style employed. In these several ways dynamic tensions are created. The responses of the reader are shaped and directed towards the central concern of the work.

Distinguishing Characteristics of Literature

Whereas design and patterning of action raise a piece of writing to the level of art, style or level of language is one of the most important elements in the composition of literature and accounts for a number of its peculiar characteristics. Language — that is, words as they are spoken or written — is the artistic medium or material of all literature, and because words follow one another in sequence, the effect is progressive or cumulative, not immediate. It takes time to listen to or read even the briefest work; the structure or design is not perceived all at once, especially in longer forms such as novels, which are not taken in at a single sitting.

The mind or imagination must register the basic elements of the construction as they occur, store them up, and later re–create the unity of the whole and the interdependence of the parts. Separate levels of consciousness are required of the reader. On the one hand an emotional and sympathetic response to the human situation of the surface level is needed, and on the other, an intellectual and analytic reaction to the form and texture (language) of the composition. The two activities must be exercised together, and the beginner should be very careful to note the features of design and technique as they become evident. Otherwise, analysis and appreciation which develops from a recognition of the relationship between an author's method and his or her subject matter is impossible.

In addition, the very way in which language is used to express subject matter is likely to differ widely from everyday usage. Literary expression depends very heavily on subtle comparisons and contrasts of register which need not even be grammatically correct, as well as on complex schemes of rhetorical or figurative devices and pervasive patterns of musical effects. Reading serious literature requires special instruction and training over and above that for reading the newspaper or writing a business letter. After all, no one believes that merely because he or she is able to walk and run, they can compete seriously with trained athletes. If the inexperienced reader is unfamiliar with techniques of composition, he or she cannot appreciate the wider significance or excellence of literature even when the work reflects a familiar view of real life. Faced with works which are frankly non–realistic, the beginner may even fail to understand the language of the surface level because stylisation and distortion of reality have been used.

It should be obvious in any case that the attempt to fictionalise a real event is bound to include a certain amount of distortion or falsification. Re–creating an incident in words involves selecting details according to their importance and relevance as well as putting them in a meaningful order. The process amounts to a refocussing of their importance and an interpretation. When constructing a complex plot, as opposed to merely recounting an incident, more distortion occurs because events and their interpretation must be regulated in order to form a coherent pattern and an ordered progression. The random and often unrelated events of real life are ordered and shaped through a reordering and reshaping of language for a definite purpose.

It is, of course, possible for the reality of a fictional world to approximate to that of real life, to create an illusion of everyday reality, but it is also possible for a writer to express an idea, an ideal or a state of being with little apparent reference or relation to the details and actions of temporal existence as we know it. A literary convention has developed in West African folk tales, for example, in which the characters are often given animal or insect names as well as characteristics. It is a kind of distancing device (a mask or stylisation) which makes it possible to poke fun at human failings or celebrate strengths without making the point at uncomfortably close range. The distortion serves to delight us through the interplay of imagination as well as to signal a figurative or metaphoric understanding of the situation. Imaginative literature may go so far as to create worlds and events which never have existed or never can. Recognisable and familiar incidents may also be combined and projected in a new and original way. The illusion of reality in literature presents neither more nor less difficulty than the conscious distortion used to focus attention on an idea, a state of being or the quality of an emotional experience. In both cases an understanding of the author's vision comes through a systematic appreciation of or response to the form and texture of the composition. The following chapters outline a scheme and method of approach for doing just this.

Comparison with Other Art Forms

Perhaps a comparison with other art forms is the best way to make the distinguishing characteristics of literature perfectly clear. Painting, for example, is two–dimensional and uses line, colour and texture as basic elements of composition. A picture is seen all at once, in a single glance. It is perceived as a unity and its design or structure is self–evident, it is right there on the canvas or wall. Of course, the viewer does examine a picture in detail, moving the eye from section to section in order to admire the technique and the interrelation of parts in addition to the effects created. Painting may or may not have 'meaning' in the conventional sense of the word, however. Visual art is readily 'understood' so long as the artist arranges recognisable objects into a composition which resembles the way in which those objects might appear together in real life. We are perfectly at home with portraits, landscapes or pictures that have a 'story' behind them, such as a representation of the adoration of the Magi or Akbar's victory over the Hindu forces of Hemu.

But other pictures exist which distort the details of real life, combining them in unnatural ways. They may contain no recognisable thing at all because the shapes that are used are abstracted and reduced to the simplest possible pattern. In the first of these instances an idea about life or an ideal is being expressed. In the second, the concern is even more technical and the artist is experimenting with individual and uncombined elements of reality; the play of light, the illusion of depth or perspective, etc. As with literature, an imitation of real life is possible, but not necessarily desirable. The realistic element is incidental to the artistic composition and execution in painting, but literature is tied more closely to reality by the fact that words have meaning and any composition of words must make at least minimal sense.

The other major arts offer a similar basis for comparison and should also be considered. Shape and texture alone are the constructional elements of sculpture, for example, which is a three–dimensional art and still more time–oriented than painting. Sculpture should not be viewed from a single point in space but rather from as many points as possible. Different aspects of a work are seen when moving around or through it, different contours and relationships of parts to the whole. In this respect sculpture is more like literature than painting is. Its unity of effect cannot be experienced all at once, but only through an effort of imaginative re–creation.

Sculpture may or may not represent natural objects, but here again, realism or naturalism is a secondary consideration. As in painting and literature, the natural object or subject matter which is presented is very likely to be associated with or representative of another and more abstract idea. On the other hand, uncombined elements of shape and texture may also be explored for their own sake.

The basic elements of dance are physical gestures as they are arranged or patterned according to definite intervals of time and the medium is the human body, just as the compositional elements of sculpture are shape and texture while the medium is wood, stone or metal, and the elements of painting are line, colour and texture while the medium is canvas, board, or plaster, and paints of various kinds. Dance, as performed for the entertainment of spectators rather than the individual pleasure of participants, is an art form which is as time–oriented as literature. The movements are experienced separately and in sequence; their relationship is perceived as an imaginative re–creation because all the sequences are not present at one and the same time. Even when the movements are captured on film and can be viewed again and again, the parts are separated from each other by time. A progressive evaluation, sequence by sequence, is necessary to an appreciation of the whole.

Dance may or may not imitate natural actions, but its mimetic possibilities are nearly as strong as those in any of the other arts. Dance can approach realism and suggest any kind of normal human activity by incorporating appropriate gestures in the basic vocabulary of movement which makes up the dance pattern. On the other hand, dance can also be abstract and directly expressive of ideas and states of mind, more so even than either sculpture or painting. Rhythmic movement of the body is perhaps more closely associated with emotion or feeling than are shapes and colours because a living human being is present. But dance is also capable of abstraction and concern for harmonies and patterns that have no other meaning or relevance to human situations than the beauty or accomplishment of their composition and technique.

The elements of a musical composition are sounds as arranged according to definite time intervals, and sound–producing instruments which are struck, scraped or blown into are its medium. Music is, of course, time–oriented and its effect is also cumulative, which means that as much effort must be put into progressive analysis and criticism while listening as is required by dance or literature. Although intimately associated with dance, music alone is much less capable of sustaining meaning or presenting a realistic imitation of life because it lacks inherent association with the human condition: actions, desires, frustrations, etc. Sounds varied in pitch and duration are themselves rather abstract and have little native relationship or relevance to everyday life, except in so far as they can approximate to natural sounds or imitate human moods and the quality of experience through design and patterning.

Like all the arts, music expresses human emotions and states of mind, but it can also turn in on itself and exhibit an intellectual, almost mathematical, sense of pattern by concentrating on the elements of its composition. If such a concept as pure art existed, it would be found at that extreme of each art form where the artist is wholly concerned with exploring the uncombined elements of his basic materials or medium — that is, with questions of artistic form and texture.

Literary Composition and Relation to Life

Literature is certainly the least pure of all arts and the least capable of such purity or abstraction. In the first place, the elements of a literary composition are not simple and direct objects of sense perception such as line, colour, shape, texture, bodily movement or sound. Rather they are very elaborate and complex expressions of actions, characters, setting, point of view and style. In the second place, these elements are not perceived directly by the reader or audience, but are re–created through the medium of words. A character, for example, is 'seen' in response to all the words relating to him or her. In addition to the time element introduced by the sequential nature of language, words have meanings in their own right, because of their very nature and being.

Words are not just sounds, but sounds which have fixed meanings and associations. Using words necessarily invokes these meanings as well as the grammatical conventions which govern the language. A number of experiments have been made in recent times exploring language itself as an element of literary composition by combining words without relation to conventional meaning. The results so far tend to unintelligibility and such experiments generally fail. Actions, characters and settings are the basic elements of literature and language merely expresses these larger entities which combine to form a literary composition. Individual sentences, compositional elements and the larger design into which action, character and setting are arranged must make sense, and they, in turn, all contribute to an even larger, unifying idea or concept (theme) which also has a direct relation to actual life. More than any other art, literature reflects or comments on actual experience; social, philosophical, psychological and moral concerns are inescapable.

Areas of Critical Judgement

Because both form and meaning are essential to literature, it is important to distinguish criticism or appreciation of the composition from that of the author's particular view of experience and its relation to society. The first question is an artistic one and concerns the effectiveness of the construction in expressing a theme, attitude or idea. The second is one of assessing the validity of that central concern as it relates to personal values and perceptions of life. The chapters that follow concentrate on the constructional elements of literature, their nature and effectiveness, but only as a first step towards understanding literature and its relation to the larger problems of social, psychological and moral truth. Literature is often said to be a school of life in that authors tend to comment on the conduct of society and of individuals in society. They either point out what they see as important issues in human affairs or propose ideal alternatives to the way things actually are. The customs and mores of a particular social group or of individuals, their aspirations and values, are explored and exposed. After evaluating the author's method and effectiveness of expression, one must ask whether or not his attitude towards and understanding of the subject is actually valid. What new insight into the psychology of a man or groups of men is advanced? Is it a truthful picture of human situations? Can one agree with the implied morality and ethical judgements of that particular fictional world? Does the work offer a view of man's place in society or in the universe which one can believe in? These and similar questions must be answered. They form part of our critical response to literature, but critics do not always agree about the relationship between analysis of internal or literary qualities and that of the truthfulness or validity of the vision presented.

Some critics hold that it is entirely possible to admire a literary composition and recognise its technical excellence, yet fail to sympathise with its theme and even disagree violently with the view of experience held by the author. One might recognise the intensity and beauty of Wordsworth's poetic expression in the early lyrics, for example, as well as admire the force and clarity of his thought, yet fail to respond to nature in anything like the same way. In fact, one's own view of nature may even be contradictory and emphasise the more violent and rapacious aspects of birds, animals and men preying upon one another while ignoring the order and harmony of landscapes and vegetable life. In that case, Wordsworth's poems can be accepted as superior works of literature because of their artistic merit, but rejected as valid philosophical statements because they are founded on a limited and unacceptable view of nature.

Other critics hold that the relevance of a work of art to actual life in the everyday world is at least as important as, if not more so than, the technical qualities of its composition. The primary importance of literature for critics of such persuasion is found in the thematic content of a literary work, in the relevance and truth of its moral discernment, social vision, philosophical perception or psychological penetration. No one, however, would deny that the two major areas of concern are interdependent or that they arise very naturally from the distinguishing characteristics of literature as an art form.

If the relationship between a work of literature and its relevance to society is important to criticism on the one hand, then that between the work and the author or act of creation is equally important on the other. Students of literature are fascinated by creativity and often address themselves to the psychology of art and of the artist. How did particular works come into being? What influences from outside sources have been assimilated? What mental process did the author go through? How does an artist's creative consciousness operate, and is it different from that of other human beings?

In order to answer these and similar questions, it is necessary to study other works by the same author and his or her unpublished papers as well as to look into biographical information and the background of the period. Here again, there is a fine distinction to be made between amassing historical evidence, which may be interesting and valuable in its own right, and recognising in that evidence material which illuminates the work or our understanding of artistic creation. The point is that the literary work itself is the centre of interest, while biographical or psychological background should be subordinated to the analysis or interpretation of the text's form and to the truthfulness of its vision.

Biographical criticism is especially awkward because of the temptation to equate facts from the author's life with parallel instances in the works, and to come to conclusions that have no real basis or supporting evidence. One must be especially careful about equating fictional characters with the author or assuming that an author is speaking personally and in his own voice through a given character. Of course, the author's views and attitudes are expressed within a work of literature as well as by that work, but characters, actions and attitudes may also be required by the plot in order that the composition be well formed and meaningful. The process by which life experience is changed into art is obscure and difficult to unravel, especially since the personality, intellect and experiences of each author differ from those of all others.

Basically, there are two opposing views of artistic creation: spiritual inspiration and conscious craftsmanship. The first holds that the mind of the artist is tuned in to supernatural sources and at certain moments receives ideas and even the entire text of a work, as though the author were but a mere recording agent. The other view holds that the artist is a careful workman who learns his craft by diligent study, exercise and criticism. Modern science and psychology lead us to believe that the two views are not so different from one another as they might appear.

The mind is now considered to operate on two levels at once: consciously and unconsciously. Ideas, images and patterns that appeal to the individual are retained and assimilated by the unconscious mind and often reappear at the conscious level, being called forward by new associations, in new and developed forms. The process should be familiar from daily life, where the mind makes free associations among the countless memories and ideas stored away in the unconscious, forming new relationships and patterns of thought which crystallise in the conscious mind wholly formed and completely detailed. Even when ideas, formulations and whole works appear to be communicated from beyond the conscious mind, the writer must exercise critical judgement and a certain amount of editorial ability in preparing the work for publication. In the same way the writer who considers himself a conscious craftsman is more often than not indebted to his unconscious (or inspired) mind for the initial conception of the work, its basic design and patterning.

However strongly one leans towards the romantic view that creation is a question of inspiration from outside the self and therefore unconscious, it cannot be said that authors are unaware of the accomplishment of their work. Complaints that Shakespeare couldn't pass a school examination on his own plays and that critics spoil works of literature by forcing interpretations which the author never intended are just not valid. Authors are supremely aware of their own subtlety with technique and composition, yet works of art cannot be limited to the significance the author had consciously in mind. Once a work is offered to the public, its meaning embraces all sensible interpretations that readers find in it, all those readings that the subject matter and composition will bear.

In any case, one can deduce a great deal about the nature of literary composition and about the workings of the human mind from a knowledge of an author's actual experience, his life, reading and personal contacts in relation to his work. Rejected drafts and personal papers can also reveal patterns of thought and of construction which help to illuminate the interpretation of both individual works and of an entire output or oeuvre.

Historical Perspectives

Historical reconstruction — another very important factor in the study of literature — gives rise to several critical preoccupations. First of all, there is textual criticism which tries to establish an accurate text based on the last known revision of the author. Editorial and printing errors must be eliminated before valid appreciation and analysis can begin. There is not much to be gained from analysing a superseded or corrupt text. The comparison of different versions published by an author as well as of published drafts is fundamental to biographical and psychological approaches. Such activity is particularly important in the case of older literature and of works which for one reason or another have had a troubled publishing history. Textual criticism is not very important for the beginner, however, so long as one takes care to read standard and authoritative editions such as those recommended in course syllabuses and listed in approved bibliographies.

The second kind of historical reconstruction is far more complex and takes into account the background of ideas, forms and styles that characterise the literature of different periods and also affect a work of art. Language, for example, changes continually from historical period to period and words now in use may well have had very different meanings in the past. Norms of personal relationships and customs also change, even within a single culture, and without an understanding of the conventions in force at the time or place in which a work was written, misreadings or total incomprehension may result. Literary forms and aesthetic ideas also develop in response to the changing conditions of society, and a good reader must acquire enough knowledge of the social, political and economic background as well as of the history of ideas and aesthetic values to place an individual piece of literature, an author's entire work or that of a school of writers in its proper context.

Reading literature with an eye to historical perspective, however, does not stop one from reassessing works according to the conventions and ideas of other ages, especially one's own. Whatever a work of literature meant to people at the time of its publication, its meaning and relationship to society is open to reinterpretation and reassessment. It may go out of fashion for long periods of time and then again become relevant depending on its relation to the changing aesthetics and ideals of a given society. The Metaphysical Poets, for example, were long out of fashion because their subjective themes and method of direct presentation through disjointed images did not appeal to an intervening literary age which preferred social satire and discursive rational presentation. When the early modernist poets turned to similar themes and methods of presentation, they rediscovered the Metaphysicals and brought them back to prominence as an important historical school.

In the same way, cultural conventions and values may differ from one ethnic group to another within a single historical period, and a thorough understanding of the backgrounds involved is necessary for comparative study and assessment of influence or assimilation. For example, the interest of European or American writers and critics in African, Caribbean and Black American literature can be easily accounted for with reference to cultural background. Contemporary disillusionment with Western society and frustration in finding new themes, forms and modes of expression inevitably welcomes a literature which mirrors those preoccupations but plays them off against a vital traditional culture while celebrating spirituality, emotion and communality in literary forms and styles derived from African oral tradition as well as modern Western norms.

In order to understand particular works of art in the cultural context of their historical periods, it is best to have a clear outline of literary history in mind — that is, the historical development of aesthetic values and world–views. Familiarity with the general outline and characteristics of literary history, especially that of English literature which is an antecedent of all other literatures in English, is a great help to students as it provides an immediate context for individual works as well as identifying the general nature of a period or age — its identifying forms and themes.

Antique Sources of Literary Tradition

Before undertaking a discussion of major historical ages and characteristics, however, it is important to understand the antecedents of literary tradition in English. The culture of Western Europe, which includes England and America, is derived from two ultimate sources, Graeco–Roman civilisation and Judæo–Christian theology. From the classical world of Greece and Rome we have inherited a highly developed sense of imagination and of expression as well as literary forms. In fact, Latin served as the normal language of education until fairly recently and has had an enormous effect on English literature from the earliest times. It should be remembered that the most productive period of Roman culture (c. 100 BC—100 AD) imitated and assimilated earlier Greek achievements. Roman culture stands between ours and that of classical Greece (c. 500—300 BC). The legacy passed on from the Graeco–Roman world also includes a full range of myth and heroic legend, a storehouse of incident, image and symbol which is still in use and still useful.

When the language and culture of Greece and Rome were known by every educated speaker of English, classical literary forms and allusions to myths or legends were taken for granted, but now the student of literature, whatever his or her cultural background, must look up references and allusions in order to appreciate the connotations and associations that are intended. It is rare in these days of expanded knowledge and specialisation to have specific courses in secondary school on Greek and Roman mythology for students of literature. No one expects the beginner to have all the historical and cultural background needed to read literature.

All that is required is the willingness to learn and some idea of where to look for the information. Even today, literatures in English rely so heavily on the classics that an effort must be made in order to enjoy the richness of texture that such references lend. A greater understanding of an author's vision and aims can also be gained by comparing a product of assimilation with its original, as in the case of J. P. Clark's *Song of a Goat* (*Agamemnon* by Aeschylus, among others), Ola Rotimi's *The Gods Are Not To Blame* (*Oedipus Rex* by Sophocles) or Wole Soyinka's *Bacchae* (*The Bacchae* by Euripides).

The Judæo–Christian tradition as embodied in the Bible has also given us a rich store of mythic incident, symbol and allusion in the heroic legends of the Old and New Testaments. Whether or not one is Christian and versed in Bible lore, it is as important for every student of literature to know his or her way about the Scriptures as it is to know Greek and Roman mythology or literary tradition. Biblical allusions abound in even the most modern literature, and the very names of characters are often chosen in order to evoke expectations associated with their Biblical counterparts. Echoes of actual words and phrasing from the King James version of the Bible (1611) are often used, even today, for emphasis and contrast in literature because the style of that translation is recognised as having distinctive cultural associations wherever it is used.

It should be remembered that when dealing with references to religion in literature, the material should be treated as objectively and unemotionally as possible. One's own belief or disbelief should not be allowed to colour or distort the author's intention. For artistic purposes the mythology and legends of the Judæo–Christian tradition are neither more nor less valid than those of any other religious system — Celtic, Yoruba, Wollof, Moslem, Buddhist or Hindu, for example. It is merely that that particular tradition has been an historical influence on English literature and is, therefore, relevant to our study in that capacity alone. Other religious systems are very often of similar importance in regional or ethnic literatures which evolved through the assimilation of literature in English and local cultural traditions. Nonetheless, the Judæo–Christian tradition is central to all literature in English.

Another legacy of this tradition is an ethical approach to man's place in the universe, a code of absolute values and morality which has pervaded every aspect of Western culture and has survived the lessening of faith among Europeans in a God–oriented universe. The ethics of the classical world were relative in their application and the behaviour of Greek and Roman gods was little different from that of man. Both noble and petty actions took place in the classical heavens as they did on earth, while human morality was determined by the actual needs and desires of society at the moment.

Christianity, on the other hand, believed in a God of absolute goodness who was incapable of imperfection and whose laws as revealed to man were beyond question. The function of the individual was to perfect himself spiritually in order to gain salvation and such activity tended to emphasise the importance of individual morality and ethical conduct, of man's relationship with God and with his fellows. The shift was from the easy–going and tolerant society of classical paganism with its man–centred view of the world to a more spiritual and self–denying society with a God–oriented view. It follows naturally that English literature reflected these basic preoccupations and developed forms and techniques with which to express them.

The Historical Development of English Literature

The historical development of English literature, or more

properly, literatures in English, can be marked off into four major periods or ages. Such a division is, of course, relatively arbitrary and merely reflects an effort to describe basic characteristics, grouping works together under useful headings. This can be done according to several different methods, and the scheme that follows is not the only one in use. You will notice that the names of divisions and subdivisions sometimes refer to the prevailing language, ruler, world–view and even literary technique or prominent writer, whatever best summarises the essential characteristics of that age.

450–1500 *Medieval*
    450–1066 Old English
    1066–1500 Middle English

1500–1660 *Renaissance*
    1558–1603 Elizabethan
    1603–1625 Jacobean
    1625–1649 Caroline
    1649–1660 Commonwealth

1660–1798 *Neo–Classical*
    1660–1700 Restoration
    1700–1745 Augustan
    1745–1798 Johnsonian

1798– *Modern*
    1798–1832 Romantic
    1832–1901 Victorian
    1901–1914 Edwardian
    1914–1939 Modernist
    1939–   Contemporary

The one aspect of literature that is not accounted for in this scheme is oral tradition, which actually transcends the boundaries of time and still exists as a living and creative force today. Oral literature is usually thought of as belonging to pre–literate societies, but in fact, even within a highly literate culture, specific groups of people who form distinct sub–cultures are still creating poems, songs and stories about their life experience that are recited and passed on orally rather than written down and published. One immediately thinks of contemporary miners in isolated regions or itinerant farm workers and also urban ghetto dwellers who often have a rich and living oral tradition which is still being developed and extended. Oral literature, however, does have a tendency to find its way into print and so becomes institutionalised as written literature.

Beowulf, the great Anglo–Saxon epic, for example, is the product of a purely oral tradition. It grew up as a series of tales in verse about a particular culture hero and was finally written down, as was also the case with works such as the Old Testament, *The Iliad* or *Sundiata.* Collections of oral tradition in England have been made in all periods and those works of literature stand in relation to their time and place, as do any works of written literature.

In both range of thematic concern and wealth of technical or aesthetic conventions, oral literature has exactly the same characteristics as its written counterpart. But one must bear in mind that a recorded version of a folk song or tale isolates it from oral tradition. The words become fixed and unchangeable; dramatic gestures and voice inflections of the performer as well as the relevant cultural setting are lost. Reading ritual incantations in a modern city library, for example, is a far cry from participating in a religious ceremony, and an imaginative reconstruction of the work's original context is as important to oral literature as it is to written forms. An objective historical reconstruction is especially necessary in studying oral tradition because the value system and world–view reflected in the literature is often at odds with our own. The customs and morals of a pagan past, for example, may upset a Christian reader who might instinctively wish to suppress or re–interpret the material according to his or her own beliefs as well as to disassociate him– or herself from that cultural past.

The Medieval Period: 450–1500

The Medieval period in European tradition is very important as an age in which the cultural values and aspirations of the Celtic and Teutonic peoples who inhabited Northern and Western Europe gave way to Christianity and feudalism developed. It was a time of cultural assimilation and political interaction, more correctly known as the Middle Ages rather than the Dark Ages, because of its position between the decorum of the ancient world and the rebirth of humanism, which we call the Renaissance. The period was characterised by the amalgamation of peoples and languages, while legendary tales of rough warrior heroes gave way to romances and allegories of refined adventure, spiritual quest and idealised love. The cultural aspirations of the age were essentially aristocratic and one can easily appreciate the role of Christianity in turning attention to an idealisation of experience which offset the brutality and exploitation of the feudal system.

In England the period is divided by the language change from Old English or Anglo–Saxon, which is related to other Teutonic (Germanic) tongues, and Middle English, a cross between Anglo–Saxon and Middle French which is a Latin–based language. In 1066 the Normans, descendants of a Northern and Teutonic people who had assimilated the culture and language of the French, conquered England and radically affected its social, political and cultural history. Because of their links with the Continent, the Normans opened the way to ever–increasing influences on English culture from the south, where refinement, rich imagination and original forms were literary commonplaces, where social (moral) observation and commentary was balanced by spiritual aspirations and idealism.

The Renaissance: 1500–1660

As wealth and political stability increased, a number of factors came into being which contributed to the rebirth of classical learning and humanism. In the first place there was the growth of cities and of a middle class of merchants and artisans who catered to the tastes of the nobility and shared their cultural aspirations. Only after liberation from the harsh life of the peasantry could the middle classes recognise and celebrate their own individualism and humanity. The more the individual controlled his universe, creating both order and beauty, the more he looked to himself as a legitimate object of study and value. The excessive spirituality and self–denial of the earlier God–centred view slowly gave way to a man–oriented conception of the universe. Knowledge and free enquiry into a formerly frightening and half–understood world opened the door to man's further intellectual development. The rebirth of learning was at hand and a highly idealistic gospel of human progress followed. In replacing the superstition of the Middle Ages the men of the Renaissance turned to classical sources of scientific knowledge and philosophy. In literature they also looked to examples of form and style used by the ancient Greeks and Romans, but not before assimilating late Medieval ideas of composition and theme to produce a new and original literature.

The Renaissance began in Italy and nearly 150 years passed before it had made its slow progress northward through France and Germany to England. By 1500 the development of the English language had reached the stage of what we call 'Modern' as opposed to 'Middle' English, and the vernacular, rather than the formal Latin of education and government, was finally accepted as the natural medium for literature. Great works such as those of Geoffrey Chaucer had been written in Middle English during the late Medieval period, but Latin still dominated the intellectual life of the country.

The general literary style of the Renaissance was a lively and richly ornamented English which made effective use of characteristics derived from Anglo–Saxon, especially the flexible ordering of monosyllabic words, heavy patterns of stress, repetitions of sound and vivid imagery. The following excerpt from *De Orbe Novo* (1511), which was translated by Richard Eden as *The Decades of the New World, or West India* (1555), shows something of the style of the period as well as one of its major preoccupations in the celebration of natural man in a pastoral golden age.

> The inhabitants of these islands have been ever used to live at liberty, in play and pastime, that they can hardly away with the yoke of servitude, which they attempt to shake off by all means they may. And surely if they had received our religion, I would think their life most happy of all men, if they might therein enjoy their ancient liberty . . . Among those simple souls, a few clothes serve the naked; weights and measures are not needful to such as can [know] not skill of craft and deceit, and have not the use of pestiferous money . . . they seem to live in that golden world of which the old writers speak so much, wherein men lived simply and innocently without enforce-

ment of laws, without quarrelling, judges and libels, content only to satisfy nature, without further vexation for knowledge of things to come.

(Eden in Kermode, 1, p. 544)

Drama and poetry were the main literary forms of Renaissance England while prose romances also had a certain following. All literatures were influenced by medieval as well as classical models, although each work was a new creation and shared the characteristics of its own age. More and more literature was being written by professionals of the middle classes rather than noble amateurs, and the audience included both the middle and lower classes, particularly in the case of drama which did not require literacy.

Fictional situations, however, concerned themselves mainly with the aristocracy and concentrated on questions of noble conduct and character. Nobility of birth or status was often contrasted with nobility of spirit, the appearance with actuality, and speculation as to the proper training or nurture for nobility of character was common. The relative merits of city life with its inevitable sophistication and immorality were often contrasted with an idealised view of country life, and questions raised as to the rightness of revenge in supporting ideals of honour and loyalty. Above all, the theme of ideal love between man and woman was celebrated, but throughout the literature of the period the fictional situations as well as the heroes and heroines were thoroughly human and realistically reflected. The normal motives and reactions of the audience were exploited, as opposed to their aspirations and ideals, which became the case later, during the Restoration.

The Neo–Classical Age: 1660–1798

Of course there were changes of sensibility decade by decade and reign by reign throughout the Renaissance. We can easily see that the differences between the Commonwealth and the Restoration are no greater than those between the reign of Charles I and the Commonwealth. Political and literary history evolve and develop continuously. Division into periods depends on recognising the moment when an evolving preoccupation or attitude of society becomes a dominant characteristic and sets a new tone, a new system of values, for the age.

The Neo–Classical period is characterised by a complete return to classical models of literary construction, style and theme, a formalisation and restraining of Renaissance exuberance and experimentation. Concern shifted from man as a feeling and passionate individual to man as a social animal, from an investigation of inner experience to that of outer relationships. Poetry became the dominant literary form and satire the characteristic mode of the period, although drama had a certain importance at the beginning of the age and the novel came into being towards its end. The period began in celebration of exaggerated heroic virtues and it ended in preoccupation with those of the middle classes and even humbler country folk. The phantasies of superhuman courage, honour, love and self–sacrifice which were exemplified in heroic tragedy quickly gave way to comic exaggerations through which the pretensions and conduct of a middle–class and urban elite were exposed and ridiculed.

At the height of the Neo–Classical age, poetry took the form of direct discussion or speculation on questions of the day rather than the expression of feeling or attitudes through fictionalised situations. Many of the greatest works of the period were frank re–creations of particular classical works, using the English language to approximate and surpass the original Latin and thereby emphasising the similarity between the antique and modern worlds by updating the subject matter to reflect contemporary conditions and ideas. Much attention was given to elevation of thought, decorum and refinement of style. Towards the end of the period, concern shifted away from urban culture to the glories of nature and the more basic values of country life. The rise of the novel derives from the same preoccupation with social commentary and interest in the actual lives of middle–class people, their aspirations and values in relation to ideal human behaviour and absolute morality.

There were, of course, a number of historical influences and factors which encouraged such changes in literary composition, style and theme. To begin with, the emphasis Protestantism placed on individuals reading and interpreting the Bible for themselves brought about widespread literacy, while the horror of the Civil War and the failure of the Puritan government emphasised the need for traditional authority, kingship, heroic or noble obligations, and the aesthetic authority of the classical past. The aristocracy was fast losing the initiative in government and throughout the period the middle classes were gaining the authority of a ruling class.

Above all, the Neo–Classical was an age of reason, one of intellection as opposed to emotion, in which an even further expansion of knowledge occurred. It was at this time that the foundation of scientific method was laid, and the premium placed on logical thought and verifiable evidence largely accounts for the shift in literary style from rich ornamentation and expressiveness to a plainer, more literal and directly discursive language. Take for example this passage from a popular journal, Richard Steele's *Spectator* (11 August 1712).

> The day of people of fashion now began to break, and carts and hacks were mingled with equipages of show and vanity; when I resolved to walk it out of cheapness; but my unhappy curiosity is such that I find it always my interest to take coach, for some odd adventure among beggars, ballad singers, or the like, detains or throws me into expense. It happened so immediately; for at the corner of Warwick Street, as I was listening to a new ballad, a ragged rascal, a beggar who knew me, came up to me, and began to turn the eyes of the good company upon me by telling me he was extremely poor, and should die in the street for want of drink, except I would immediately have the charity to give him sixpence to go into the next alehouse and save his life. He urged with a melancholy face, that all his family had died of thirst. All the mob have humour, and two or three began to take the jest; by which Mr. Sturdy carried his point, and let me sneak off to a coach.
>
> (Steele, 4, p.101)

Concentrating as it does on contact with the lower classes and the wisdom of frugality, the passage exemplifies a major current in Augustan writing. The word choice is almost invariably simple and the sentences are loosely constructed in a series of brief phrases and clauses tacked on to one another without much regard to formal and elaborate structures. The effect is that of colloquial speech, while the prose rhythm of educated English is maintained by altering the length of the independent units within a definite pattern

One major concern of the age was to fix the English language and legislate against incorrect or unacceptable word usage, grammar, spelling, etc. Because it was also a Neo–Classical age, the efforts that were successful in this direction were arbitrarily based on the rules of Latin grammar, and the resulting confusions have reached almost to the present day.

Another significant notion that also influenced literature involved a change of attitude towards the nature of God. Being an age of reason, the old idea of faith in God was no longer sufficient, nor was the conception of deity as a passionate, angry father who requires homage to keep him happy. A more rational view was based on the elaborate interrelationships and properties of nature, on an absolute and scientific order then being deduced from verifiable evidence. God was held to be an abstract and depersonalised force for absolute order and goodness, whose ultimate manifestation was the created universe, and man's duty or function on earth was to imitate that order and decorum for the good of society and the salvation of one's own soul.

The authority of classical literature and the love of ancient Rome for order and decorum were essential features of the Neo–Classical age, but one can also see that the deistic view of the universe and the expansion of scientific knowledge also led to a preoccupation with nature. At first nature was seen as a manifestation of deity and later in its own right as a moral force or model to be contrasted with the immorality and degradation of city or court life.

René Descartes' formulation, 'I think, therefore I am', is another outgrowth of the age of reason and it acknowledges the dominance of intellect over both individual emotion and religious belief. It also confirms the older individualism of Protestant Christianity which held that each human being was ultimately responsible for a personal covenant with God and the interpretation of Holy Scripture. Saying that a human being only exists in so far as he or she thinks, makes reason and judgement the highest achievement possible and reserves both activities to the individual rather than to society. The fact that each person thinks and judges for himself accounts for the emphasis on individual questioning and reassessment of all knowledge in European education, and for the preoccupation both with character development in literature as well as with works that put individual characters in conflict with society. If thinking determines one's existence, then one must exercise the intellect in order to exist properly.

Beyond concern for reason, the Neo–Classical period was interested in travel, adventure and discovery in exotic lands. The imagination of England was stirred by first–hand knowledge of Africa, Asia and the Americas; by knowledge of their cultures, climates, plants and animals. A measure for comparative analysis of European preconceptions and manners was at hand and the journey or voyage of a fictional hero became a major feature in the literature of the period. Although the age offered a wide range of new ideas and literary ideals in its earlier years, the principles of reason and plain language gave way in the end to an even more romantic posture than that which had characterised the Renaissance.

The Romantic and Modernist Periods: 1798–1939

Romanticism is a complex concept and besides its usage as a proper noun to refer to a particular group of English poets — especially William Wordsworth, Samuel Taylor Coleridge, Lord Byron, Percy Bysshe Shelley and John Keats — it denotes a specific range of subject matter and attitudes which are in much wider general use. Perhaps the primary feature of a romantic attitude towards life is a concern for the emotions or feelings of individuals, and especially of artists. Love between the sexes is, of course, a related subject as is a preoccupation with the supernatural, because the Christian view of love and marriage holds that sexual relationships between men and women are intimately connected with those between individuals and God. Romantic delight in a world of imagination also leads to the fictional representation of all kinds of supernatural agents from fairies to ghosts and demons.

Imagination is of central importance to a romantic view of the universe because it is capable of transforming natural images into representations of ideal states or conditions. Since the act of artistic creation is the most highly prized of all human activities within this system of thought, it follows that it is directly influenced and inspired by the supernatural which speaks through the imagination of the artist. Man is said to be essentially good in his natural state and merely corrupted by the evil which exists in the world. A parallel belief holds that it is possible for individuals and societies to perfect themselves by aspiring to an ideal. In fact, almost every facet of romanticism involves an ideal condition in one way or another, and even the love of adventure or exotic and imaginative settings shows a desire to replace the disordered and often degrading incidents of real life with perfected views of ideal encounters. In all its forms, romanticism offers an ideal alternative to actual life, and we think of a work as being romantic or an incident as romanticised when an exaggerated extreme of emotion or mood is dominant instead of the interplay of opposed forces or qualities of everyday life.

The following passage from John Stuart Mill's *Autobiography* (1873) offers a good example.

At first I hoped that the cloud would pass away of itself; but it did not. A night's sleep, the sovereign remedy for the smaller vexations of life, had no effect on it. I awoke to a renewed consciousness of the woeful fact. I carried it with me into all companies, into all occupations. Hardly anything had power to cause me even a few minutes oblivion of it. For some months the cloud seemed to grow thicker and thicker. The lines of Coleridge's 'Dejection' — I was not then acquainted with them — exactly describe my case:
  A grief without a pang, void, dark and drear,
  A drowsy, stifled, unimpassioned grief,
  Which finds no natural outlet or relief
  In word, or sigh, or tear.
In vain I sought relief from my favourite books; those memorials of past nobleness and greatness, from which I had always hitherto drawn strength and animation. I read them now without feeling, or with the accustomed feeling minus all its charm; and I became persuaded, that my love of mankind, and of excellence for its own sake, had worn itself

out. I sought no comfort by speaking to others of what I felt. If I
had loved anyone sufficiently to make confiding my griefs a
necessity, I should not have been in the condition I was.

(Mill, pp. 113–14)

One must be careful, however, to distinguish a romantic
view of life from a sentimental one. As romantic idealisation
moves further and further away from the realm of possibility
or actuality, it approaches sentimentality, a tendency to be
swayed by feeling alone and a nursing of emotion for its own
sake. When characters and actions are too good (or evil, etc.) to
be true, the threshold of sentimentality has been crossed.
Another criterion of judgement might be the justification of all
actions as the product of strong and spontaneous feelings, the
extension of romantic love to insist on the rights of passion and
the belief that all love, by its very nature, is pure.

Sentimentality appears in English literature, especially
during the late Neo–Classical and Victorian periods, and also
in Anglo–Indian literature of the present time. A brief example
from *So Many Hungers* (1947) by Bhabani Bhattacharya in
which a newly delivered, middle–class mother endures
unreasoned fears should make the point fairly clear.

He had slept well, freed from the strains of the night before.
Moju twisted in agony; her wide eyes haunted by fear — and
the evil omen of a cat moaning eerily in the dark street, close to
the house door, made the fear a certainty: that she would not
live to see her child. Oh, she would hate to die so young — just
over twenty — and so many dreams unfulfilled. With
advancing pain, clutching her husband's arm, pressing his arm
hard against her bosom, she made her despair flow out into his
nerves, till he felt in him the whispered echo of her pre-
monition, and he edged close to her and took her head in the
crook of his arm, enveloping her, shielding her from some
mortal hurt. He saw the pupils of her eyes dilate, strained with
deepening dread, as though Yama had tramped out of the
night and stood at her bedside, in his hand the soul–holding
tube into which he slipped life–sparks as he collected them,
bits of phosphorescence.

(Bhattacharya, p. 7)

Later in the nineteenth century, after the bitter disillusionment in both progress and the benefits of the Industrial Revolution, a contrasting philosophy or view of life experience developed and greatly influenced the presentation of experience in literature. An attempt was made to document actual life, especially that of the working classes, to reflect its exact qualities and character without too much concern or comment for an illuminating or universalising theme. The method employed was a literal or matter–of–fact style and the direct presentation of accurately observed detail which built up a picture of the unspoken, unknown or unconscious forces at work within either the individual or society.

Two short examples demonstrate the method: the first is a description of the heroine of George Moore's *Esther Waters* (1894) which suggests a contrast between her actual situation in life as a servant and the qualities of her character. The second shows her later on in her career as an unwed mother, forced to work as wet nurse in a middle–class family for someone else's child and searching for someone to care for her own baby.

An oblong box painted reddish brown and tied with a rough rope lay on the seat beside her. The movement of her back and shoulders showed that the bundle she carried was a heavy one, and the sharp bulging of the gray linen cloth that the weight was dead. She wore a faded yellow dress and a black jacket too warm for the day. A girl of twenty, firmly built with short strong arms and a plump neck that carried a well–turned head with dignity. Her well–formed nostrils redeemed the some-what thick, fleshy nose, and it was a pleasure to see her grave, almost sullen, face light up with sunny humour; for when she laughed a line of almond–shaped teeth showed between red lips. She was laughing now, the porter having asked her if she were afraid to leave her bundle with her box.

(Moore, p. 1)

Esther visited many streets, always failing for one reason or another, till at last she found herself in Wandsworth, in a battered, tumbledown street, no thoroughfare, only four houses, a coal–shed, and some broken wooden palings. In the area of No. 3 three mites were playing, and at Esther's call a short, fat woman came out of the kitchen, her dirty apron sloping over her high stomach and her pale brown hair twisted into a knot at the top of her head.

(pp. 136–7)

Among realistic writers emphasis naturally fell on the more sordid and degrading aspects of the human plight as the period progressed, as industrial exploitation and inhuman conditions became undeniable. First known as realism, this objective view developed into naturalism which held that man's actions and character were determined by both heredity and environment, and that the individual fights for survival against a mechanical universe, against its social, economic and political pressures. An example might be taken from Yambo Ouologuem's *Bound to Violence* (*Le devoir de violence*, 1968).

'He sits down by the fire. He too has an ax, ropes, a game bag, just like me. But he's going north. He chews his millet drugged with *dabali*. He takes quantities of it. He asks me for a handful of my millet. To compare, he says. I object, I say I'm out of it. The man bargains. I give him a little millet for a little information. About my future boss. About the working conditions. About life in the South, where he's come from. "You'll see," he says, "They won't ask you any questions. Work, eat, work: don't say anything. Don't talk back. Good morning, good night, that's all. You'll have your women and your drugs."

'The man laughs. He cries. A long time, in silence. As if he were trying with his tears to recover from his exhaustion, from the mental anaesthesia that made him resemble an animal. He needed to resume contact with the core of himself. Deep in thought, he talks. He explains; he listens to himself speak.

' "We'll never get through."

' "What?"

' "The wall."

' "What wall?"

' "That wall . . . there . . . there," he raves.

"Don't you see, a nigger is nothing; a nigger woman is good enough to fuck. We're helpless; we haven't got the law on our

side. There's Saif, it's a country without many witnesses: so
they sell us." '

(Ouologuem, p. 107)

In reading modern literature one must distinguish the philosophical view or attitude to life from the method of presentation as
well as distinguish romantic from realistic modes of expression.
In the twentieth century a basically romantic or idealising
conception of man and his universe might be presented with a
realistic style and a naturalistic view might also be presented in a
rich and refined romantic style — that is, highly ornamented with
figures of speech, rhetorical devices and rhythmic patterning.

The evil excesses of the Industrial Revolution also gave rise to
socialism, labour unions and the growing influence of the
working class in politics, encouraging other events to affect the
sensibility of the age. Certainly one of the distinctive features of
the period was the interaction between the middle and the lower
classes. Perhaps a more important factor, however, was the
dominance of scientific methods of investigation which brought
together as much factual evidence as possible and then by
analysis discovered a coherent pattern which explained or
described the original phenomenon.

The most disturbing of the early scientific discoveries was
Darwin's theory of the origins of man which held that human
beings had evolved over long periods of time from less complex
species. For the first time, serious doubt was cast on the literal
truth of Christian teaching which held that man was created by
God in a single act at a specific moment in time. Together with
the obvious immorality and oppression which were produced by
industrialisation at its worst, faith in absolute goodness and a
God–centred universe began to fail. As the Modern period
progressed and world wars confirmed man's worst fears about the
situation, systems of government and economics became more
complex and inhumane. The individual was obviously no longer
in control of his environment, but rather controlled by forces
which he little understood.

A great part of the dilemma was brought about by strides in
scientific discovery and the general expansion of knowledge,
while being continually reinforced by the awesome presence of

mass communication which makes one more than ever aware of man's inhumanity to his fellows through instant reporting from the furthest corner of the earth. Natural disasters and their aftermath, urban crime and even scenes of actual battle and bloodshed, however distant, are brought into one's very home by newspapers, radio and television.

The Contemporary Age: 1939–

As opposed to the romantic aspirations and belief which prevailed at the beginning of the Modern age, contemporary literature generally reflects disillusionment and disbelief. In between there were a number of alternative views and attempts to come to terms with life. At first, there was recourse to both a classical and medieval past, then a celebration of Celtic culture, as well as the use of themes and techniques deriving from a revival of interest in symbols as a means of representing qualities and states of mind that were either abstract, ideal or supernatural. Finally, there was a preoccupation with human psychology on the one hand and the exploitation of artistic material on the other which turned art in upon itself. Methods of presentation became increasingly difficult and disjointed, relying for the most part on distortions of normal sequences or conventional expectations, and placing dissimilar but related incidents or images next to one another in an effort to express the quality of inner life experienced rather than the mere facts or immediate outward actions of that life. Virginia Woolf's *Mrs Dalloway* (1925) provides us with as good an example as any novel of the period.

And Lady Bruton went ponderously, majestically, up to her room, lay, one arm extended, on the sofa. She sighed, she snored, not that she was asleep, only drowsy and heavy, like a field of clover in the sunshine this hot June day, with the bees going round and about and the yellow butterflies. Always she went back to these fields down in Devonshire, where she had jumped the brooks on Patty, her pony, with Mortimer and Tom, her brothers. And there were the dogs; there were the cats; there were her father and mother on the lawn under the tree, with the tea–things out, and the beds of dahlias, the hollyhocks, the pampas grass; and they, little wretches, always up to some mischief: stealing back through the shrubbery, so as not to be seen, all bedraggled from some roguery. What old nurse used to say about her frocks!

Ah dear, she remembered — it was Wednesday in Brook Street. Those kind good fellows, Richard Dalloway, Hugh Whitbread, had gone this hot day through the streets whose growl came up to her lying on the sofa. Power was here, position, income. She had lived in the forefront of her time. She had had good friends; known the ablest men of her day. Murmuring London flowed up to her, and her hand, lying on the sofa back, curled upon some imaginary baton such as her grandfathers might have held, holding which she seemed, drowsy and heavy, to be commanding battalions marching to Canada, and those good fellows walking across London, that territory of theirs, that little bit of carpet, Mayfair.

(Woolf, pp. 123–4)

The dominant view of life as expressed in contemporary literature is absurdist, however, and holds that human life or endeavour is essentially devoid of meaning. Because literature has always been a means of ordering experience into meaningful patterns, the novel and drama, especially, are now used to project meaningless patterns through unresolved ironies and paradoxes. The frustrations, disillusionment and alienation of modern man is demonstrated by creating fictional worlds in which our most widely held and deep–seated assumptions about human conduct and social order are challenged, exposed and ultimately denied. Samuel Beckett proves himself a master of this method in *Watt* (1939).

We are the Galls, father and son, and we are come, what is more, all the way from town, to choon [tune] the piano.

They were two, and they stood, arm in arm, in this way, because the father was blind, like so many members of his profession. For if the father had not been blind, then he would not have needed his son to hold his arm, and guide him on his rounds, no, but he would have set his son free, to go about his own business. So Watt supposed, though there was nothing in the father's face to show that he was blind, not in his attitude either, except that he leaned on his son in a way expressive of a great need of support. But he might have done this, if he had been halt, or merely tired, on account of his great age. There was no family likeness between the two, as far as Watt could make out, and nevertheless he knew that he was in the presence of a father and son, for had he not just been told so. Or were they not perhaps merely stepfather and stepson. We are the Galls, stepfather and stepson — those were perhaps the words that should have been spoken. But it was natural to prefer the others. Not that they could not very well be a true father and son, without resembling each other in the very least, for they could.

(Beckett, p. 67)

While various themes, modes and techniques have been experimented with, the mainstream of English literature has also broken up into a number of related ethnic literatures, each with its own thematic and aesthetic values or standards. In the nineteenth century the most notable developments were in American and Irish literatures, and these were later followed by Indian, Australian, Canadian, African and Caribbean writing. The conditions, values and aspirations of the different peoples caused them to develop literatures of unique and distinctive characteristics. The traditional range of English or British writing has continued to focus on social behaviour and moral commentary, while American literature, for example, because of the original desire to create a new social and political order in a new and unspoiled land, has also raised questions as to the nature of truth, the meaning and function of man's place in the universe. American literature has also passed through all the phases of the Modern period, yet it has developed its own particular themes and values. In the nineteenth century its romantic preoccupation with nature merged with the celebration of the pioneer hero and folk culture. Romantic interest in the more terrifying aspects of the supernatural gave way to philosophical idealism known as Transcendentalism in which the God–like aspect of man was considered to be the only reality as well as the moral source and guide for human conduct. As the Victorian period wore on and socio–economic disillusionment set in, the themes and styles of realism (including naturalism) became dominant and reflected the displacement of the pioneer folk hero by the tragedy of men and women who were either corrupted or destroyed by economic forces and the power of social pressure derived from ruthless financial success. One response to the growing alienation of thinking men was the effort of T. S. Eliot and Ezra Pound, among others, to revive classical and Renaissance European culture in order to reintroduce its ideals into the intellectual and moral wasteland of modern life. The mainstream of American literature, however, continued to concern itself directly with the actual perversions and distortion of earlier ideals which are still obvious in American life and thought.

The latest development in American literature has been the rising importance of minority literatures which celebrate the separate identity and values of important sub– or counter–cultures, especially those of women, American Indians, Chicanos and Black Americans. Such minorities reject the values and artistic forms of the traditional male–dominated, white or European culture and offer a new literature based on their own cultural experiences and aesthetic sensibilities.

In the same way, African literature in English is a new and exciting force in literary tradition, one which has captured the imagination of an international readership because of its relevance to contemporary problems of cultural alienation and the search for new modes of expression. In general, black literature is based on socio–political protest and the rejection of European tradition, but it also raises perennial questions of ethnic and individual identity in a dehumanising modern world. To one degree or another each ethnic or national group in Africa is still in touch with an older cultural tradition whose manifestations are different from the social, personal and aesthetic conventions mirrored in traditional English literature. A conflict of cultural values has become the main subject matter or theme in African literature, while the assimilation of forms and literary techniques from both European writing and African oral tradition have added a new aesthetic interest. With an understanding of the individual elements of all literary construction, the forms, techniques and cultural conventions which determine literary composition, any and all these literatures in English are accessible.

2 Narrative Fiction and the Printed Word

Definition of Genre

There are many ways of classifying or defining works of literature and the conventional categories are known as 'genres', a French word meaning kind or type. Distinctions are made according to features of construction, subject matter and theme, on the one hand, as well as function or mode of expression on the other. Calling a work of literature a novel describes its general form or composition, and it might be further identified as an historical novel, because its subject matter is derived from historical fact or conditions. The same work might also be characterised by theme; a political power struggle, a domestic tragedy, a tale of adventure, etc. Both the internal or aesthetic characteristics and the external relationship of the work to real life, its truthfulness and validity of representation, are also taken into consideration when classifying a work by genre. For example, a novel and a play may have the same subject matter and theme but their distinctly different construction and form account for distinguishing genre names.

Major genres are classified and subdivided still further, and again according to recognisable constructional features or forms as well as characteristic subject matter. The epistolary novel constitutes a distinct sub–genre, for example, as does historical fiction or literature about adolescents entering adulthood (Bildungsroman). The function or purpose of a work may also place it in a familiar category or subdivision. A novel, a play and even a poem may all be examples of social satire or of political protest, for example, and at the same time differ widely in mode or tone of expression as well as in their essential literary form. The novel might be light and comic, the play serious and sad, while the poem might be savage and aggressive in exposition of subject matter and theme. With a clear understanding of existing categories a student of literature is better able to recognise essential characteristics and place individual works in relation to others of the same kind. The thing to remember is that any work of literature will have several characteristics or possible genre classifications and each one can be examined and discussed in detail. A novel, for example, which is primarily a work of social protest may also constitute a tragedy. Every feature of a given work should be recognised and commented upon.

Genre Divisions

Narrative fiction, drama and poetry are the three major genre divisions of literature and the fundamental differences between them are constructional. The distinction between prose and verse, however, is not an identifying or defining characteristic of these genres. Any of the three, in fact, can be written in either prose or verse. The epic, for example, is primarily a narrative in verse, as is a long poem such as *The Idylls of the King* (1859) by Alfred Tennyson. Depending on its subject matter and theme, the dramatist also chooses between prose and verse in order to give his work an appropriate stylistic vehicle of expression. In modern times the prose poem has become fairly common as a genre, while poetic prose and the structuring of prose fiction or drama according to the principles of poetic composition has also become an important stylistic technique.

The really distinguishing feature of narrative fiction is that it is basically a story or meaningful sequence of events. Characters and actions are so organised and presented that an idea or attitude (theme) becomes evident. With the exception of folk tales and the earliest epics which were memorised and recited publicly, other forms of narrative fiction in the English tradition are conceived as written literature. In fact, narrative fiction is the only genre that is meant to be written down for private reading, although a work may be read out to an audience.

Drama and poetry, on the other hand, are conceived for public performance although they may also be written down and read privately. The conceptual difference has a great deal to do with the characteristics of each genre. For example, in fiction the physical absence of a performer who provides an interpretation or understanding of the author's attitude towards the action or theme, gives rise to the importance of the narrator and narrative point of view. Because narrative fiction is basically a story which is written down and therefore 'told', the manner of the 'telling' is of great importance to the total effect of the work. The story–teller is the centre of consciousness in the tale; his or her personality, moral values and attitudes, as separate from the story itself, must be taken into consideration while reading the tale. In the same way drama derives its most characteristic features from the effectiveness of stage presentation, a factor which does not depend on language, while the distinguishing features of poetry are rhythmic movement and musical devices.

Traditional Subdivisions

There are a great many subdivisions of narrative fiction, but they group themselves roughly into antique or outmoded forms: the folk tale, epic, romance, allegory and satire on the one hand; and contemporary forms: the short story and novel on the other. Because students are often required to read older forms of literature and modern works also preserve many of their characteristics, it is wise to have an idea of their basic features before attempting to define and characterise the modern forms.

1. *The folk tale.* Because the folk tale belongs to oral tradition it is limited in length by the requirements of memory and of performance. Folk tales are common to most cultures and vary enormously in terms of themes, subject matter, degree of artistic development and social function. One of the most widely known sub–genres of the folk tale is the beast fable which is particularly common among African cultures and was first introduced to Europe through Aesop's Fables. In this version, the tale is used to illustrate a moral precept or judgement of human conduct but it does not follow that all folk tales are conscious instruments for educating the young of a cultural group. The same tale might be used to dramatise several different moral axioms or proverbs, and then again might well be told under different conditions merely to entertain by exciting the imagination of the audience. The decision to include a moral or summation of ethical theme, as

well as which one to include, depends entirely on the story–teller and the immediate circumstances under which the story is being told.

Folk tales, like all literature, serve to celebrate or examine basic human experience — birth, love, war, death and supernatural intervention — as well as the morality of human conduct. A thorough appreciation of performance techniques as well as the social context of the tale is necessary to a complete understanding of the form. Take for example the Uncle Remus stories of the American south. Here we have an extended series of African beast fables developed by Black Americans during the time of slavery which celebrate the wiliness and cunning of Br'er (Brother) Rabbit who consistently outwits the strength and authority of Br'er Fox. The social and psychological relevance of the stories to the experience of that cultural group is fairly obvious. Consciously or unconsciously, Br'er Rabbit was and is a very inspiring and sympathetic character to a people deprived of all political, social and financial power or authority and driven to survive by wit alone.

Other examples are the Paul Bunyan tales of the northern forest regions of the United States at about the same time, or the Davy Crockett cycle of the Appalachian mountains, both of which celebrate culture heroes of a dominant pioneering society, one imaginary and the other historical. These tales entertain through imaginative exaggeration without so much as a glance or serious reflection on the morality of the conduct they take for granted.

2. *The epic.* An epic is a long and complex work which celebrates a culture and an idealised hero who exemplifies the virtues and values of that society. In most cultures the epic originated before the existence of writing, and developed orally into cycles of tales which were slowly elaborated into an artistic unity. Later on, the finished epics were written down, much admired and then imitated by highly learned and sophisticated poets. In addition to control over the natural world in terms of success in war, hunting, athletics, drinking and womanising, intercourse with the supernatural is also suggested by the participation of gods in human affairs. A successful descent into the underworld on the part of the hero and/or the defeat of super-

human enemies is a characteristic feature of epics. In the classical European tradition they also contain repeated invocations to a muse for poetic inspiration, a plot which opens at a high point of excitement towards the middle of the story, and catalogues of art treasures, warrior's names and war machinery as well as scenes of single combat, massed battles, consultations of elders, set speeches of worldly advice and formal lamentations over defeats and losses. When we use the word 'epic' to describe the quality of another work — a novel or film, for example — the reference is to its scope or grandeur, its accomplishment in presenting a similarly all-inclusive or encyclopædic view of human experience.

In form, the epic is a verse narrative interrupted by scenes of dramatic presentations and interspersed with lyrical passages of description and personal emotion. In style it is serious, decorous and elevated. There is also a great deal of comedy to be derived from the application of the serious style of epics to actions and characters of an ordinary and unheroic nature. It is always funny to treat the foolish and trivial with exaggerated formality and heroic courtesy. In English literature the Neo–Classical period saw a great revival of interest in the epic, both serious and comic, and the novel, which developed in the latter half of that age, assimilated something of its form and character.

Beowulf is the national epic of England. It was composed in the Old English language (Anglo–Saxon) and reflects the values and world–view of a Germanic culture prior to the ninth century when the tale was first written down. Although it is different in several respects from the classical models of *The Iliad* and *The Odyssey,* it has many features in common with them. It would be foolish, however, to say that *Beowulf* is not an epic merely because it does not conform in every detail to the Greek texts. Allowance must be made for those characteristics which naturally arise from differing cultural conventions of subject matter and principles of composition.

In the same way that *Beowulf* shows enough of the essential features of the primary or folk epic form to be classified within that genre, so do such works as the *Ramayana,* for example, or *Sundiata: an Epic of Old Mali* as recorded recently from oral tradition by D. T. Niane. Secondary epics in English, that is, those which were written by a single author in conscious imitation of a natural or folk epic, include such works as John Milton's *Paradise Lost* (1674) and Hart Crane's *The Bridge* (1930).

3. *The romance.* The romance is also a classical form, but rather than generally derived, it was specifically developed by the Greeks and later adopted by the Romans. It is a prose work of no great length and its name refers to a characteristic subject matter which is highly imaginative, rather than being a reflection of practical everyday life. Simple stories of mythical or legendary happenings which show human sympathies with nature, adventures involving superhuman conduct, or figures, and sexual love are perhaps the most common topics of the romance in classical times. The form was taken up again in the Middle Ages with the added interest of the period in physical or martial adventures as ends in themselves, and in spiritual or idealised love. Features of the classical romance tend to find their way into both Renaissance and Modern literature in English.

4. *Allegory.* Closely related to the romance and sometimes combined with it, especially in Medieval times, allegory is a narrative in which each element of the story (its actions, characters and images) has a metaphoric or representative meaning and the interrelationship of these elements (the plot) makes sense on both the surface or stated level and on a secondary or unstated level of meaning (see p. 172). The point of allegory is to emphasise the secondary or unstated references and meaning by creating an entertaining and satisfying story at the surface level and inviting the imagination of the reader to see through to the unstated or allegorical level.

Biblical parables form a specific sub–genre of allegory directed towards teaching moral truth. Medieval allegories were far more complex and sophisticated, however, having to do with the heroic, spiritual and aesthetic aspirations of a highly developed society. Long tales of love and adventure were written, usually in verse, in which characters, action and even settings represented either individuals or abstract ideas, virtues, states of mind or conditions of being.

For example, a noble knight who seeks the Holy Grail (an image of the individual's search for spiritual salvation) might fall in with another knight who leads him to a castle for shelter where quarrelling and fighting continually break out. Such a detour from the path of virtue into a condition of anger and violence as opposed to serenity and forbearance becomes an ethical object lesson as well as an exciting tale of adventure. In the course of such an allegorical episode, the hero or heroes might encounter a vast number and range of situations or experiences which could account for a complete system of values or an evaluation of familiar human conduct.

Under cover of its metaphorical machinery, allegory also allowed for the exposure of folly and vice in actual historical personages and could easily investigate the real political, social or moral circumstances as well as the ideals of a given historical period. In England the form was used to great advantage during the late Medieval period and the early Renaissance, especially in Edmund Spenser's *Faerie Queene* (1589, 1596) and John Bunyan's *Pilgrim's Progress* (1678). The indirectness of its method, however, forms a marked contrast with the straight-forward and outspoken satire of classical times which was taken up again in the Neo–Classical period.

5. *Satire.* Allegory was certainly used for satirical purposes as well as for political and social commentary, but satire as a recognisable genre is a distinctively separate form. Satire developed among the Romans as a prose composition of undetermined length and complexity whose subject was an undisguised and open discussion of human affairs. The tendency was to examine the ills of society or errors of men, and later classical writers further dignified the form with verse composition. In its classical form satire is rarely a subdivision of narrative fiction because it has little or no plot. It does not present fictionalised life experience for the reader to analyse and interpret, but rather communicates the considered judgement and attitudes of the author directly and discursively. Jonathan Swift's *Gulliver's Travels* (1726) is a good example of a loosely fictionalised satire while Alexander Pope's *Essay on Man* (1733–4) or Samuel Johnson's 'London' (1738) conform more closely to the original genre classification.

At its purest, satire is related to the essay and other kinds of expository or argumentative writing, but its end or goal is often incorporated into forms of narrative fiction and gives the work an added quality or characteristic. Such a supplementary quality should not be confused with the distinctive and dominant character of the entire work, however. It is possible for a man, let us say, to have certain aspects of mind or character which are normally associated with women. He may be said in that respect to be feminine, but he remains a man in all others. In literature there is often a mixing of qualities and the dominant form should be distinguished from other characteristics which are derived from other genres. An historical novel or a novel of protest, for example, may be satirical in effect, while in other works the conception and form of satire may predominate, as in *Gulliver's Travels*.

6. *The novel.* The modern or living forms of narrative fiction are the novel and the short story. They often share constructional features, subject matter and themes derived from the epic, romance, allegory and satire, but they remain distinctively separate from them. The novel was the first of the two to develop and from the end of the Neo–Classical period it was recognised as a major literary form. It is normally a prose work of quite some length and complexity which attempts to reflect and express something of the quality or value of human experience or conduct. Its subject matter may be taken from patterns of life as we know it, or set in an exotic and imaginative time or place. The work may create the illusion of actual reality or frankly admit the artificiality of its fictional world in order to direct our attention to an imaginative relationship between the subject matter or theme of the work and the real world in which we actually live.

The pattern of construction is not fixed in any way; any number of developed techniques and devices may be selected and arranged by an author so as to express his or her particular conception of a chosen subject matter and theme. The one requirement of construction in a novel is that it should combine a number of episodes or events and provide a reasonable, developed view of its subject or subjects.

The novel originally developed towards the middle of the eighteenth century as a realistic reflection of middle–class life and experiences, while the spread of literacy through Bible study at that time provided a very wide audience. The first novels were especially concerned with moral behaviour and tended to incorporate a good deal of social satire. The forms then in fashion were epistolary on the one hand, and picaresque on the other.

In the first the plot unfolded through a series of letters, usually written by the main character to friends or relatives, which provided an excuse for the formal but seemingly realistic narration of events. Samuel Richardson's *Pamela* (1741) is an excellent example. In the picaresque novel (*picaro* is the Spanish word for a fictional antihero who is a scoundrel of low birth and evil ways), a roguish but attractive central hero or heroine undergoes a series of unrelated adventures, usually while journeying through the countryside to or from the city. Actually, the episodes have a common concern or theme and examine different aspects of human behaviour in contemporary society. Henry Fielding's *Joseph Andrews* (1742) and *Tom Jones* (1749) are good examples of the form and each happens to be modelled on the plot of a classical epic, *The Odyssey* and *The Iliad* respectively.

The novel of manners which investigates social behaviour and ethics is another recognisable form of this period as is the novel concerned with the education of a young man or woman (Bildungsroman). Early in the Romantic period themes of passionate love and supernatural intervention in real life gave rise to new genres such as historical romances and the Gothic novel, which exist to evoke emotional excitement for its own sake. The two forms are independent of one another but Edward George Bulwer Lytton managed to mix them together in a work such as *The Last Days of Pompeii* (1834).

In mid–Victorian times (c. 1860) disillusionment with worsening social conditions and alienation gave rise to novels of protest and moral as well as psychological investigation. Interest in society and human conduct never waned and the characteristic form of the period was a long novel with two or even three parallel plots which spanned the various social levels of contemporary life. George Eliot's *Middlemarch* (1872) is perhaps the best known of the triple–decker novels.

As disillusionment and alienation grew to dominance after the First World War, the modern novel in England turned to experimentation with form and technique while in America novelists tended to pursue themes and subject matter of obvious social or moral relevance. In both cases, however, authors became more interested in capturing and expressing the quality or psychological truth of human experience than in the bare realistic facts of external happenings. Plots become fragmented and inconclusive, as in Joseph Conrad's *Heart of Darkness* (1902) or James Joyce's *Ulysses* (1922), while the burden of interpreting the patterns of associated ideas and images is left to the reader.

In the same way, the contemporary novel is composed more in the manner of a poem than that of a traditional prose narrative. The ambiguities and ironies often cancel one another out and insist on the meaninglessness or futility, if not merely the impossibility, of understanding. Yambo Ouologuem's *Bound to Violence (Le devoir de violence)* (1968) and Wilson Harris's *Palace of the Peacock* (1960) are examples of this kind.

7. *The short story.* The short story, on the other hand, is a particularly modern conception and did not gain recognition as an important literary form until the last half of the nineteenth century. It is similar to the novel in all characteristics except that it limits itself to a single, complete episode and makes up in compression and intensity for what it lacks in scope and breadth of vision. The short story is an outgrowth of the modern concern for the examination of artistic materials and forms. In it we see the basic unit or building block of the novel isolated for examination.

It is almost impossible for the novelist to succeed with the larger constructional problem of unifying various episodes into a harmonious and meaningful whole unless the episodes themselves are successful in form and expression. The short story is therefore the logical place to begin a serious study of narrative fiction as it offers almost all the characteristics of the novel but permits a simplified pattern of construction and a limited number of elements (characters, actions, setting, etc.).

Aesthetic Elements of Narrative Fiction

In order to take up the question of construction in narrative fiction, it is best to review the basic features or aspects of a work which must always be taken into account, and then examine the various devices and techniques under each as they appear. After all, there is a finite and definable number of possible constructional elements or techniques which make up any work of literature, and a satisfactory analysis requires only the recognition of the author's actual choice together with an appreciation of the particular way in which he or she has woven them together.

In a very real way it is like appreciating the effectiveness of an outfit of clothing chosen from a known wardrobe for a particular purpose. The questions to ask are: Is the outfit suitable in cut, colour and texture for the occasion? Are the individual elements of the costume as well suited to each other as they are to the occasion? Are there other combinations of garments from the stock available that would have been more suitable? In the case of narrative fiction the initial choices of the author have to do with the following:

Conceptual Elements (surface facts)
actions — events and their sequence of occurrence
character — agents of motivation and of reaction to events
setting — points of reference for character and action

Mode of Narration (expressive devices)
point of view — focus of the narrator's knowledge and values
style — focus of the author's attitudes and values

The conceptual elements express both subject matter and theme while the method of narration is wholly concerned with suggesting or indicating the theme. For example, the events themselves constitute a major part of the subject matter, but the order in which they are revealed and their relationship one to the other helps to focus attention on the main preoccupations of the author.

Action — the Ordering of Events

There are a number of ways in which events can be ordered or interrelated but in each case the relationship must be logical. Narrative fiction is not made up of a series of incidents which merely follow one another in time. The laws of cause and effect govern their relationship and provide a logical plot progression.

E. M. Forster makes a distinction between 'The queen died and then the king died' and 'The queen died and the king died of grief'. The first is merely the recounting of an incident taken from life, the second constitutes a plot because it clearly distinguishes cause and effect, the motivating force and its outcome. In the modern novel where the logical progression of action is often fragmented, logic still prevails, but of a kind which is usually associated with poetic composition.

1. *Chronology.* Chronological sequences are often thought to be the natural and most realistic way to tell a story: that is, recounting events in the order of their supposed happening according to the conventions of time as measured by a clock. But narrative fiction is not always an actual record of what really happened. In the first place, events are fictionalised by the author's selection and re–creation even if they were once real; in the second, a great many literary events are wholly imaginary. In any case, it is not the events themselves which are important, but rather the idea or theme which they exemplify.

In order to express a desired quality, emotion or attitude, the author may wish to alter the strict sequence of clock time. For example, a very different focus of attention can be obtained in literature by opening a story with an indication of its outcome. If the reader knows what is going to happen from the beginning, he or she immediately understands that the significance of the tale is to be found elsewhere and will concentrate on how or why such an ending should have come about. In the same way, suspense can be created by beginning a story at a high point of the action or by withholding a sequence of action in order to arouse curiosity and reader–participation. The missing information can be made more striking and effective if introduced later to reinforce another action or idea by being placed near it.

The way chronology is used, therefore, indicates a great deal about the author's focus of interest or preoccupation in the story. If strictly chronological, the author is obviously concerned with creating an illusion of documentary reality for one reason or another; if the events and episodes are shifted about in time, it is to focus attention on some aspect of the plot other than its outcome, and if an episode from a distant and seemingly unrelated past is introduced as though it were happening in a present time (a 'time machine' or 'flash–back' so–called), it is to give some relevant information as to character formation or motive on the one hand, or to refocus attention towards a resulting pattern of ideas on the other.

Ralph Ellison's *Invisible Man* (1952) is a good example of strict chronology, except that the whole story is told by the narrator after he has lived through all the experience. We already know that he has opted out of society and then we relive those experiences in their natural sequence in order to learn why. James Baldwin's *Go Tell It on the Mountain* (1953), on the other hand, tells the story of a boy growing up, but in order to understand the experiences he undergoes and the pressures brought to bear on his life, the author provides several flash–backs to show us what kinds of people his mother and stepfather really are and what forces shaped their personalities. In this way we get a wider historical and sociological perspective on those immediate pressures which affect the central character's life.

2. *Logical sequence of events (cause and effect).* A structural pattern in which events are ordered according to their logical relationship is merely an alternative to a chronological arrangement. As an author determines a strategy for expressing theme and subject matter, the need to join one episode with another depends on their interrelationship, their association with a central theme, and the logic of the story as a whole, not on the order in which events might actually have taken place. Even in everyday life events do not necessarily have a direct relationship with those that are close to them in time, and, since fiction concentrates even more heavily on the logical and thematic relationships between events or episodes, an extra–chronological order of events is to be expected.

Only significant incidents are included in fiction and they are so arranged as to lead the reader to a particular understanding of the action. The question to ask is: What understanding does the order of events lead to — what is the pattern of logical relationships? The best method to follow is to evaluate the work, episode by episode in outline form, jotting down each relationship as you see it, and before long a pattern will appear.

The Guide (1958) by R. K. Narayan is a good case in point. It is the story of a disarmingly roguish tourist guide who seduces a beautiful dancer away from her husband and makes a celebrity of her just as he had conned or gulled his tourist–clients up to that point. He loses the fortune he made from her success, goes to jail and ironically becomes one of India's great holy men after his release. The novel, however, is not told chronologically, but rather opens with Raju, the hero, coming out of jail. Through the course of the work he narrates his past and the circumstances which led up to his imprisonment. Interwoven with the narration of his past worldliness is the progress towards sainthood through the simple life he is leading at present, detached from worldly concerns and dedicated to the good of the people around him. At every stage in the story, scenes from his past contrast sharply with those of his present life and a point is made which would otherwise have been lost if the plot had been arranged in the order of the actual happenings. Raju's clever manipulation of people and situations for his own ends in the past are both exciting and amusing. They add interest to the story, but the theme is discovered in the comparisons of that past with his present peace and contentment in a life of spirituality and service to others. The rearrangement of the chronology accounts for the focus of interest and effectiveness of expression in the novel.

3. *The well–made plot.* A more highly developed form of organisation is to create an aesthetic or constructional pattern that has a logic of its own, and is at the same time tied to the logical sequence of the plot incidents themselves. In the latter half of the nineteenth century, a form of popular drama known as 'the well–made play' came into fashion. It is a useful concept by which to measure basic structures found in novels. The well–made plot, like the classical models from which it is derived, always contained an introduction, a development section of rising action, a crisis or catastrophe, a resolution or falling action,

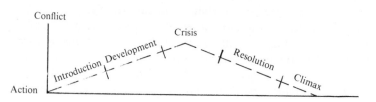

and a climax or unravelling of the original conflict that had set the plot in motion. The effect is to organise subject matter into a logical and expressive structure which also has the benefit of a balanced and satisfying external pattern or shape. A well–made plot can always be represented graphically since its outline is so pure and unity as well as decorum are so essential to it.

Of course, the well–made plot is only possible when dealing with a subject matter and theme which can be expressed by a linear or straightforward development of events: because A happened, B followed, and because B happened, C followed, etc. The logic of events in a well–made plot is a pattern of progressive consequences, of cause and effect, of expectation and fulfilment. It is largely an aesthetic concern and appeals to a delight in abstract patterns of construction as well as in the satisfactory expression of theme.

Narrative fiction need not have an obvious, external pattern or shape such as the graph above, or that of a circle or an hourglass as is also common, but the presence of such forms calls attention to structure as an obvious and major feature in the communication of meaning.

4. *Discontinuous episodes.* Rather than a cumulative effect built up by a sequence of episodes or actions leading inevitably through the development and unravelling of a conflict, it is also possible to organise a narrative using discontinuous or seemingly unconnected episodes which are, however, linked by thematic or other means.

In Jonathan Swift's *Gulliver's Travels* (1726), for example, we have four separate and independent sections, each a voyage to some exotic and wonderful place. The first is an island where Gulliver is many times the size of the tiny inhabitants and he looks down on their insignificance, laughing at their petty affairs and institutions. The reader, however, sees that they behave pretty much as do the English of Swift's time. The second voyage is to a land of giants where Gulliver is tiny, but here he is repelled by the unpleasant physical characteristics of the people, their rough, oily skin, stinking breath and lascivious sexuality. Of course, the giants are nothing more than normal human beings and their grotesqueness is an exaggeration caused by Gulliver's changed point of view. In this section the satire concentrates on the physical nature of human beings but the relation of the land of giants to England is also seen in the conversations Gulliver has with the King of Brobdingnag who is horrified by Gulliver's proud descriptions of his homeland, its conduct and institutions.

The third voyage finds the hero on a floating island where supposedly learned men are completely occupied with impractical and ridiculous knowledge, completely divorced from the real affairs of everyday life. Here Swift gives a satirical view of the learning of the day, just as he had done earlier with political or social institutions and the animal nature of mankind. The fourth voyage is to yet another island where horse–like beings live an enviable life of sweet reason and simple goodness while creatures resembling men live as beasts, wallowing in their own filth and stupidity.

The point throughout is that each culture is meant to be compared and contrasted with the England of the period, although the comparison is never stated, and the reader is indirectly challenged to re–examine his or her assumptions about political conventions, social aspirations, the animal nature of man, the relevance of intellect and reason to everyday life, and the practice of public and private morality. On a secondary level the discontinuous episodes do relate to a multi–faceted theme of satirical intention, but only when analysed and appreciated by the reader.

5. *Allegorical structures.* Perhaps the most complex method of plot organisation is that which combines the concern for external shape or form which is emphasised by the well–made plot and the analysis of thematic relationships which link discontinuous episodes. In this sort of plot structure the interrelationship of themes forms a recognisable pattern which has meaning in its own right. There are two major kinds of such compositions: the allegorical and the mythic.

Since allegory as a historical genre has already been discussed there is little more to add, except to distinguish between works in which the surface action is so unrealistic and unremarkable that the secondary level gains our immediate attention and those in which secondary levels are very much submerged or hidden. *Pilgrim's Progress* (1678), for example, by John Bunyan is a work in which the characters and situations are obviously mere personifications of abstract ideas. One is only interested in the surface level in so far as it provides a vehicle for the secondary level. The hero, Christian, is not so much a real human being as he is a concept on legs, as it were, and the point of the story is to dramatise the doctrine of salvation. Warned by Evangelist, Christian flees the City of Destruction and encounters much difficulty on his journey to the Celestial City. He meets such characters as the giant, Despair, for example, and passes through Vanity Fair, but he also receives help and support from such characters as Faithful and Hopeful along the way.

On the other hand, there are allegorical fictions such as Herman Melville's *Moby Dick* (1851) in which the surface action is both real and believable. On this level the novel is a whacking good story of whaling in the nineteenth century, but there are also obvious implications in the novel that there is more to it than just that. In fact, the characters, images and events can be interpreted as being representative of the qualities, conditions of mind and states of being which turn the story into a tale of obsessive conflict between men in society and the existence of evil in the universe. The secondary level is no less true or significant than that of the hero's quest for salvation in *Pilgrim's Progress*, but it is far less obtrusive and certainly more artful or aesthetically pleasing. One takes pleasure in both levels of narration as well as the relationship between them.

6. *Myth patterns.* The idea of a mythic plot can be viewed in several lights, but essentially it is a pattern of events or relationships which parallels a known or recognisable cycle and reassures or satisfies readers because of its natural associations. The generative cycle of a day or year provides a very elementary example; that which is born (comes into being), develops, declines, dies and is reborn in a subsequent cycle. It is only a short step to other kinds of resurrection myths and the stories which imitate or parallel that pattern tend to share the authority of their models.

In fact, common patterns or motifs which have great psychological appeal are usually embodied in historical myths or legends which are exploited over and over again because of their inherent authority. The jealousy and rivalry of children and parents in small European families is now spoken of in terms of the myth of Oedipus, a Greek hero who is said to have killed his father unknowingly and begotten children upon his own mother. The story strikes a European reader, at any rate, as one which is entirely possible since the confusion of sexual roles and antagonism between fathers and sons is now accepted as being natural among that particular group of people. The tale is particularly shocking because the latent desires are actually carried out. In the classical play, *Oedipus Rex*, by Sophocles, the pattern is made acceptable by leaving Oedipus ignorant of the relationships, rendering him heroic or worthy of our sympathy, and having him accept responsibility and punishment for his actions even though fated by the gods to carry them out. We are meant to identify ourselves with the actions and yet distance ourselves from them: There but for the grace of God go I. The known pattern of events is thus incorporated in a work of literature and, at this remove from everyday reality, we are reconciled to the tendencies of our own lives as well as to the very dangers of human desires and relationships.

Sin, punishment, expiation and regeneration constitute another acceptable pattern that calms and reassures the European. The first two elements are present in *Oedipus Rex*, the second pair in the sequel, *Oedipus at Colonus*, in which the hero is raised to a superhuman state of spiritual power before he dies and joins the immortals. The same pattern is present in many disguises in the Bible, but perhaps best known in Exodus where the Israelites, after their release from bondage in Egypt, are condemned to wander in the desert for forty years before they enter into the promised land because they fell away from the proper worship of Jehovah.

A modern novel such as John Steinbeck's *The Grapes of Wrath* (1939) makes good use of the pattern by incorporating its outline or scheme of events exactly, thus adding the force of the original with all its associations to what is being said. In *The Grapes of Wrath* a group of poor farmers, through no fault of their own, are forced to leave the land of their fathers in the middle part of the United States because of economic changes and pressures. They decide to travel to California, where they believe they will find honest work and a life of comparative ease and plenty. Their trip across the plains and deserts of America is a story of great courage and hardship, but instead of reward and a promised land, they find far worse exploitation and oppression in California than that which forced them to leave their homes in the first place. In Steinbeck's story, the central figures have not sinned, but the sin for which they suffer exists in social and economic institutions. Instead of a spiritual theme (man's relationship to his God) Steinbeck focusses on a social and economic problem, man and his relationship to his fellows. In doing so he brings in the moral values and certainties of the Exodus myth by using its narrative pattern or outline as a basis for the new plot. The recognition of such patterns and uses, wherever they are present, is an important element in understanding the nature and force of a literary composition.

Not all myth patterns are complete narratives, however, and some are difficult to recognise at first. For example, the appeal of a fairy story such as *Sleeping Beauty* seems to come from the alternation of good and evil which plays a large part in the success of the work. The unhappy king and queen who have no child are finally blessed with a daughter, but as they celebrate, an evil fairy places a curse (death) on the child, which is then rendered less harmful but not altogether cancelled out by a good fairy. The parents try to alter the child's fate, but the princess does prick her finger on a spindle at the age of eighteen, does fall asleep for a hundred years, and a brave, handsome young prince does penetrate the barrier of forest that grew up around the castle to awaken her with a kiss. Good eventually triumphs after a certain amount of adversity, and an aesthetically pleasing rhythm is set up within the story of alternating joy and woe which is particularly effective.

But there is an even stronger mythic element in the narrative, a pattern that imitates a natural and personal sequence of events in everyday life. What happens to the princess is said to happen to every human female whose mortality is offset by the promise of sexuality and reproduction. On reaching physical maturity, a man comes along, penetrates the physical barrier and awakens the girl sexually to a fuller and more functional life as an adult woman and mother. The fairy story contains a mythic projection or fictionalised representation of a conventional pattern. It builds a narrative around a single incident or episode of experience as it is seen by a given group of people.

A last example of mythic pattern in fiction is the use of a

traditional rite of passage as the organising principle or basis of plot. A rite of passage is a ceremony which celebrates a change of status, usually from childhood to adulthood. In social terms among Europeans much used to be made of twenty–first birthdays for boys and coming–out parties for girls. In spiritual terms the Christian sacrament of Confirmation proclaims that passage as does the Jewish Barmitzvah, but in the traditional cultures of Africa, for example, such a rite is more communal in nature, and sexual as well. The individual is prepared by the community to take his or her place as a worker and a parent. Camara Laye's *African Child* (*L'enfant noir*, 1953) is a story about the education and development of a boy who begins by being at one with his people and ends separated from them. The novel opens with descriptions of the intimate life of a family and clan, easy intercourse with the supernatural, and communal harmony in a rural setting. The boy is given a European education and by the middle of the story, which centres on a description of his initiation into adulthood, he is already different from his fellows, set apart from them and their lives. He goes to the city for more schooling and on returning discovers that he has lost all sense of closeness with the community. A friend of his dies mysteriously, his illness being far too advanced to be cured by either traditional or European medicine. Finally the hero leaves for Europe to further his studies with a map of the Paris underground railway in his pocket to guide him in that strange unnatural world. The point is that instead of being reborn to full membership in the community through its traditional rite of passage which he undergoes at the very mid–point of the work, he dies or is separated from it because of his initiation into European culture. As in the earlier example, an identifiable pattern of human experience provides the basic structure for a narrative fiction; in recognising its presence, we appreciate the significance of the work more fully.

7. *Mixed methods of construction.* In all cases of plot structure discussed so far, it is easy to see that the method or methods employed by authors are strong indicators of major areas of interest and meaning within individual works. The thing that has not been pointed out, however, is the common practice of

compounding methods of construction. For example, in a three–decker Victorian novel such as *Middlemarch* (mentioned above) we find the landed gentry, professional townspeople and yeoman farmers of a particular place represented in separate yet parallel plots which revolve around the emotional lives and values of three heroines who are far from identical in character. In fact, the stories are not repetitions of one another, but variations on a single theme in which the different facets or aspects of similar actions and relationships might be played out. Such a complete rendering of experience could not be achieved within a single plot, however fully developed.

Another form of complex plot mechanism involves the use of sub–plot which was first developed in Renaissance drama. A sub–plot is a frank repetition or minor echo of incidents and relationships contained in the main plot which is particularly useful in emphasising and reinforcing thematic concerns. Of course, both the Victorian triple–decker and sub–plotting rely on logical sequences of cause and effect, but the multiplication of similar events and relationships through thematic parallels comes close to that of discontinuous episodes.

The two modes are not incompatible, however, and can be mixed in the same work with excellent effect. Nellie Harper Lee's *To Kill a Mocking Bird* (1960) is a good case in point. The story centres on two young children in the American South who learn about tolerance, kindness and human understanding through a series of separate experiences. There are a number of complete and discontinuous episodes, each with its own lesson for the children. There is also a continuing or repeated involvement with a strange and frightening young man who has locked himself away from human contact in a neighbouring house for many years. He comes out only at night and intrudes on the lives of the children. In between any two discontinuous episodes or object lessons, there is a chapter which involves the mysterious man, but these chapters make up a continuous story or plot with its own climax and resolution. The independent episodes are brought together by the presence of the hero and heroine as well as by a similarity of themes just as in a picaresque novel, and the connected sequence of chapters which centre on the mysterious man is tied in with the others in the same way. In the end both methods of construction come together to deliver up the same theme, while the novel gains in diversity and interest because of the varied constructional patterns.

Form — Outward Shape of Construction

In order to come to terms with the method of construction in a given work and to appreciate its effect on the subject matter and theme, the form or outward shape of the author's divisions of the work into parts should also be considered. Novels, and to some extent short stories, are subdivided into sections. Every identifiable part acts as an independent unit in relation to the whole, and each should also be examined closely to see how that unit functions internally. The question here is one of recognising subdivisions, their internal composition and relative inter-relationships. Narrative fiction is most often subdivided into books, volumes, or parts, as well as chapters and sections, and the constituent units may or may not be uniform in construction.

There are two general methods of creating form or shape in literature. The first is to allow the subject matter to dictate the size or length of divisions. The author merely writes as much as he or she needs to about each event in order to express the theme. The second method is to adjust the natural shape of events and so create a more regular or ideal sense of balance and symmetry. In the case of organic growth or development, each section of a narrative will be as long as it needs to be and will fall in sequence by virtue of logic and the requirements of total effect. In the same way the outline or form of the plot will develop as it needs to, without special attention to the creation of architectural symmetry and balanced patterns. The relative length of subdivisions will either be an indication of emphasis and the importance of the material in the scheme of the whole work, or a function of the subject's complexity and the difficulty encountered in expressing it clearly and completely.

If Camara Laye spends several chapters telling us of his young hero's idealised but unconsummated love for Marie in *African Child* and the mysterious death of his friend, something central to the theme is being suggested. In this case it is the unnatural situation the hero's European education has led him into. On the other hand, the discussion of mythic structures in the paragraphs above is given a good deal more space than other patterns because such structures are more complex and harder to explain, not because they are more vital than other kinds of structural features. In both cases the material is important, as the space given to them shows, but the reasons differ. It is not difficult to come to a correct conclusion about those reasons since they are reflected in the relationship of the part to other parts and to the whole.

The formal development of a narrative, however, as opposed to an organic one, will alter and trim the external shape of units and their relationships within the larger whole in order to obtain an elegant and more mathematical pattern or design. For example, a formal construction might be divided into twenty–five chapters of roughly equal length and each group of five might be interconnected to form a major subdivision of the action, each corresponding to one of the five–fold divisions of a well–made plot. To do this the author would have to place major turning points in chapters 5, 10, 15 and 20, the crisis in chapter 12, and the climax, perhaps, in chapter 22. Such a formal construction calls attention to itself as an aesthetic feature and invites admiration for the author's ability to create a living fictional world in which a viable theme is well expressed within the additional restrictions of a limiting and formal composition.

This is not to say, however, that a formal composition is in any way preferable to or better than an organic one. An author chooses one or the other method of construction according to the effect he or she desires and the suitablity of the method to the subject matter and theme. Both students and critics are expected to recognise and evaluate the effectiveness of the composition in relation to the subject matter and theme.

First of all, one looks at the subdivisions indicated by the author. It is best to analyse them in outline form, one at a time. The questions to ask are: What happens in each sub–section and what is its effect on the whole story? Looking at the outline, one can then make larger deductions and generalisations about unifying features and interrelationships — such as, for example, describing the outer form or architectural shape of *To Kill a Mocking Bird*, discussed above. The close analysis of structure is not a mere mechanical exercise which destroys our enjoyment, but rather a valid tool which helps us to understand how the author's effects were achieved.

Character

So far I have spoken of action and the ordering of events, as though character either does not exist or is not pertinent. It is, of course, not possible to have action without characters; events are determined by character and character is also defined by events. The conception and presentation of character, therefore, has as great an effect on the significance of a work as the selection of events and their ordering. Techniques of presentation offer little difficulty, in fact, so long as one remembers that indirect methods are just as useful as direct ones.

A character in a novel or play is not a real human being and has no life outside the literary composition, however well the illusion of reality has been created by the author. A character is a mere construction of words meant to express an idea or view of experience and must be considered in relation to other features of the composition, such as action and setting, before its full significance can be appreciated. An author first conceives of a fictional framework, then selects and organises incidents from the random and shapeless accidental details of life according to an interpretative principle, in order to build up a coherent pattern and express a theme.

In the same way, elements of character must be selected and combined within a coherent mode or convention of presentation: tragic, comic, epic, satirical, romantic, realistic/naturalistic, dialectic or absurdist. Since each mode or convention has a distinct view of human experience, characters are generally created according to the relevant needs of these aspects, views or outlooks. For example, tragedy involves an investigation of desires and motives, and tragic characterisation centres on the psychological study of destructive inner conflict and frustration. A dialectical novel, on the other hand, requires more loosely representative characters — voices, as it were — which will advance an argument or thesis plausibly, but not vitally realistic and complex personalities with whom the reader will necessarily become involved. Stylisation and distortion is inevitable in the creation of literary characters and it may be necessary to control or limit the reader's knowledge of a given figure or figures. But then, we cannot know another person perfectly or completely in real life either, rather we see only those characteristics which are brought out by immediate circumstances or situations.

1. *Methods of characterisation.* The rendering or creation of character involves far more than the commonplace ideas of direct description and reported dialogue: what the character says and does or what others say about him. Indirect methods are more effective and useful. Many of them are derived from the ways in which we normally perceive and understand human character: by direct observation of people in real life, self–observation and also knowledge of inherited or traditional literary types. Of course, direct statements of character analysis and motive are often stated by authors or narrators, but more subtle methods are also used in every work of fiction.

The simple fact of choosing a name is a very telling indication of character. Take for example the dried–up old maid in Virginia Woolf's *Mrs Dalloway* (1925), who is called Miss Kilman, or Mr Jaggers, a jolting (abrupt and disconcerting) and jagged (sharp–edged and ruthless) lawyer in Charles Dickens's *Great Expectations* (1861). Names can also allude to prototypes in earlier literature or history as in the case of Stephen Daedalus (the Christian saint, Stephen, and Daedalus, the artificer, from Greek mythology) in James Joyce's *A Portrait of the Artist as a Young Man* (1916). Names can also suggest the allegorical (representative) nature of a character as in Everyman, Fellowship and Good Deeds from the medieval play, *Everyman*.

Repeated mannerisms, such as oddities of speech and movement or an obsession which is peculiar to one figure alone, also tend to characterise people as do their clothes or possessions. The faces and physiques of individuals are generally explicit indications of character or personality and an author may even include physical elements which have conventional associations or meanings in order to build up the desired qualities of personality. In European tradition, for example, red hair is associated with a passionate temperament; high–domed foreheads with intelligence, etc. Dialogue and conduct, whether directly presented or reported through another consciousness, is a most powerful technique for characterisation, but here again it is not merely the fact or detail that is effective, but rather the deductions that the reader comes to concerning the unspoken and unseen well–springs of character. The personality and value system of characters can often be suggested through carefully controlled word choice and habitual turns of phrase. A hesitant and indecisive personality, for example, can be established by the exclusive use of modal auxiliaries (might have, could have, etc.) and piling up qualifying phrases in sentence after sentence.

Characterisation through association with physical setting is another effective method for authors who wish to imply and suggest qualities of personality, while the use of figurative language and patterns of images associated with different characters is still another indirect way of investing a fictional creation with character. The use of the wild, wind–swept heath, for example, in Emily Brontë's *Wuthering Heights* (1847) helps to emphasise the passionate nature of Catherine and substantiate the demonic character of Heathcliffe. The recurrence of such imagery as the sun (reigning planet), the rose (lord of flowers) and the lion (king of beasts) in Shakespeare's *Henry IV, Part I* (1598) testifies by constant association with Prince Hal that he is really worthy of the crown.

Rendering the inner life of characters, on the other hand, requires more complex methods, especially if the author wishes to retain the illusion of reality. Journals, diaries and letters were used in the first novels and the direct interior monologue borrowed from the soliloquy of Renaissance drama was also employed. At first the monologue was only reported by the narrator, but later the idea of a character analysing his or her thoughts became fashionable and, finally, stream of consciousness techniques were perfected in which an unbroken flow of thought or awareness in the waking mind is carefully re–created.

Take for example the following passage from *Go Tell It on the Mountain* which describes the quality of the hero's consciousness or mental processes during the spiritual possession of a religious experience. The vision of his parents is particularly revealing as it shows us his unconscious awareness of the actual relationship which exists between him and them as he sees it. The colours scarlet and white in this context are conventional representations of sin and purity.

Ah, down! — what was he searching here, all alone in darkness? But now he knew, for irony had left him, that he was searching something, hidden in the darkness, that must be found. He would die if it was not found; or, he was dead already, and would never again be joined to the living, if it was not found.

And the grave looked so sad and lonesome.

In the grave where he now wandered — he knew it was the grave, it was so cold and silent, and he moved in icy mist — he found his mother and his father, his mother dressed in scarlet, his father dressed in white. They did not see him: they looked backward, over their shoulders, at a cloud of witnesses.

(Baldwin, p. 228)

It is also possible to render the inner life of characters through external action and dialogue, or even through figurative language, imagery and setting (see the example from *Mrs Dalloway* above, p. 35), but it is better to look at a work you are now studying and see the devices at work in context than to discuss such techniques in the abstract.

2. *Degree of character development.* Regardless of what methods are used in characterisation, all characters are not developed to the same degree or depth. For the purpose of a particular plot and theme, the author may need a character or characters of great psychological complexity, or, on the other hand, characters who are of little interest in themselves but who represent a particular attribute or quality. E. M. Forster's distinction between round and flat characterisations is useful here. The first include those fictional creations who have complex many-faceted personalities and an independent inner life which itself invites our interest, while flat characters are those who exhibit only one character trait or motivation and whose main claim to our interest is in the actions they perform or the quality they represent. The point to remember is that fictional characters cannot be rigidly divided into one or the other group. As with all pairs of critical terms, flat and round indicate the limits of possibility in characterisation; there is an almost infinite range of combinations and points in between. One does not ask: Is this character flat or round?, but rather: How fully developed is the characterisation and what effect does this have on the author's conception of life experience or on his expression of subject matter and theme?

Since the question is relative, one of degree rather than an absolute (either/or) proposition, one way to answer it is to jot down the qualities of the actual characterisation which belong under each heading and weigh them on balance. Such and such a character, for example, is rounded out in so many ways within the work and flattened in so many others. Another method is to make comparisons with other characters from the same work in order to demonstrate an understanding of where the figure in question belongs on the scale or range of possible characterisations. Such and such a character, for example, is more rounded than characters X and Y but flatter than Z.

A common misconception is to attach critical value to characterisations of one type as opposed to another. Students often believe that fully developed characters are somehow superior to flat renderings. A formal ballgown by its very nature is not superior to a bathing costume, except as the appropriate dress for an important dance. In the same way the most successful rendering of character is the one best suited to the realisation of an author's vision of life. Flat or little–developed characters are often required in fiction to direct attention towards action and ideas rather than psychological development and depth of inner experience. The whole range of allegorical characters comes to mind, for example, as do the prolific comic conceptions of Charles Dickens or the main characters in contemporary African fiction in English who are often only slightly individualised so that they better represent a social generality.

In the same way the idea of character development as a question of change or growth of personality and awareness is often misunderstood. Both round and flat characters are equally capable of changing their natures, depending on what happens to them, but neither type is required to undergo such a development in order to be considered a successful creation. A stereotype of evil, for example, may or may not reform as a consequence of some unique occurrence, while a fully delineated or developed creation may, for one reason or another, never grow or develop, although the main characters in realistic narratives sometimes do.

The deciding factor is always the effect to be achieved within the fiction. One particular plot and theme may require a certain combination of character development and degree of self–revelation or change. A different plot and theme will require another. The reader and critic should recognise the actual degree of development which does exist as well as its relation to the subject matter and theme. The more fully developed characters will always draw our attention to inner conflict and psychological complexities, while the flatter creations will direct attention away from themselves and towards the ideas and forces at work in that particular fiction.

3. *Archetypes and stereotypes.* All fictional characters, as we have seen from the above, are verbal stylisations of real people, but there are degrees and kinds of stylisation which distinguish one group of characters from another. The recognition and identification of such usage in a given piece of literature tells us a great deal about the forces operating in that fictional world and leads to a fuller appreciation and interpretation of the work. There are, for example, archetypal characterisations (models or typical specimens of character) which often provide the basis and prototype of individual creations; the hero, villain, rebel and seeker are all types of men who are seen in relation to their fate, passion, desires, heredity or environment. In European literature archetypes of women, on the other hand, tend to be seen in terms of their function or effect on others: the virgin (victim or bride), mother (nourisher or protector) and witch (source of knowledge or destroyer).

Other kinds of archetypes are peculiar to one or another of the conceptual modes or philosophic views of literature. For example, in romantic fiction there are satanic heroes, demon lovers, innocent victims and destroying temptresses. Still other kinds of archetypes may represent qualities rather than relationships and they are very often individualised as paired opposites or conditions representing virtues and vices: for example, wealth and poverty, etc. Archetypes of recognised social figures and professional classes also exist: for example, the social climber, the absent–minded professor, the cynical aristocrat, the unscrupulous lawyer or the depraved lecher, but at this point the idea of archetype, a model or abstract essence of a given characterisation, is likely to be submerged in stereotype, a fixed and familiar characterisation which may or may not reflect reality, yet fulfils an established function.

The difference between the two is that a character who can be identified by archetype is capable of development, of growing or diminishing in stature according to his or her reaction to experience, while a stereotyped character never rises above the accepted role and associations of his kind. An author may even show great skill in creating an interesting variant, but it is the basic type, none the less, which operates in the work through the individual. Stereotypes are particularly effective when attention is being directed to action and patterns of experience, as in a broadly comic conception of life, while the great archetypes are more common to a tragic view and psychological investigation. In the case of the archetype, it is the individuality of the character which predominates, a quality of uniqueness and force of personality which communicates itself, while the universality and representational nature of the figure remains a secondary consideration.

4. *Caricatures.* Beyond stereotypes one comes to frank distortions of character known as caricatures, generally used for satirical effect. Caricature should be familiar to everyone from newspaper cartoons in which the exaggeration of a single feature of a well–known personage's face or figure dominates the representation and comes to stand for that person. General de Gaulle's nose, Konrad Adenauer's wrinkles or Richard Nixon's hooded eyes come easily to mind. Caricatures are immediately recognisable although they are not faithful and accurate portraits of their subjects. They are almost always funny because of their grotesqueness and the sharp contrast they make with reality. On the other hand, they can also be cruel and unjust if the features chosen are already beyond reasonable normality, for example, or not really representative of the subject at all.

Within the arsenal of literary techniques there are even certain types of recognisable or established caricatures which have acquired historical authority. During the English Renaissance, for example, the Comedy of Humours was founded on the idea that individuals are motivated by a dominant humour or quality of character. For this reason literary creations were sometimes denied realistic complexity of personality and presented as possessing an exaggerated obsession or characteristic. Within this genre a work might be peopled by characters who exhibit nothing but overblown aspects of avarice and covetousness, for example, as in Ben Jonson's *Volpone* (1607, acted 1605). Among the figures in the play we find the main character, Volpone (a name derived from the Italian word for fox), his servant, Mosca (fly), and the merchant, Corvino (crow). The plot turns on their concerted efforts to dupe one another of worldly goods.

During the Restoration, when the manners and mores of the middle classes were being further scrutinised and exposed, many works appeared in which caricatures and stereotypes rather than fully developed characters were used. Each figure presented some consistent form of vain or foolish behaviour as in the case of John Horner, the seducer, and Mr Pinchwife, the over–cautious husband, whose innocent country wife provides the catalyst for the action of *The Country Wife* (1675) by William Wycherley.

The effectiveness of caricatures and stereotypes is not limited to comedy alone, however, and such characterisations also figure in the dialectic argument of novels of purpose (thesis novels). However, caricature in narrative fiction is almost always associated with deflation or inversion of actual human conduct. The exaggeration of caricature produces a parody or travesty of everyday life which succeeds in amusing and instructing us in so far as it is able to reduce and ridicule the assumed stature or dignity of individuals by exploding pretentiousness and exposing the sub–human quality of man's folly or vice.

Setting

Whatever conception of character and action may exist in a work of literature, those characters and actions must be located with reference to time and place; setting is a major factor in the formulation of subject matter and a direct influence on the expression of theme. As in the case of the other factors, however, setting need not be realistic, nor, in fact, even physical. Historical time (past, present or future) is very effective for certain narratives and an accurate geographical location advisable, but it is also possible to set a fiction in some vague undetermined time, omitting historical references altogether in order to achieve a sense of timelessness and universality. Physical setting may be localised in a particular and known place or an unspecified and unfamiliar region, depending on the author's particular need. Each choice, however, indicates the aim or end of the work, and the analysis of setting in relation to character and action is always revealing.

In fact, setting need not even be physical in terms of time and space, but may well be constituted of psychological or moral conditions which are common to a given time, place or set of circumstances. For example, when Arthur Miller wrote about the individual in conflict with the conformist pressures of society he chose to place the action of *The Crucible* (1953) in the restrictive context of puritan New England during the seventeenth century. It was not the physical or temporal associations that he relied upon, but rather the moral conventions and sanctions of the period.

1. *Relation of setting to action and character.* Setting is usually a subordinate or secondary consideration in the formulation of subject matter; it is generally thought of as an adjunct to action or character, either by comparative association or contrast, but at times, setting rises to the status of a character and as such can condition or determine the action itself. At its most common-place level, setting merely provides a proper background, as in Ali Mazrui's *The Trial of Christopher Okigbo* (1971) which sets out to examine the relationship between the personal responsibility of the artist to his craft and his public responsibility to political commitment. The narrative is set in a very imaginative afterlife with specific characteristics which reflect the essence of African experience as understood by the author and which help to substantiate the action more vividly than a conventionally realistic setting could do.

It is also possible for setting to become a more active factor in narrative, as in ghost stories, for example, where setting characterises action. The scene may be just as haunted and scary as the action which takes place there, while shifts of scene (changes of setting) often signal a contrast or comparison between actions and/or character. Setting, of course, need not be consistent in a work of fiction and may shift from episode to episode as required by the subject matter and theme, just as characters who begin as caricatures may be further developed later on into more rounded conceptions and vice versa. The emphasis given to the description of setting usually makes it very clear whether or not the setting is merely a context for the action or has a larger significance in the expression of a given theme.

Setting may even dominate action and character, as in the case of Joseph Conrad's short story 'The Lagoon' (1898). Here, almost as much space is devoted to a physical description of the scene as to the action and characters, and the placing of the two men and dying women on a stilt–house in the middle of a forest–ringed, mirror–still lagoon under a star–lit sky gives a physical picture which reinforces the isolation of the central figure and his passionate nature within a vitally alive yet impassive universe.

Not only is the setting an active force in the story, but the language which the author uses to describe it also indicates a system of values or judgements through patterns of verbal figures, images and musical devices. A moral view is being suggested as to the nature of the universe against which the action of the narrative is measured. The jungle is natural and alive, but unpredictable as well as unknowable. Its will to life and growth generates conflict and destruction. The story then shows us that man has similar qualities and tendencies.

> The narrow creek was like a ditch: tortuous, fabulously deep; filled with gloom under the thin strip of pure and shining blue of the heaven. Immense trees soared up, invisible behind the festooned draperies of creepers. Here and there, near the glistening blackness of the water, a twisted root of some tall tree showed against the tracery of small ferns, black and dull, writhing and motionless, like an arrested snake. The short words of the paddlers reverberated loudly between the thick and sombre walls of vegetation. Darkness oozed out from between the trees, through the tangled maze of the creepers, from behind the great fantastic and unstirring leaves; the darkness, mysterious and invincible; the darkness scented and poisonous of impenetrable forests.
>
> (Conrad pp.188–9)

Setting is a very powerful feature of narrative fiction, particularly in the scope it allows for fine writing and an indication of moral values, as well as perceptions and observations on life in general. No criticism or appreciation of literature can be complete which does not recognise an author's use of setting alongside that of action and character.

Point of View

On a different level of operation altogether, the modes of narration (expressive devices) called point of view and style serve to place emphasis on and interpret the conceptual elements or surface facts (subject matter) already discussed, and thereby suggest the theme. Point of view, for example, is wholly concerned with theme, or more accurately with the relationship between subject matter and theme. Narrative fiction presupposes a narrator or story–teller, especially as it is published and read privately. The presence of a fictional narrator who acts as an intermediary filter to focus attention and who introduces his or her consciousness and values into the story as a moral touchstone is, in fact, the distinguishing feature of narrative fiction, setting it apart from the more direct presentation of drama or poetry.

Point of view actually operates on two different levels within a narrative. The first is structural and has a direct influence on the action by determining the degree of knowledge or understanding given to the reader. For example, we are bound to get a different account of an action from someone who was actually present than from someone who was not, and we must take this into account when evaluating the report. One does tend to rely on the word of a narrator who gives evidence of being a knowledgeable and balanced judge of human psychology, while preferring to make independent judgements based on actual evidence when the narrator appears to be unintelligent or biased in one way or another. The second level is stylistic or textural, and therefore indirect. Its aim is to give an indication of values or judgements which may stem from the fictional narrator, the author, or both. For example, the use of language, especially word–choice and imagery, to indicate values and attitudes when describing the setting of 'The Lagoon' as discussed above can be legitimately seen as an expression of narrative point of view through style. In every aspect of a work the author may use stylistic devices to suggest an attitude towards or evaluation of actions and characters. In the same way, of course, the attitudes and values of the fictional narrator can also be indicated.

It should be obvious, especially from the following discussion of point of view as a structural concern, that author and narrator do not necessarily share the same conception or philosophy of life experience. In fact, their views and attitudes may even contrast sharply at times. The point of view an author actually uses for a story helps to direct our response to the work as well as to suggest or express the story's theme.

1. *Narrative method.* The choice of narrators, and therefore of the kind of consciousness through which the story is filtered, has an enormous effect on the degree to which action or character is knowable or understood. There are only two possible modes of narration: direct or objective ones, in which the narrator merely presents details and facts without attempting to influence the reader's perception of them very much; and indirect or subjective ones, in which the narrator colours and shapes the presentation of details in such a way as to imply a definite attitude towards them.

In direct narration there is a tendency to identify the author with the fictional narrator. Even so, one should remember that this is not the actual writer with all of his or her personal concerns and preoccupations, but rather an abstracted and objective aspect of that complex personality. In the case of indirect narration it is even more important to distinguish the author from the narrator very clearly, because the particular subjectivity and emotional experience of the fictional narrator is the actual device that the author is using to colour or express his subject matter and theme.

2. *Direct narration: omniscient view.* It is possible to identify at least two different kinds of direct narration. The omniscient narrator is a god–like presence who stands aloof from the action but sees and knows everything there is to know about that fictional world. He knows of all past and present as well as future events, even those which happen at the same moment but in different places, and he knows what goes on in the mind of every character. Such a narrator is in no way bound by the normal limitations of human beings.

The omniscient narrator, however, is under no obligation to tell all, even though he knows all. The decision to withhold information is the author's and it is his function to choose and organise the action in order to direct our attention towards significant ideas or perceptions. Wole Soyinka, for example, introduces Monica Faseyi in chapter 3 of *The Interpreters* (1965) in the act of disgracing herself and her social–climbing husband at an Embassy reception by forgetting to buy gloves for the occasion and asking for palm wine after refusing champagne. At first the reader sees her as her husband fears others will see her, ill–bred and unsophisticated, but later it becomes clear that she is not a village bride caught out of her social depth, but rather a sophisticated foreigner, and her conduct is being used to expose her husband's colonial mentality in trying to be more English than the English.

In omniscient narrations the difference between what the narrator could tell us at any moment and what or when he actually reveals it is always a sure pointer to what the author holds to be important or significant. Whenever the reader is thrown back on his or her own deductions to fill in missing material or answer questions which have been raised, he is surely at the story's centre of interest.

3. *Indirect narration: personalised views.* An alternative to omniscient narration is the adoption of a personalised point of view: that is, a closer identification of the narrator with a particular human being. Often the term first–person, as opposed to third–person, narrative is used to distinguish a personalised point of view. The omniscient narrator normally uses third–person pronouns (he, she or they) in referring to characters and this tends to emphasise their separate existences. A first–person method (I or me), on the other hand, tends to identify the fictional characters with the narrator. The implications of the shift from omniscience to a personalised point of view should be obvious.

The third–person narrative suggests a greater distance between the reader and the fictional world presented to him, because the omniscient narrator is not subject to the same human limitations as the reader in perceiving action and character. Instead of passively accepting the omniscient narrator's view of things, the reader of a first–person narrative is invited to sympathise with both the narrator and the other characters, sharing with them their human limitations in perceiving and understanding the action. The reader may not be told about the past or personal motives of the other characters, but must deduce such infor-mation about everyone other than the narrator whose consciousness approximates his own. The omniscient point of view, however, is certainly more artificial and creates another kind of realism while it allows both a wider selection and combination of actions and a more direct (stated) penetration or analysis of character.

In the earliest novels the frank admission of an artificial point of view was common. In William Godwin's *Caleb Williams* (1794), for example, the first–person narrator and hero of the work explains his knowledge of Squire Falkland's past which takes up all of Book I as being partly the account of his friend and protector, Mr Collins, a retainer in Mr Falkland's household.

> I shall interweave with Mr Collins's story, various information which I afterwards received from other quarters, that I may give all possible perspicuity to the series of events. To avoid confusion in my narrative, I shall drop the person of Collins, and assume to be myself the historian of my patron. To the reader it may appear at first sight as if this detail of the preceding life of Mr Falkland were foreign to my history. Alas! I know from bitter experience that it is otherwise. My heart bleeds at the recollection of his misfortunes, as if they were my own. How can it fail to do so? To his story the whole fortune of my life was linked; because he was miserable, my happiness, my name, and my existence have been irretrievably blasted.
>
> (Godwin, p. 10)

Even in later Victorian times when authors were more interested in guiding their readers to experience fictional characters and actions from the inside, it was still common for a narrator to break into the fictional world and address the 'dear' or 'gentle reader' directly, either offering a judgement on a particularly dramatic scene or turn of plot, or asking the reader to disengage himself from the action and make an objective judgement about it.

It is not that first–person narratives give a more accurate or believable illusion of the real world, but they do invite the reader's direct participation in the action through close identification with the fictional narrator. First–person narration is perhaps better suited to a comic view of life because of its immediacy and closeness to reality in which limited human beings tell us their stories. Third–person narration is more appropriate to the expression of a heroic and tragic world because of its formality and distancing effect. A first–person hero cannot be altogether flat, but a third–person hero can.

As with setting and characterisation, however, narrative method need not be consistent within a given story or novel. It is perfectly normal for an author to slide from one point of view to another depending on the desired effect of the incident or character, and a good reader will note both the pattern of the changes and their effect in evaluating or analysing the work. For example, a first–person narrator may reveal a great deal about what is in his or her own mind and then introduce another character, action or description with the objectivity and detachment of a third–person point of view. In the same way a third–person narrator might shift from external description to internal examination of character and motive. In both cases the narrative as such, may also be interrupted by dramatically presented scenes of direct dialogue in which the narrator disappears altogether and we have the impression of actually being present, a party to the action or conversation.

The effect of such shifts and changes should be noted as they colour or influence our responses as well as determining our perception of character, action and setting. It may even be that a consistent pattern of associations is being created; for example, related figures and actions being seen from an external point of view and others from an internal one. Such a scheme could have a profound effect on the expression of theme.

4. *Indirect narration: persona.* Whereas direct narration emphasises the story and its significance is usually discovered in the observable relationships between action, character and setting, indirect narration is a far more complex and sophisticated technique, leading the reader's attention further and further away from the surface level of action towards an area of investigation or world of ideas that lies behind it. Indirect narration is essentially subjective: that is, the personality, views and values of the narrator are called into play and have a definite influence on the reader's response to the subject matter.

The distinguishing feature of indirect narration is a purposeful rendering of the narrator's character, and this may be either directly stated or hidden and merely suggested. In other words the normal techniques of characterisation may be employed, on the one hand, or the narrator's character may be deduced from the attitudes and values exhibited as the story is told, on the other. Because the narrator of a story told by indirect method has a definite or definable personality and name, he or she is often called a 'persona' in order to distinguish the technique from a more depersonalised variety of direct method narration.

The term 'persona' is borrowed from Latin, but it is used to refer to the mask or artificial personality of a fictional narrator through whom the author 'tells' the story. The persona of an indirect narration is less readily identifiable with the actual author than any story–teller in a direct method narration, even when the work pretends to be autobiographical, as in the case of Camara Laye's *African Child (L'enfant noir,* 1953) or James Joyce's *A Portrait of the Artist as a Young Man* (1916).

Because aesthetic and structural requirements of literature filter out and alter many of the random and unorganised incidents of real life, the actual person the author is and the one he represents himself to be in an autobiography are not necessarily the same. When discussing indirect narration, it is always better to speak of the persona or the narrator's character and attitudes rather than that of the author. However highly fictionalised the narration is, the effect of indirect narration is to increase the illusion of real life and the reader's direct involvement in it over that of a third–person direct narration. Indirect method concentrates, for the most part, on first–person narrative technique, depending on the extent to which the narrator is actually immersed in the action, and encourages the reader to accept the reality of the narration because it comes from an identifiable and recognisable source.

We are all used to being told stories about other people and incidents which, in the end, we must judge according to our understanding of the motives and values of the narrator, however omniscient and objective that narrator claims to be. Such a tale, when written, is accepted as real, but by virtue of being distanced from the reader's direct experience (that is, observed indirectly through a persona rather than perceived dramatically, or directly through omniscient narration) attention is focussed on the need for exercise of a critical or evaluative faculty. Most readers are more at home with indirect narration even though more participation in reconstructing and evaluating the facts is required. Direct narration places more emphasis on action and its outcome, while indirect methods raise more complex questions concerning analysis and meaning.

The choice of persona has a very telling effect on fiction. Imagine, for example, the consequences of selecting a character who is innocent, immature or simply unintelligent to tell a story that he or she incompletely or inaccurately understands. The reader would be required to exercise a good deal of judgement and imagination to reconstruct the badly disfigured or unstated reality of the case. In order to emphasise value judgements, on the other hand, a persona who is unsympathetic to the moral or ethical implications of characters and actions might be created. If the central interest in the work were the relative or subjective understanding of an event by each of the characters involved, it would be necessary to shift the point of view from which the action is recounted so that each character could retell the same event according to his or her view of it.

The point of view in indirect method need not remain constant any more than in direct narration. In fact, it is as normal for an author to move from persona to persona as it is to slip from indirect to direct method and back again, even if doing so suspends the illusion of reality for the time being. For example, in a first–person indirect narration where the narrator is a major or central character, the author may describe exactly what is going on in the mind of another character. The narrator or persona could not possibly have this information in real life, but for the purpose of the narrative, the reader must know it. In addition to the information given the reader must also be aware of the manner or method of its presentation, as this indicates a great deal about the literary composition and the relationship of subject matter to theme.

5. *Multiple points of view.* In addition to the use of a single narrator, there are also cases of multiple points of view which compound and intensify the impact of a story. Take for example the method of Emily Brontë in *Wuthering Heights* (1847) where Mr Lockwood is said to be writing down the story of the Earnshaw family, a good deal of which has been recounted to him

by Mrs Dean, an elderly woman who had been housekeeper in the family at the time of the action some years before. Mr Lockwood is, of course, a fairly neutral intermediary, but Mrs Dean is obviously biased towards Catherine Earnshaw and the children of the next generation whose lives are dominated, as Catherine's was, by Heathcliffe. Mrs Dean is a woman of a well–defined moral vision, whose class sympathies and character traits influence her judgement.

The story itself often shifts to an immediate and dramatic presentation of action which no housekeeper could have known about as it involves very private and intimate conversations, etc. The combination of very different points of view is admirably suited to this particular story of human passion as the narrators tend to substantiate and verify the reality of the sometimes bizarre action with their very ordinary and solid presence. These personæ not only lead us into the action, but they also complement one another and call attention to the author's theme by differing in understanding or evaluation of the action. Mr Lockwood is driven to speculate about what is told him and questions Mrs Dean's views, while she gives her own account of characters and actions which the reader later perceives more directly and can make his or her own judgement about. Comparison of the differing views helps us to understand the action in all its complexity by pinpointing the very problems which form the basis of the tale.

Other uses of complex points of view can be found in *The Turn of the Screw* by Henry James (1898), 'The Jumping Frog' by Mark Twain (1867) and *Heart of Darkness* by Joseph Conrad (1902).

In *The Turn of the Screw* there is also an elaborate framework of narrators which establishes and tends to verify the facts. The ostensible narrator is writing down a story he heard told by a middle–aged acquaintance after dinner at a London club. The man who told the story is not actually involved in the action but knew the details from his little sister's governess who is the principal character in the action. In his youth this man had fallen in love with the woman but because of the difference between their ages and social stations could not marry her. The action of the actual tale took place much earlier still, in the first youth of the governess herself, and throughout her account, written some years later, she is the sole narrator of those events. Yet the story raises the question of her responsibility for the catastrophe which took place. She believed that she was saving the children in her care from the machinations of evil ghosts, but the reader comes to suspect that she is given to hysteria and self–delusion; in fact, that she generated the crisis herself. Because the actions are so distanced from us and presented with such testimonials of truthfulness, the ambiguities of those happenings are emphasised and left to the reader's judgement for resolution.

In 'The Jumping Frog' the author purports to be writing a critical or documentary essay to show that one of his humourous sketches, 'The Notorious Jumping Frog of Calaveras County', has been misrepresented and divested of all its art by being translated into formal and pompous French. In order to prove the point, he prints the original story, the so–called French text, and his own literal translation from the French back into English. The clever satire on French pretentiousness and intellectual snobbery is not the main point of the exercise, however, for the reader is also struck by the degree to which the humour and art of the original sketch depends on the rich and imaginative dialect of rural America as used by the principal character. The sharp student will also notice that within the original tale that dialect is also heightened or emphasised by contrast with the formal and pompous style of the city–bred and self–satisfied narrator.

In *Heart of Darkness* there is an anonymous narrator who recounts a story mostly told by Marlow of his own journey up the Congo to rescue a man called Kurtz, an adventurer who has cut himself off from his background and acts in a strange and unaccountable manner. The focus of interest is on Kurtz and what happened to him in a place where the social constraints he was used to and the guide–lines of European culture no longer applied. The 'heart of darkness' is both the unknown, uncharted Congo as it appeared to Europeans at the turn of the present century, and the unknown, uncharted depths of man's individual soul or consciousness. Kurtz's experience is not presented directly but must be intuited or deduced from peeps and glimpses of similar experiences as they occur to Marlow. There is never a question of reconstructing what actually happened to Kurtz but rather of imagining or conceiving those conditions which caused the deterioration of Kurtz's humanity and morality from the evidence of hints and parallels. Much real information is actively suppressed because action for its own sake is not the point. The extremely indirect method is meant to focus attention on the quest for understanding of the situation, not merely what happened to Kurtz and how his experience changed him, but what happens to any individual who challenges the deepest and most unspoken convention of his universe, his reliance on the fixed patterns of society or civilization.

6.   *Style as a reflection of the narrator's value–judgements.* Narrative point of view as a structural feature — that is, the choice of a consciousness through which the narrative is perceived and presented — is certainly a most important device in narrative fiction, but it is also true that point of view, in the sense of the author's attitude towards the action, is also present in the style or quality of language used throughout the work. As suggested earlier, values and judgements are normally implied by conventional associations of sentence structure and imagery, figures of speech and sound patterning.

Style is an all–pervasive influence on a work of literature and it is without any doubt the most difficult element of composition to analyse because of its infinite possibilities. Style informs all other considerations, giving texture to the whole and influencing the reader's value–judgements on action, characters and setting. The language used by the narrator or ascribed to him or her is as effective as the tone and moral judgement implied by the point of view. A work of literature is made up of language, of words in infinite combinations and patterns, while the general quality or nature of the pattern contributes to the characteristic texture of the whole and affects the structure or organisation of the subject matter directly. The study of style requires a complete textbook on its own, but there are a few general conventions which can be outlined to give an indication of a general critical method to be used when considering literary style and discussing its impact on subject matter.

Style — an Expressive Device

Style is a function of the way one uses language: it involves word choice and arrangements or patterns of phrasing. Of course, there are correct or accepted ways in which words must combine to give meaning, but within recognised limitations wide variation of expression is possible, not to mention the effectiveness of unconventional but meaningful and expressive combinations. Each word choice and turn of phrase which is used affects the overall quality or balance of characteristics which finally allows us to generalise about and identify that particular style, to give it a name and compare its characteristics with recognisable and established registers of language.

Any discussion of style or of its relationship to subject matter must begin with an acknowledgement of its characteristic vocabulary, sentence construction and expressive devices or techniques, and this cannot be accomplished without an awareness of the basic categories of style which already exist and from which literature chooses and borrows both techniques and stylistic devices.

1. *Formal and informal styles.* To begin with, spoken and written language must be recognised as very different entities. In English, for instance, there are words, phrases and even grammatical patterns which are normally spoken, but not written, unless actual spoken language is being written down for one reason or another. In writing a letter to a friend one might well write exactly as one speaks, even ungrammatically and with colloquial expressions or slang, if that is the normal level of language used between the two individuals. A friendly letter couched in very formal terms, making use of elaborate sentence patterns and figurative ornamentation, would certainly be artificial and absurd. Formal and informal English can be distinguished from one another with ease because of such variables as in the following examples:

INFORMAL/COLLOQUIAL	FORMAL/EDUCATED
Word Choice	
place of origin	provenance
to give in / surrender	to capitulate
to get a letter	to receive a letter
Contractions	
he isn't here	he is not here
she can't find it	she cannot find it

Relative Pronouns

I hope he comes	I hope that he comes
the book that I want	the book which I want

who do you want to talk to	to whom do you wish to speak
Mary, who he asked	Mary, whom he asked

Subjunctive Mood

I wish I was dead	I wish I were dead
if only I was able to go	would I could go
impossible for him to visit her	impossible that he visit her

Polite Formulæ

I'll (I'd) be grateful	I should be very grateful
thanks a lot for	I cannot thank you enough for

Both formal and informal English display other features which are difficult to fit into a simplified table such as the one attempted above. For example, informal writing often includes interjections and asides — that is, phrases, questions and comments which interrupt the flow of the basic sentence, yet are incorporated into it. One can also expect longer, looser constructions with phrases and clauses tacked onto one another, as often happens in speech, the ideas being added as they occur to the speaker. In formal or educated writing there is a tendency to make tighter, more unified statements, often balancing a construction by placing a subordinate clause before the main subject and verb, rather than having all qualifiers follow. Informal writing is basically organic and declamatory, statement following statement, while formal writing is more consciously designed and shaped so that its aesthetic features add a measure of emphasis to the bare meaning. For this purpose rhetorical figures (see below) and figures of speech (see below and also p. 165 *f)* play a much more important role than in informal writing.

It is often the case, however, that a passage under investigation falls somewhere between the two extremes and the degree of the mixture between the two must be noted before the style can be placed with any degree of accuracy. Of the three examples which follow the first is by Stokely Carmichael, former chairman of the Student Nonviolent Co-ordinating Committee, and is clearly formal and serious. The second was recorded during a street interview by Calvin C. Hernton and is obvious informal spoken language, while the third is Hernton's comment on the quotation and employs both formal and informal elements.

> The major limitation of this approach was that it tended to maintain the traditional dependence of Negroes, and of the movement. We depended upon the goodwill and support of various groups within the white community whose interests were not always compatible with ours. To the extent that we depended on the financial support of other groups, we were vulnerable to their influence and domination.
>
> (Carmichael p. 127 in Jones)

> The only way Negroes like me are going to get a chance to live like human beings instead of like niggers — yeah, niggers, that's what we live like — the only way is if some foreign country comes over here and put the white man in his place, put him out of business. Before we ever get our freedom Sam's got to be conquered by a foreign power.

> The man who made that statement has a wife and three daughters, and has worked as a department store janitor for ten years. He goes to church, he is not flat broke, he earns sixty dollars a week, and he has a hustle on the side — you know, he can get you a television or maybe a studio couch for a third of the price. The thing that keeps bugging this man, and millions like him, is that every time he encounters himself in the mirror, or in his thoughts, or in the face of someone else, or in the smile of one of his daughters, he encounters a symbolic thing which is the object of perpetual rejection, hatred and violence of white America.
>
> (Hernton, p. 97 in Jones)

2. *Historical and personal styles.* Historical styles are perhaps the most obvious and easily identifiable register of a language. We all recognise that each period or age has evolved a convention of language which sets it apart from all others. Certain words and turns of phrase tend to be peculiar to the style of a given period while that fixed fashion of sentence construction and rhythm provides a common ground for both the formal and informal language of an era. As the student becomes more and more

familiar with style, he or she should be able to date the writing of an unseen passage within twenty years or so merely by the evidence of the language used. For example, the following is taken from James Fenimore Cooper's *The Prairie* (1828) and is characteristic of its period.

'Listen,' said the trapper when he had succeeded in making Middleton see the moving column of birds. 'Now you hear the buffaloes, or bisons as your knowing doctor sees fit to call them, though buffaloes is their name among all the hunters of these regions. And I conclude that a hunter is a better judge of a beast and of its name,' he added, winking to the young soldier, 'than any man who has turned over the leaves of a book instead of traveling over the face of the 'arth in order to find out the natur's of its inhabitants.'

'Of their habits, I will grant you,' cried the naturalist, who rarely missed an opportunity to agitate any disputed point in his favorite studies. 'That is, provided always deference is had to the proper use of definition and that they are contemplated with scientific eyes.'

(Cooper, p. 205)

As one reads more literature, it should also be possible to recognise the individual style of a particular author or speaker who has developed a unique and individual way of using language within the common style of his age or period. It is not unusual, for example, to see a suit or hat in a shop and think that it is just right for someone you know well. Individuals often have a marked preference for certain shapes, textures or colours within the limits of possibility offered by a current fashion. This is also true of language or style and accounts for the development of individual or personal styles which emphasise a particular combination of elements from the general style of the period. Take the following passage from *As I Lay Dying* (1930) by William Faulkner, for example:

In the afternoon when school was out and the last one had left with his dirty snuffling nose, instead of going home I would go down the hill to the spring where I could be quiet and hate them. It would be quiet there then, with the water bubbling up

and away and the sun slanting quiet in the trees and the quiet
smelling of damp and rotting leaves and new earth; especially
in the early spring, for it was worst then.

(Faulkner, p. 134)

3. *Occupational registers.* When thinking of the origins of words
and phrases, or the appropriateness of their usage in connection
with a particular kind of human activity, we leave aside such
distinctions as formal and informal levels, historical and personal
styles. While speaking or writing about religion, science, or the
administration of government and business, for example,
different collections of words and phrases are used which are
peculiar to each activity and to no other. Particular stylistic
devices are often associated with a given discipline, as in the case
of long–disused Elizabethan pronouns and verb forms (thou
goest, etc.) in prayers and sermons, while key words such as
salvation, resurrection, original sin and 'blood of the lamb' are
also characteristic of a religious register. In scientific writing such
a phrase as 'eight fixed open–hearth steel–smelting furnaces' is
common because the style is characterised by its tendency to
prefix a number of noun modifiers before the head–word of a
phrase. And in most cases the words themselves are rarely in
common use except among the professionals or students of that
discipline. The language of administration, on the other hand,
tends to be formal and impersonal, with emphatic sentences of
balanced construction and middle length which are often
couched in the passive voice to avoid indicating the agent of
responsibility. For example, 'A statement was issued concerning
the company's economic growth and development.'

Since so many spheres of influence or occupational activity
have recognisable forms of language or style, it is a simple matter
to bring in wider associations and emphases by echoing the
appropriate elements of one such register when creating a
fictional world. For example, an author who wishes to emphasise
the irony of a situation might choose to narrate the tale using all
the stylistic devices of objective newspaper reporting. By association the reader would be inclined to believe in the reality of
the facts and, at the same time, would feel free to draw his or her
own conclusions, especially when contradictory or illogical statements and facts are being presented. In this way the fictional

world draws upon the authority and values of a familiar activity in the real world where the same kind of language is used.

On the other hand, it may even be that the associations brought into play are contrasted with the actual situation. For example, supernatural and heroic characters or actions can be emphasised by echoes of religious and archaic language which are normally associated with them, while a particularly frivolous and comic character might be further exaggerated by the unnatural contrast of a similarly elevated and formal style.

4. *Synthesis of styles in literary expression.* The point to remember about expository writing is that it is in no way limited to a particular style but tends to make use of any and all stylistic characteristics which are useful. Expository writing is primarily interested in the clarity and logic of its analysis or argument. Rhetorical figures may be used, even metaphorical language, images and musical devices, in so far as they help to communicate information directly to the intelligence of the reader or listener. For example:

> In Nigeria, as in other developing countries and particularly those in Africa, the major tasks for government are to maintain stability and promote rapid economic and social development. Both of these tasks call for the right type of political leadership — dynamic, dedicated and development – oriented. The development process has to be induced, and the maintenance of political stability and of law and order is primarily a political function. The misfortune of the first Republic was that politicians failed dismally to provide the right type of leadership. Although they paid lip service to economic and social development, they were more interested in pursuing their selfish ends and in amassing wealth at public expense.
>
> (Adedeji, p. 14)

Literary presentation, on the other hand, endeavours to present fictional action, characters or emotions and to force the reader to deduce or intuit the idea behind them. Instead of stating that a heroine is tired and depressed, for example, a physical image of fatigue and depression may be created in whatever words or style is suitable in the context. 'She entered the room without noticing the flowers on the table and slumped into a chair, closing her eyes against the sunlight.' Notice that the flowers and sunlight are only present to mark the limits of, or make a contrast with, the heroine's state which is also directly expresssed by actions suggesting that state (slumped, closing her eyes).

A very complex interrelation of context and presentation of images or actions is used to build up a work of literature, and a high level of observation and deduction is needed by the reader. One must be a keen observer of life, and especially of the way people act, react and talk; of the relationship between outward actions or objects of everyday life and inner feelings. Take for example the following scene from *The Autobiography of Malcolm X* (1965).

> Then we were looking up at the judge in Middlesex County Court. (Our, I think, fourteen counts of crime were committed in that county.) Shorty's mother was sitting, sobbing with her head bowing up and down to her Jesus, over near Ella and Reginald. Shorty was the first of us called to stand up.
> 'Count one, eight to ten years —
> 'Count two, eight to ten years —
> 'Count three . . . '
> And, finally, 'The sentences to run concurrently.'
> Shorty, sweating so hard that his black face looked as though it had been greased, and not understanding the word 'Concurrently', had counted in his head to probably over a hundred years; he cried out, he began slumping. The bailiffs had to catch and support him.
>
> (Malcolm X, p. 244)

Writers are under no constraint in choosing vocabulary or sentence patterns, and the response of readers must be open and receptive to stylistic variations from the written or formal norm. There is no such thing as a literary style, at least not in the same sense that we accept the existence of a legal or medical register of language usage. Literary style varies considerably. Rather than depending on province or register for its characteristic features, it relies on grouping techniques or devices which have been selected for their expressive qualities in relation to the individual subject matter of the work and its theme.

5. *Identification of dominant style.* In order to generalise about the style of a given literary work, it is necessary to assess or analyse the dominant characteristics of the writing. A disciplined understanding of technical devices (word choice, images, figures of speech, rhetorical devices, etc.), including their emotional overtones and associations in context, is required, however, because that is actually what determines the nature or character of the style. In order to describe or identify a given level of writing, the elements or stylistic devices employed must first be recognised as well as the relative weight and balance of their combinations.

The first distinction to be considered is a question of level or register and the second is the related one of emotional tone or tenor. In addition to the difference between formal and informal or colloquial styles which has already been discussed, there is also a contrast between elevated or inflating and deflating styles. Both formal and informal registers can be inflating, just as they can both be deflating, or even neutral and objective. For example, characters and events can be given a certain amount of formal elevation, even majesty, by constructing sentences of balanced rhythms and regular intervals between points of emphasis. Multi-syllabic and full–sounding words may also predominate and sound patterns developed with frequent intonational stresses evenly distributed within balanced (parallel) grammatical phrasing. Such a style would suggest authority and firmness of purpose because people who exhibit these characteristics normally use that kind of language and the same qualities of measured dignity and authority are called into play. For an example, one has only to think of the serious and measured style of a political speech by a world leader. By the same token a general sense of warmth, familiarity and human sympathy can be gained by a somewhat more informal or colloquial style, so long as the subject matter remains serious and morally attractive.

Depending on word choice, images, figures of speech, rhetorical and musical devices, any number of attitudes towards the subject matter can be established. The exact emotional overtone which is created, as opposed to the degree of formality or informality of style, depends even more specifically on the relation between style and content. Context alone carries meaning, and style merely underlines or emphasises it, reinforcing value judgements. Rhythm and sound pattern, for example, may imitate or reflect the movement of an emotion such as happiness or sadness by varying the speed, length and/or texture of the sentences. Styles can be described as sombre, meditative, light (joyful) and even lyrical, depending on the total effect of rhetorical figures, metaphorical language, rhythm and sound patterning as they emphasise and elaborate upon qualities already present in the subject matter. Such generalisations, however, are no substitute for the examination of specific examples in their original contexts.

In addition to raising the level of importance or completeness of expression through parallels of stylistic devices and subject matter, it is also possible to create an ironic style in which figurative inversions or oppositions of words and phrasing as well as of ideas, situations and even expectation or outcome, predominate. If the techniques of inversion occur over and over again, on each page as it were, the cumulative effect of irony will further express and emphasise the author's attitude towards his subject matter.

Another method of deflation is to create an opposition or inversion between language and action, that is, to use linguistic patterns normally associated with actions above or below the actual occasions of the fictional world and so indicate contrasting values. In *The Rape of the Lock* (1714) Alexander Pope makes great fun of social pretensions in his own time by describing a world of card parties, teas and love intrigues by using the language and apparatus of epic tradition which is usually reserved for mythic heroes, war and actions of great cultural significance.

The effectiveness of style is always seen in its relation to subject matter and theme, and stylistic analysis is founded in a detailed knowledge of normal language usage and available literary techniques. There are far too many facets of language to attempt a complete study here, but a few general distinctions can and should be made.

(a) *Word choice.* Word choice is certainly one of the first concerns of any literary language. English, in particular, has developed over a very long period of time and has been heavily influenced by both French and Latin which were for a time superimposed on it. It has one of the largest and most diverse vocabularies of any language, and numbers of words overlap one another in meaning, but differ in the range of their overtones or associations. The choice of a particular word for expository or factual writing is itself difficult, since words are not interchangeable; the word which perfectly expresses a particular idea or fits best into a combination of other words must have both a precise and suitable literal meaning (denotation) and appropriate overtones and associations of usage (connotation).

For example, the words 'woman', 'female' and 'lady' all denote the same biological entity, but they each connote different values and attitudes towards human beings of that sex. 'Woman' is a fairly neutral word and can be applied to any individual so long as only a distinction of sex is intended. 'Female' has a more technical or scientific use and emphasises sexual function at the expense of the humanity or individuality of the person. If used in a social rather than medical or administrative context, the effect is degrading or dismissive. The whole woman is reduced to a sexual object, dehumanised and depersonalised. In some, but not all contexts, therefore, the word 'female' is derogatory, it has a negative emotional charge or aura. Used in this way, the response of the reader is influenced through the indication of an unspoken value judgement. 'Lady', on the other hand, refers to a person who is more than either biologically or individually significant: in fact, one who is also of some social status or importance. A lady is a woman who is either refined in character and manners or occupies a social position in which refinement is expected. To say, 'A lady is a female who . . .' introduces a certain shock value or force because of the sharp contrast between the words 'lady' and 'female'. Much more is at stake in word choice than mere root meaning. The word in relation to both its context and the effect desired is of much greater importance than the word alone.

(b) *Connotation.* There are many ways in which words derive connotative values. For example, 'serpent' is a more highly charged or emotional word in English than 'snake', partly because it carries with it associations of diabolical evil and guile from the Bible story of Eve's seduction by Satan who disguised himself as a serpent. 'Doubloon' has far more romantic overtones than any contemporary unit of money because of its historical and literary associations with pirates and treasure. Both denotation and connotation are important to literature, particularly the emotive force of words, their normal associations and the emotions they arouse.

Words of neutral value, for example, generally give the impression of objectivity, simple diction the impression of sincerity, and those words borrowed from professional registers can be reassuring in their suggestion of rational and impersonal judgements. A highly charged vocabulary, whether positive or negative in force, suggests a highly emotional reaction to the subject matter, and its effect on the expression of the theme is equally pronounced. Consistent patterns of connotation are often built up in literature as an element or building unit of meaning. The good reader looks out for these patterns and the effects they create in establishing an idea, attitude or quality about a person, place or thing.

(c) *Images.* Words, however, do not function alone, they combine to form phrases and ultimately sentences in which other forces are brought into play. At the level of the single word or phrase in its relationship to a context, images and figures of speech must be considered, and at the level of the whole sentence, rhetorical devices and syntax (the combining and ordering of words and phrases in a sentence). Because literature re–creates the known universe through words, the image is one of the author's most effective tools.

Very simply, an image is a word or phrase which calls up a sensory response in the reader's imagination. Chopping, crash, perfume, scratchy and sour, for example, are words that appeal to the sense of sight, hearing, smell, touch and taste. Each is a simple image and capable of elaboration or expansion into more complex entities. The physical description of a person may extend over several paragraphs, yet function in literature as a single image or representation. On the other hand, words such as sad, beautiful and intellect are not images, but rather qualities, states of being or abstractions. They constitute information which can be more concretely expressed and communicated through examples of specific instances which constitute images.

Images are not always taken as literal facts, however. If an author says that a particular character wore a green shirt, we accept the mental picture summoned by the words, but should he say that the character turned green with envy, we know that this cannot be literally true because our experience of life tells us that people do not turn green for any reason whatever. It is true that blood can suffuse and darken the face or drain away and cause the person to look pale or grey when caught up in a strong emotion. Green, however, is the colour which in Europe is traditionally associated with jealousy, as red is with courage or passion and white with purity, etc. What we do understand, then, is that a jealous emotion showed on the face, but instead of an accurate and realistic description we have an associated image substituted for it, an image that cannot be taken literally. Rather it is an obvious exaggeration or distortion of the original. A comparison is being made, but all the parts are not stated. The idea of blushing or blood rushing to the face has been left out and it is that idea which connects the change in the person's appearance with jealousy.

A simpler way of looking at it is to accept the image 'green' as representing jealousy by conventional association. To say that the person turned green merely emphasises that his primary quality or characteristic at that moment is jealousy: man — green —jealousy. In either case we understand the sense of the statement to be contrary to fact but still meaningful, and we call such devices figures of speech.

(d) *Figures of speech.* Figurative language is as common in everyday speech as in literature, and has the effect of compounding or condensing ideas as well as underlining or emphasising them. It is a highly prized device because of the inventive and creative possibilities in linking several ideas together. At least two images are suggested in every figure of speech, a primary one which is compared or contrasted with a secondary image because of a shared, associated, representative or opposite quality. Very often the secondary image is merely substituted for the primary one.

In order to understand figures of speech, the three basic elements of their being must be reconstructed, especially if one or more is not actually stated; the primary image which arises from the subject matter, the secondary image to which it is related, and the basic quality which links the two together. If, for example, one says of a man that he is a bull or that someone is a bull of a man, we understand that his size and strength are being stressed.

Figurative devices are usually classified by types according to the relation of the primary to the secondary image (see p. 165 *f* below), but it is foolish to think that one understands a passage or scene any better for knowing the name of the device used in it. What should be identified is the quality or attribute that underlies the comparison or contrast, for it is the frequently unstated basis of the association which is emphasised by the figure of speech. Such devices focus attention on particular qualities of the primary image, and more often than not, these figures occur in patterns which repeat and reinforce a given set of ideas, values or attitudes relevant to the theme and meaning of the work as a whole.

Striking effects can be achieved by drawing a number of secondary images from related sources, and supplying each figure with a parallel quality or attribute which includes its relation to the primary image. In *Girls at War* (1971), for example, Chinua Achebe describes the bombardment of a bridge and makes use of just such a creative pattern.

> They drove on in silence for the next half–hour or so. Then as the car sped down a slope towards a bridge someone screamed — perhaps the driver, perhaps the soldier — 'They have come!' The screech of the brakes merged into the scream and the shattering of the sky overhead. The doors flew open even before the car had come to a stop and they were fleeing blindly to the bush. Gladys was a little ahead of Nwankwo when they heard through the drowning tumult the soldier's voice crying: 'Please come and open for me!' Vaguely he saw Gladys stop; he pushed past her shouting to her at the same time to come on. Then a high whistle descended like as spear through the chaos and exploded in a vast noise and motion that smashed up everything. A tree he had embraced flung him away through the bush. Then another terrible whistle started high up and ending again in a monumental crash of the world; and then another, and Nwankwo heard no more.
>
> (Achebe, pp. 117–18)

The screaming shattering of the sky is, of course, the noise of low–flying planes and the high whistle descending like a spear, the noise made by a bomb or shell. The tree couldn't fling Nwankwo away but the impact of an explosion does and the second explosion knocks him unconscious. The pattern being built up is animated by sounds as well as physical action or movement which is consistently presented as being automatic and inhumanly motivated. The description of events is indirect and particularly immediate to the imagination of the reader as the screech, scream, engine roar and human yelling merge into the whistles and shattering explosions.

Because individual figures of speech and the larger patterns they often form bear so closely on attitudes and meaning they must be recognised and evaluated as they appear. Distortions and displacement of normal language usage within the figure sometimes makes this difficult, however, especially when the reader is not familiar with the meanings of the words, their usual contexts and associations. The temptation is to guess at unknown meanings, using an immediate context as a basis for deduction, but such efforts almost always lead to disaster.

In literature words are very likely to be used in a different sense or in combinations different from the way in which they are used in literal or expository writing. If a statement is figurative rather than literal, its meaning depends on the relationship between the primary and secondary images, and, since the primary image may also be unstated, each word must be fully understood before its relationship to the others can be deduced. It is just not possible to guess the meaning of an individual word with any degree of success from an unknown or misunderstood context.

(e) *Rhetorical devices.* As distinct from images and figures of speech, rhetorical devices and syntactical patterns also exert a heavy influence on style. Rhetorical principles exist in all languages and govern the way in which emphasis is made within the possible limits of a grammatical sentence. Rhetorical devices are common to all kinds of writing, but since there are many textbooks which outline a full range of devices, both historical and contemporary, there is little need to go into great detail here. The most common and effective figures are extended series, inversions, subordination, co–ordination and parallelism.

Extended series is particularly effective in elaborating and exemplifying an idea through a sequence of developed instances or examples as in the following:

[Culture] includes all the characteristic activities and interests of a people: Derby Day, Henley Regatta, Cowes, the twelfth of August, a cup final, the dog races, the pin table, the dart board, Wensleydale cheese, boiled cabbage cut into sections, beetroot in vinegar, nineteenth–century Gothic churches and the music of Elgar.

(Eliot, *Notes,* p. 31)

Inversion places emphasis on a word or idea within a sentence by displacing normal word order and the conventions of expectation shared by all speakers of the language. 'I was left to work for my living and work I did.' Although the verb is out of its normal order, the sentence is perfectly understandable, and coupled with the repetition of the word 'work', the statement becomes very strong indeed.

Subordination and co–ordination are terms which refer to the ways in which larger grammatical units that might stand as independent ideas are linked together to emphasise their actual relationship. It is possible to use one or the other method almost exclusively, or to mix them, and they have a direct effect on meaning through the association of emotion and response. Co–ordination is the linking together of two or more separate but comparable words, phrases or clauses with no other relationship but comparison or contrast.

He was an intelligent man, but he made a serious error of judgement.

Subordination links together two or more unequal ideas or clauses while specifying and even emphasising the exact relationship of dependency between them, one action being the result or necessary prerequisite (time, place, agency, cause, effect, etc.) of the other.

Although he was an intelligent man, he made a serious error of judgement.

Normal word order, especially in spoken English, begins with the subject or actor followed by the action and then one or more qualifications of the action in sequence. A more harmonious balance and rhythm is achieved by placing some of the qualifying phrases or clauses first. Instead of sentences running downhill, as it were, towards a single heavy stress at the end, the qualifications and modifications are distributed more evenly throughout.

Two very distinct styles can be developed from these different methods of construction. In one, a number of simple declarative sentences either stand on their own or are loosely linked together as clauses in larger sentences by the co–ordinate conjunctions 'and' and 'but'. The effect is one of simple presentation and objectivity with a matter–of–fact tone and it serves to distance the author or narrator from the situations described:

> The candle made shadows on the wall behind the men and Anselmo stood where he had come in to the right of the table. The wife of Pablo was standing over the charcoal fire on the open fire hearth in the corner of the cave. The girl knelt by her stirring in an iron pot. She lifted the wooden spoon out and looked at Robert Jordan as he stood there in the doorway and he saw, in the glow from the fire the woman was blowing with the bellows, the girl's face, her arm, and the drops running down from the spoon and dropping into the iron pot.
>
> (Hemingway, p. 50)

Subordination, on the other hand, emphasises logical relationships and rational thought, suggesting the presence of a controlling consciousness or intellect:

> Laboring in the soil had never been congenial to my grandfather, though with his wife's help he prospered by it. Then, in an era when success was hard to avoid, he began to invest in stocks. In 1922 he bought our large white home in the town — its fashionable section had not yet shifted to the Shale Hill side of the valley — and settled in to reap his dividends.
>
> (Updike, p. 43)

Parallelism as a rhetorical device is very closely related to co–ordination in that grammatical units are multiplied and balanced against one another in order to emphasise the parallelism and relationship of the ideas contained in them. Two words, phrases or clauses in parallel generally give a sense of logic, an impression of reasoned thinking, while three emphasise a further sense of stability and accomplishment, especially one of things worked out or completed.

> His followers were the poor and the dispossessed: share-croppers, migrant workers, unskilled laborers.

When three words or phrases open a sentence and are joined to a common verb (a rhetorical device known as a periodic sentence), the sense of completion is accompanied by a feeling that a circle has been completed, a confusion resolved.

> Subsistence agriculture, a falling death–rate and scanty employment opportunity outside farming implies widespread underemployment in crowded rural areas.

In the case of phrases in strict grammatical parallels the emphasis shifts from the words repeated to those which are not.

> This is a government of the people, for the people and by the people.

Four words or phrases and more in parallel suggest an emotional or unstable situation.

> As in the days of the alchemists and necromancers, science is again awesome, threatening, uncanny and sinister.

Even the length of the sentence and the comparative roughness or smoothness of phrasing as well as similar qualities of sound patterning have a decided impact on its emotional character and meaning. A long line, for example, multiplies the sensation of length in either time or space. When smoothly phrased with long open or rolling sounds predominating, such a sentence gives a strong feeling of calmness, tiredness, passiveness or sickness, depending on the subject matter. On the other hand a short line or sentence which is broken up into short phrases and further emphasised by sharp, quick or explosive sounds gives a strong impression of vital activity, agitation or roughness. The following excerpt from the court scene in *A Passage to India*

(1924) by E. M. Forster shows an effective modulation from one style to the other.

> The Superintendent moved to the support of his friends, saying nonchalantly to the Magistrate as he did so, 'Right, I withdraw'.
>
> Mr Das rose, nearly dead with the strain. He had controlled the case, just controlled it. He had shown that an Indian can preside. To those who cold hear him he said, 'The prisoner is released without one stain on his character; the question of costs will be decided elsewhere'.
>
> And then the flimsy framework of the court broke up, the shouts of derision and rage culminated, people screamed and cursed, kissed one another, wept passionately. Here were the English, whom their servants protected, there Aziz fainted in Hamidullah's arms. Victory on this side, defeat on that – complete for one moment was the antithesis. Then life returned to its complexities, person after person struggled out of the room to their various purposes, and before long no one remained on the scene of the fantasy but the beautiful naked god. Unaware that anything unusual had occurred, he continued to pull the cord of his punkah, to gaze at the empty dais and the overturned special chairs, and rhythmically to agitate the clouds of descending dust.
>
> (Forster, p. 224)

Syntax and its relation to meaning raise questions of devices such as rhythm and sound patterning — that is, stress, intonation, metre, assonance, consonance, rhyme, etc., which are discussed in more detail in the chapter on poetry (see p. 151 *f*) — but their influence is just as great on prose writing. In general, they tend to reinforce subject matter by imitation, contrast or emphasis by creating a striking stylistic contrast to that of the surrounding language.

Conclusion

In every respect, style is a highly technical affair and the response one has to the language of literature can be traced back to a series or combination of conscious devices used by the author. If close attention is paid to the various areas of style already discussed, it should be possible to characterise or identify the general style of either a given passage or of a work as a whole, in its relationship to subject matter and theme.

Style is nothing more than the choice and ordering of words with particular emphasis on connotative association, images, figures of speech, rhetorical devices, rhythm and sound patterning. In discussing style, however, the mere isolation of technique is futile. It is only in the impact on what is being said at both the surface and deeper levels that the analysis of style has any meaning or use. Style certainly does influence each of the other aesthetic elements — events, characters, setting and point of view — but all work together to express various truths about human experience.

3 *Drama and the Theatre*

Drama as Re–creation of Action

Instead of re–creating actions through the imagination of the reader who interprets the language of narrative fiction, drama re–creates action immediately and physically on a stage in front of an audience. The producer or director interprets the literary text and the audience is invited to immerse itself in the action, to respond to the effectiveness of production techniques (acting, costume, scenery, etc.) which make the action both believable and meaningful as well as to the literary techniques of composition and expression. Since drama is played out before an audience it must necessarily present a whole or complete action and it is also limited in time by the attention span of the viewers. Because of its private and personal nature as well as the length and complexity of its action, a novel is read in bits and pieces.

A book can be put down and picked up again by an individual reader without much loss of sense or continuity, but drama involves so many people, so much effort to organise a performance and collect an audience, that practical considerations as well as aesthetic ones demand a complete presentation at each sitting. A series of plays with interrelated action may be given at intervals of days or even weeks, but each unit must be relatively complete in itself, as are the subdivisions of a single play when it is interrupted by intermissions or intervals in which the audience walks about and talks until the next act or scene is ready to begin. In the English–speaking world, the maximum playing time for drama is conventionally limited to about three hours, after which an audience tends to become restless and inattentive, but the limit is arbitrary and likely to shift from period to period and from society to society. In Japan, for example, going to the theatre can be an all–day affair and performances last up to ten hours without any failure of concentration on the part of the audience.

Characteristics of Drama as a Performing Art

In fact, nearly all the characteristics of drama which distinguish it from other genres of literature derive from the fact that it is basically a performing art. For example, the limitation in time requires drama to be condensed and streamlined in construction. It is shorn of incidental action, digression and unnecessary illuminating detail. The novel, on the other hand, attempts to present human experience in as much detail as possible and admits of complex constructions extended over a longer reading time in order to capture and reflect the interaction of events and characters. Because the action of a novel is perceived externally by a narrator, there must be room for the elaboration of his or her attitude towards those events. On the other hand, the action of drama is directly observed by an audience and its significance is immediately obvious. Whereas the central conflict of a novel is more diffuse and is registered cumulatively by readers as they become increasingly aware of the work's basic patterning, the conflict of drama is compacted and heightened, almost over-emphasised. Some even argue that concentration of effect is the intention of drama and that its conception as a performing art, as well as limitation in time, is a consequence of this fact rather than a cause. In any case, the sharpening or heightening of conflict on the level of subject matter is a major feature of drama.

Good theatre requires action and characters which are, to some extent, exaggerated, striking and larger than life. That is just what is meant when we say that someone has a dramatic personality or that an action is theatrical. In fact, it is not so much the nature or character of actions which makes them dramatic or theatrical, but rather the treatment employed in presenting them. An action or theme is suitable for drama so long as it benefits from condensation, intensification and explicit interpretation on a stage. Nor is the function of drama different from that of any other kind of literature; the object is always the observation and judgement of human experience in a satisfying aesthetic composition and the presentation of some particular truth relative to that fictional world.

The Illusion of Reality

The immediate and physical re-creation of action before an audience introduces certain limitations as well as offering creative possibilities. One of the most serious limitations is the risk of unthinking absorption into the imaginary action on the part of an audience. The question is really one of degree; the relationship of an action to its limitation on a stage and the illusion of reality which is created.

To take part in a situation or action is to participate in its reality and the next closest one can come to that is to be an eye-witness. One step further removed from the reality of the action is to see it as a documentary, re-enacted by real people before one's eyes, as objectively and completely presented as possible, while the next is to see it fictionalised as a play with the inevitable selection of elements and restructuring to express a theme. Beyond this point there are film versions, where only the images or pictures of people are seen, and finally oral or published versions which are related by a narrator whose controlling influence distances the listener or reader even further from the original action.

The theatrical projection of an action, however, can also turn the audience into eyewitnesses of the event. The power of drama to create the illusion of reality, even for actions which never did take place, is very great, yet the total immersion of an audience in an imaginary action emphasises only the events themselves and their outcome, whereas serious literature also wishes to direct attention from subject matter to theme. Illusionism may be both natural and desirable, but it must also be tempered to one degree or another by distancing techniques which have the effect of arousing the audience to evaluate and comment on the action.

In the novel the method and style of narration accomplishes the task; in drama the elements of theatre production, the methods of staging the play, are used. Point of view and style can be employed as in narrative fiction, but in the larger number of plays such elements as mime, dance, music, song, scenery, costume, lighting and variation of the playing area are responsible for the vital interplay of illusionism and distancing which mediates between subject matter and theme, provoking an audience to participate imaginatively and critically while also being immersed in the action played out before them.

Literary Text v. Production Technique

Whenever the subject of drama is discussed, the relationship between a play as theatrical performance and as literary text is bound to create problems. Although drama is a theatrical experience and requires interpretation in physical terms before an audience, one tends to read and study the literary text on its own. The danger, of course, is in reading a play as though it were a novel and thus imagining only the stated details of the text. In the case of the more realistic presentation of a psychological study or social satire, which depends primarily on language for its effects, not too much is lost by ignoring production, but for a whole range of plays which gain their prinicipal effects in other ways, the exercise is vain. Some plays, called 'closet dramas', are meant only to be read and in many cases are impractical or unsuccessful on the stage.

In the case of the medieval mystery plays, for example, which developed from ritual presentations in the great churches of Europe during celebrations of the Mass and showed incidents from the life of Christ connected with particular high feast days of the Christian calendar, the text alone is of little interest compared with the spectacle and pageantry of a full production or cycle of plays, publicly shown outside the cathedrals and including scenes from the Creation to the Resurrection. Later they were mounted on separate wagons, pulled through the streets, and performed several times over in different parts of the city. The emphasis was on costuming and decoration as well as on dialogue and action.

The Elizabethan dramatists, on the other hand, chose more secular material or subject matter and were far more limited in the stage effects they could achieve because they wrote for a professional theatre which had to make a profit. Their plays were largely concerned with public or social morality, especially with questions of good government, universal justice and individual worth or value on the one hand, and love or natural order on the other. As in the work of William Shakespeare, Christopher Marlowe or John Webster, the language was rich and forceful, with full descriptions of place and appearances, since elaborate

settings and stage effects were not possible in the open courtyards or on the bare platforms in the open air where they were
normally performed. Instead of an actual illusion of stage realism
the Elizabethans appealed directly to the imagination of the
audience through the elaboration and completeness of the text.

As drama developed and was taken up by the ruling classes,
plays retreated indoors and audiences became more select or
elite. The proscenium stage was developed and complicated stage
settings with decorative backround designs in full perspective
dominated theatre art. Subject matter and themes were idealised
and exotic effects predominated, as we can see in the plays of
John Dryden where the realistic characterisations and believable
human experience of Shakespeare gave way to impossible and
exaggerated archetypes of heroic virtue and passion such as we
find in *Tyrannic Love* (1669), *The Conquest of Granada* (1670) or
Aureng–Zebe (1675). Later Restoration comedy returned the stage
to a more realistic form of representation which suited the direct
exposure of contemporary, middle–class social values and
conduct.

At the beginning of the Romantic period, however, dramatists
experimented with non–realistic verse plays in which supernatural figures or mere personifications of abstract ideas engaged
in poetic dialogue, as in Percy Bysshe Shelley's *Prometheus
Unbound* (1820) where gods, phantasms and the spirits of sun and
moon as well as various echoes, fauns and furies take part. In
such poetic closet drama action is minimal and often so un-
theatrical as to make a successful production difficult, although
not impossible. Later romantic drama turned again in the
direction of a qualified realism although empty stages with
painted backdrops tended to predominate. Subject matter and
themes were still somewhat idealised versions of everyday life or
aspirations and much emphasis was laid on literary construction
and style. Not until the end of the nineteenth century and the
perfection of lighting techniques, however, was it possible to have
either a full–blown realism or an alternative imaginary reality.
The modern revolution in theatre arts has also benefited
immeasurably from the new–found freedom to manipulate the
shape and style of the playing area (stage) and an equal freedom
from a dominant aesthetic fashion or stage convention. In our
own time, play production can reproduce that of any historical

period or combine features from various ages in order to achieve a meaningful degree of realism or representational anti–illusionism.

Contemporary plays are often merely the basis for interpretation through performance and make little sense when read on their own. However much different plays may vary in their reliance on literary construction or production method, one must always read or study them with an eye to their possible existence on stage. The presentation of action and characters as a theatrical experience through performance must be imagined, not the action as it is supposed to have happened in real life. Drama only comes alive in actual performance, and reading a play without imagining a production is to deprive it of the medium in which the dialogue and action was meant to find its existence. Writing is, after all, nothing more than an easy means of preserving the material and even that is being superseded by such direct methods as film, tape recordings, etc.

Traditional Subdivisions

The major subdivisions of drama are ritual, history, comedy and tragedy, and each admits of further sub-genres within its particular view of human experience or form of organisation and presentation. Drama originally developed from ritual and often retains the quality of its ancestor, if not the form. In its original state, ritual is concerned with sacrifice and magic which ensures the continuance of vegetable life. It is the unchanging repetition of a formula or series of actions which have proved themselves over a period of time to be effective. In other words, re–creating the exact circumstances re–creates the effect that they originally had or are believed to have had. Rituals have been developed to celebrate natural cycles, such as changes of season or rites of passage, and to affirm the things in life that 'are' and 'must be', such as birth, procreation and death. Solemnity and dignity accompany such ritual re–creations and special formulae of words, clothing and accessories as well as rhythmic movement or dance become an indispensable part of the performance. Ritual still survives in such secular activities as school graduations, the opening of new buildings and inaugurations of governments, to mention only a few instances. A pattern of acceptable and aesthetically satisfying actions is woven from elements borrowed from the traditional religious rituals of a society and the dignity or quality of the occasion is ensured by heightened ceremonial gestures or patterning which is also borrowed from older forms.

Any action in real life can be turned into a ritual if it is performed with ceremonial gestures and speech inflections. Breaking bread, lighting candles or drinking wine are perfectly ordinary acts which can be ritualised by a slight exaggeration or stylisation. Another way to ritualise an everyday act is to repeat the sequence of its parts on successive occasions in exactly the same order with identical movements and intentions, either with or without exaggeration and stylisation. Putting a child to bed or preparing one's desk for work can easily be raised to the level of ritual, and any process so institutionalised comes to represent and to ensure the inevitability as well as the effectiveness of that action. The example of a graduation or convocation ceremony is a good case in point. The standard of education and personal success of a graduate would not be adversely affected if the diploma were sent in the post or even delivered at the door by a ragged dirty youngster casually hired for the job. The actual decorations, musical accompaniment, costumes, processions, speeches, etc. which make up a graduation ceremony are merely ways of ritualising or heightening the symbolic importance of the occasion, marking the successful completion of a long and often arduous process and the transition to a new and different life which the graduate is about to make.

Ritual Drama

Ritual drama is distinguishable from other kinds of theatre in that it directs the attention of the audience towards the inevitability and representative meaning of the action, rather than towards the inner conflict of tragedy or the reassertion of outward order after a comic inversion or intervention. Ritual drama is not so much an identifiable form in that it has characteristic subject matter, plot line or characters; rather it is recognised as a quality or idea which exists within another form, usually tragedy. Ritual drama is a direct presentation of inevitability, an affirmation of its necessity and rightness, as in *The Bacchae* of Euripides

(480–406 BC), John Milton's *Samson Agonistes* (1671) or J. M. Synge's *Riders to the Sea* (1904), where characterisation and action are limited in development so that attention may centre on the working out of an inescapable conclusion: the fall of Pentheus (tyrannical reason and temperance) who defies the god, Dionysius (passion and spontaneity); the glorification of Samson who overcomes temptations to regain a state of grace; and the transcendence of Maurya who is reconciled to the inevitability of human mortality. Pentheus does not show right understanding of his universe while Samson and Maurya do, but the ideal of mastery in each case is affirmed, accepted and surrendered to by the audience as a result of participating imaginatively in the ritual performance.

Another case in point is J. P. Clark's *Ozidi* (1966), a drama based on a longer dramatic poem taken from the oral tradition of the Ijaw people of southeastern Nigeria. The original Ozidi saga is acted out as a ritual drama once every twenty–five years and tells the story of a warrior who was born after his father's death and brought up to avenge the treachery of his father's murderers. The boy's grandmother is a sorceress and with her help he emerges as a powerful warrior who avenges his father, overcomes evil monsters who threaten the countryside, and in the end even illness which would have carried him away is outwitted and leaves him in peace. There is another strand to the story, emphasising the risk of overweening pride which must always be held in check, but in general we cannot help but recognise the ritual basis of the plot. The time–lapse between performances and the idea of a son born to replace his father immediately suggests a cyclical view of life. Ozidi's progress is that of an archetypal culture hero, a model for every male in the community. This particular ritual drama as it is traditionally performed is really a kind of dramatised epic and the shorter, more consciously shaped play which J. P. Clark has fashioned from it retains just these characteristics. The ideals and aspirations of that community are reaffirmed, accepted and surrendered to by the audience.

History Plays

In the same way that ritual implications are usually incorporated with tragedy, either ritual or tragedy is often fused with historical drama. Ritual drama is a kind of direct presentation, while history plays are essentially a form of documentary, a celebration of national life and events rather than of myth cycles and inevitability. The action of history plays was originally conceived as the objective presentation of actual events, a kind of pageant or narrative, but as the form became fictionalised it gave way more and more to the dominance of hero and theme.

Ola Rotimi's *Kurunmi* (1971) is a good case in point; it uses incidents from the civil war between the Ajaiye and Ibadan peoples for a plot, but tends to search into the hero's character and exposes the forces of rivalry and jealousy in Yorubaland at that time, which contributed to the hero's downfall, rather than to rely solely on the history of events. Shakespeare's *Henry IV, Part I* (1598) is another good example of historical drama. The facts of history, as the author knew them, are somewhat altered to suit the dramatic construction, and the focus of interest is directed to an examination of Prince Hal as a monarch–in–the–making rather than to a mere retelling of the events or the presentation of a history lesson. Character investigation and thematic concerns enliven an otherwise dull history lesson and lend intellectual excitement by suggesting some larger truth about human experience.

Classical Tragedy

Ritual drama is equated with direct representation of mythic action and history plays with narrative documentaries, but the mainstream of literary drama as a fictionalised representation of human experience is found in tragedy and comedy. These forms are far more common than the others, and in fact often include or subsume them. The names 'tragedy' and 'comedy' derive from the Greek words *tragos*, meaning goat, and *komos*, meaning revel. In the case of tragedy, which developed from rituals of sacrifice, one expects a tempered experience, a serious and death–denying progression of action, while in comedy one expects a joyous experience, a wild and life–affirming sequence of events.

As literary terms, the words are essentially technical and refer to the distinguishing characteristics of plays, but they have also passed into common usage where their meanings have been reduced to 'sad' on the one hand and 'funny' on the other. The tragedy of an aeroplane crash is a very different thing from a literary tragedy, as is the comedy of funny stories and jokes told by a television entertainer from what takes place in a play. As a serious art form, comedy is generally concerned with situation rather than character, what happens to representative people and the relationship of those happenings to normal patterns of conduct. In comedy the improbable and unexpected happens, surprising us and exciting laughter at the ridiculousness of human situations. When the inversions or exaggerations of the circumstances are settled and normality prevails, we are somewhat reassured that a natural order exists and will always tend to reassert itself.

Tragedy, on the other hand, presents a world in which a different kind of distortion occurs and the return to normality is based on punishment or expiation for the original inversion of values, a sin against society or against the supernatural. Tragedy is primarily interested in characters and those situations which act upon their natures, ultimately destroying them. If, as in classical tragedy, the main character has been responsible for his or her sin, his punishment and death are a satisfying confirmation of absolute morality, while his own stature as hero is renewed and reasserted by the way he faces responsibility for what he has done or its consequences. In tragedies that which is noblest in human nature is redeemed and rendered imperishable, however fragile and prone to error that nature may be, and the audience is reconciled to the inevitable downfall and death of even the most heroic characters simply because the downfall is always qualified, the heroic possibilities of human nature are reaffirmed. Acceptance of the individual's defeat at the hands of life experience is the object of tragedy and that end or goal is directed towards the attitude or world–view of the audience, not towards their physical well–being.

A good deal of misunderstanding and confusion, however, has arisen from repeating Aristotle's statement that tragedy purges the audience of fear and pity. No one is quite sure what the term *katharsis* means in that context, but drama certainly should not be mistaken for medicine. Like all literature it appeals to the mind or intellect by evoking an emotional response, a greater awareness of the human condition in the audience. Physical relief, such as that engendered by defecation or ejaculation, is not really the point.

Not all sub–genres of tragedy balance an acceptance of the individual's defeat with a vision of heroic renewal, however, and there are further distinctions between classical and modern tragedy, between heroic tragedy, on the one hand, and anti–heroic tragedy, on the other. Classical tragedy requires a hero of high political and social status as well as of moral distinction who is placed in a situation which acts upon an undiscovered flaw in his character and diminishes his moral stature. The basis of heroic tragedy is the effect of the situation on character and the investigation is generally more psychological than thematic. Recognition or confirmation of the flaw occurs at the climax of the play and the hero descends to his inevitable end as the action develops towards the ultimate catastrophe.

In Elizabethan or Renaissance drama there were other kinds of heroic tragedy besides the straightforward plays of political revenge, ambition, etc., and the distinguishing feature is subject matter. Domestic tragedy — for example, Shakespeare's *Othello* (1605), *Romeo and Juliet* (1595) or John Webster's *The Duchess of Malfi* (c. 1614) — takes for subject matter some distortion and defeat in a world dominated by romantic love, but more often the structure of tragedy as a form was combined with other sub-genres, such as the history play or comedy. A tragic conception of experience is very well suited to historical documentary, lending form and depth to an otherwise uninteresting recital of national events, while tragi–comedy combines the best of both fictional worlds in assuming that the tragic flaw or error can be expiated without defeat, that the hero can be redeemed through the acts of others, and even by natural events or the mere passage of time. Shakespeare's later plays such as *The Winter's Tale* (1612) and *The Tempest* (1611) are excellent examples of the genre.

Unqualified tragedy, however, only occurs where characters of the first rank are involved ·and the action concerns absolute morality. In domestic tragedy we have lesser figures because the subject is love or personal relationships and therefore supposedly inferior to questions of state, but in tragi–comedy even kings and princes are regenerated through love. Later on in the seventeenth century, love became an acknowledged virtue and a legitimate subject for high heroic tragedy in the work of John Dryden and others, but interest in psychological depth of character and investigation had already given way to the idealisation of characters and actions. Yet another sub–species of tragedy had thus come into being.

Modern Tragedy and Tragi–Comedy

Modern tragedy, on the other hand, has characters of quite bourgeois origins and even less than average pretensions. A more fundamental difference, however, between classical tragedy and the problem play, which developed in late Victorian times, is that it is no longer the effect of situation on character which destroys the hero but rather those very heroic qualities of character are inevitably defeated by social evils and the predominance of debased human nature. Such an attitude towards life is obviously related to the naturalistic view which held human nature to be basically corrupt and denied the possibility of spiritual or heroic development of personality. Social problems and modes of conduct which limited individuality were very often the subjects of such plays and suggested the name given to the sub–genre. In Henrik Ibsen's *Enemy of the People* (1882), for example, the hero is a doctor in a seaside town who discovers that the sewage system is contaminating the waters of the public mineral baths which are the local tourist attraction. He tries to confront the situation openly and honestly, but the pride and self–interest of the town's leaders finally defeat him and he becomes a figure of the radical individualist isolated by a hostile society.

As the modern period advanced, however, all attempts to present heroic aspiration ceased and the anti–hero became the main character of tragedy, a figure who has no heroic qualities whatever, who in fact often embodies the opposite or contrary characteristics. Rather than a person of high status, the anti–hero is usually of below average achievements or even a conspicuous failure, a beggar or tramp. Instead of having courage, refinement and moral stature, he is usually defeated, coarse and weak, no better than his condition or situation in life calls for. For example, Willy Loman in Arthur Miller's *Death of a Salesman* (1949) is a failed commercial traveller and family man who has been exploited by an uncaring economic system and discarded in middle age with no reason to go on living, no meaning in his life but the bitterness of his failure and victimisation.

The anti–hero is not always a tragic figure, however, but also lends himself readily to a comic view of life. In fact, one of the most interesting literary developments since the Second World War is the introduction of a modern tragi–comic form, absurdist drama, which depends on the anti–hero as a central character. The hero of an absurdist play is often a social outcast, a tramp, madman or petty criminal, and the tragedy of his defeated condition in the grips of a meaningless existence is treated as a remorseless joke. The two tramps, Vladimir and Estragon, in Samuel Beckett's *Waiting for Godot* (1955) stand about, endlessly waiting for an event that is supposed to be meaningful but never happens, and in the meantime they set up a number of word games and arguments which are both funny and nonsensical in an effort to fill in time and give their situation some meaning. Laughter and patterned events balance a bleak view of man's ultimate defeat and the unalleviated anguish of the human condition in modern life.

Comedy

In general, comedy presents endless inversions of normal conduct; nothing is as it should be in a comic play. The expected thought or action never takes place, but its opposite or contrary almost always does. In the end there is generally a reassuring return to normality; the inversions of both action and character are exposed, if not actually righted, and the faith of the audience in an ordered universe is reaffirmed. Take for example *The Trials of Brother Jero* (1963) by Wole Soyinka, which satirises the gullibility and materialist values of representative Nigerians through the roguish self–styled prophet who plays on the compelling desires of his victims: a hen–pecked husband, a childless woman and an aspiring politician. At the same time that Jero appears to be omnipotent in the eyes of his followers, we also see him deflated as the victim of a sharp–tongued market woman to whom he is in debt for the robe of office he is so proud of. In *The Lion and the Jewel* (1963) Soyinka also makes fun of half-assimilated European or Western culture in the clownish figure of Lakunle, a village school teacher, and reaffirms the strength and cunning of African tradition through the success of Baroka, the head of the village, in taking the beautiful young Sidi to wife. The older man has let it be known that he is impotent as a way of disarming Sidi so that he may seduce her and prove his worth.

In comedy the expected order of things suffers a distortion and returns to normality by emphasising the funny or non-sensical side of the action. After all, it is the difference between what one expects and what actually happens which makes one laugh. Whenever our expectation is surprised by an unexpected opposite, especially when exaggeration or unreality is involved, we respond with delight, because it is an imaginative leap which tends to deny serious consequences. The themes of comedy are serious, however, and the recognition or resolution of inversion and inflation are as fundamental to the genre as its joyous and life–affirming spirit.

Comedy also offers a wide range of sub–genres which are distinguishable by subject matter. Renaissance drama developed a number of love situations into comic forms and also investigated the wider implications of human folly and vice in a comedy of character types known as the Comedy of Humours. In comedies of romantic love, for example, there are usually several pairs of lovers who are highly idealised and little developed in character so that they might be played off against one another. One of the major devices for inflating action is a change of roles or disguise required by the initial situation which upsets the normal course of events, but when the impediment is removed and proper roles resumed, each pair of lovers falls into one another's arms and they marry.

A notable version of romantic comedy is the pastoral, in which love plots are played out in idealised natural settings, a forest or pasture–land, where the pretensions and artifices of the sophisticated characters can be contrasted with simpler and more straightforward emotions and values. Shakespeare's *As You Like It* (1600) and *A Midsummer Night's Dream* (1596) are just such conceptions. In the first, political rivalry and consequent exile occasions the disguising of Rosalind and her life in the Forest of Arden with Celia, while in the second, two sets of lovers, who have escaped being mismatched in marriage to unsuitable mates by fleeing to a wood outside Athens, fall under the spell of a mischievous fairy which causes one of the men to fall in love with the other girl. At the same time the queen of the fairies is also enchanted and falls in love with a clownish tradesman from the city. In the end, of course, the spells are broken and order is re–established.

The Comedy of Humours, on the other hand, depends on dominant characteristics in people such as fiery or melancholy tempers and employs characters of the middle classes, rather than those of the lesser aristocracy who figure in romantic comedy, to expose and ridicule all manner of human error. Each character tends to represent some particular vice or folly and the presentation is somewhat flattened in order to focus interest on that representative type of folly or vice. Ben Jonson was the leading practitioner of the form and *The Alchemist* (1610) is a good example. Subtle and Doll Common pretend to be alchemists whose powers can turn base metals into gold in order to trick money and goods out of such gullible and grasping characters as Sir Epicure Mammon, a voluptuous and greedy knight, or the hypocritical puritans, Tribulation Wholesome and Ananais. The vision of human pretension and foolishness is very funny and the tricksters, of course, are finally discovered, but are allowed to escape unpunished.

The distance between the Elizabethan Comedy of Humours and the Restoration Comedy of Manners is very small. Again we find the urban middle classes presented and characters are representative types, but the action centres on social conduct or comportment rather than personal motivation. The characters tend to be stereotypes and their actions wholly in keeping with their images. Not what is done, but how it is done claims our attention, and emphasis falls heavily on wit and elegance of language. The plots usually turn on love, but money and social status vie with romantic passion for supremacy in a world of artifice and hypocrisy. William Wycherley's *The Country Wife* (1675), for example, makes great fun of both excessive suspicion and credulity in a corrupt society through Mr Pinchwife who brings his artless young bride to London for the first time. His suspicions put ideas of adultery into her head, while Mr Sparkish is so trustful and credulous that he loses his fiancée to another suitor. The pivot of the action, however, is Mr Horner, who spreads the rumour of his own impotence in order to allay suspicion and play on the credulity of husbands, thus facilitating his own adulterous affairs.

In the Comedy of Manners situations and characters are often mocked and ridiculed for their own sake, but with no particular thematic interest other than general social satire. A strong farcical element is always present — that is, the presentation of wit and laughter for its own sake — but as a quality contributing to the serious rather than becoming a dominant interest, and consequently an independent form. Farce as a sub–genre of comedy does exist on its own and was very popular in Victorian times as well as in the early twentieth century, but it involves broad or low humour as an end in itself and lacks a significant theme. It is not much admired at the present time.

Aesthetic Elements of Drama

The same elements which featured in the discussion of narrative fiction operate in drama, but, in this case, must be expanded to include relevant aspects of production method. There is no need to repeat the material already discussed under the same heading which also applies directly to drama and only new or different information is included.

Action — the Ordering of Events

The order and structure of action in drama is little different from that of narrative fiction, but because of the desire to economise on exposition and compound effects, the devices of parallel and sub–plotting, first developed in the Renaissance theatre, are particularly useful. Because drama is brief and more tightly structured than the novel, for instance, divisions into component parts or groupings of significant action is particularly relevant to the effect of a given play. Act and scene divisions depend on a number of factors, and historically a number of conventional patterns have arisen.

In the plays of the ancient Greeks, for example, there was a division into five episodes or scenes, each marked off from one another by the appearance of a chorus, which not only commented on the action but also sang or chanted and danced before the next sequence of action began. In Elizabethan times plays were made up of a series of shorter scenes, often irregular in length, which followed one another without interruption from the beginning to the end of the play. One knew when the scene had ended and another began even without a chorus because all the characters would leave the stage and a new set appear, introducing a new topic or action. During the Neo–Classical age and through the early Modern period, most plays were conventionally broken into three acts and intervals or intermissions were introduced to allow for changes of stage scenery and relaxation for the audience. Within each act, scene divisions were often observed, either by leaving the stage empty, bringing down the curtain, or later, turning out the lights (blackout).

In contemporary drama almost any method of combination might be used, depending on the construction of the play being performed or the facilities of the theatre itself, because questions of composition and production method are now generally held to be organic considerations rather than formal ones. The limiting conventions of earlier periods have been avoided. Both playwright and producer choose freely from among a wide variety of forms and styles. If an intermission does occur in a new play, it is usually about half way through the performance and more a question of audience convenience than of dramatic construction. It was only in the Restoration period, for example, that Shakespeare's plays were divided into numbered acts and scenes, a later and more formal view of play construction being superimposed on an earlier and more organic form. All such divisions are not arbitrary, however, and like their counterparts in narrative fiction, emphasise the author's perceptions of constructional units and their interrelationships.

Another feature of organisation which comes down to us from the classical Greek theatre is the unity of place, time and action. The original conception was that the action of the play should conform as closely as possible to a documentary re–creation of the real or actual action. All the events of a drama, therefore, were set in one and only one place, usually before a palace or temple. The action was also limited to the actual length of time it would take for a normal performance, and in this way the play exactly coincided with nature, as though one were watching life and not a re–creation of it. No break or interruption in the action was allowed and no secondary or related sequence of events. One and only one action or plot was permissible.

Elizabethan and later conceptions of drama, on the other hand, have departed widely from such restrictions as they have been free to depart from the effort to create an illusion of reality. Each scene of a play may occur in a very different place, depending on the ability of a given stage to reproduce or suggest those places, and the segments of action may be widely distanced from one another in time. A lapse of months or even years is allowed between one scene and another, while several actions or plots may be woven together to reinforce a common theme. In fact, such departures from the classical unities are necessary in order to achieve an imaginative or anti–illusionistic effect.

1. *Expressive movement and mime.* Because the method of presentation in drama is not confined to language alone and includes physical action on the part of living actors, there is an additional range of expressive devices available to both author and producer. For example, an actor's movements and facial expressions can imitate and reinforce the action or state of being which is suggested by the dialogue, and they may also contradict or belie the literary text, even adding actions which are not actually specified by the author. For example, in *King Lear* (1606) when the central character confronts his ungrateful daughters and demands a sign of outward respect due to his station, it is possible that the palace guards menace the former king as he refuses to return to Regan's castle and Goneril says: 'At your choice, Sir' (Shakespeare, p. 1090). His loss of power should then be insisted upon and his flight from the castle seen as a direct result of his daughters' tyranny rather than of his petty rancour at being denied a train of state. There would also be a corresponding sympathy in the reaction of the audience to his character and predicament. The representation of actions, either for the purpose of furthering the plot or expressing a comment on the action, may even be carried on without dialogue. This is known as mime: indicating actions and reactions by movement of the body alone.

Lady Macbeth, for example, may act out the murder of Duncan during the scene in which she urges her husband to the deed, and strolling actors in *Hamlet* (1603) mime the murder of a fictional king by his wife's lover in front of a real king who gained the throne by the same means. In addition to furthering the plot, mime can also be used to introduce and dramatise relevant background material, adding life and colour to the play. The spontaneity and humour of the mimed sequences in Wole

Soyinka's *The Lion and the Jewel* (1963), for example, add a great deal to the texture of the work as well as to its structure and significance.

2. *Dance.* Mime, as a para–literary device, is taken one step further in the scene of Sadiku's dance of victory over her husband, Baroka, whom she believes to be impotent. Bodily movement, when intensified and regularly patterned in space and time, becomes dance in the same way that random speech can be raised to the level of verse, chant and finally song. Dance is an extremely expressive art form, capable of presenting states of being or emotions as well as mimed narrative. Some cultures are more receptive than others to dance as a form of expression and have evolved highly sophisticated forms and conventions. Dance is often a very normal part of religious ritual, as it is of social entertainment, and its effect on literary drama has always been electric. For some modern authors, especially, certain emotions are beyond expression in words, or even in normal bodily move-ment. At such moments of heightened tension a character might break into a dance and leave the audience to participate imagi-natively in the mood thus created.

The relationship of dance to drama, however, has not always focussed attention on the importance of dancing as a symbolic form or representation of meaning. The chorus of ancient Greek drama danced or moved rhythmically as a visual accompaniment while intoning its songs, and Shakespearean comedies often end in a circular or ring–dance performed by characters whose conflicts with one another have been resolved. Groups of dancers representing abstract qualities or ideas such as evil or justice, etc., also performed at the courts of Renaissance princes in entertain-ments known as Interludes and Masques which combined poetic texts with music and dance, while ballet developed in Europe as a form of pure dance drama in the Neo–Classical and Modern periods with a fixed vocabulary of movement and conventions. Classical ballet, however, is a very rigid form and admits of no literary text. The story or idea of the ballet is expressed through dance alone. With the development of free-style or expressive modern European dancing at the turn of the present century, dance as a theatrical technique again became available to both playwright and producer.

3. *Music and song.* Dance normally presupposes music although it certainly can exist on its own, and in the same way music and its close relation, song, are also independent devices which can be used as desired in the composition or construction of a play. The effect of music and song is to underline and assert the emotions or feelings which already exist in the text, just as mime and dance do, but they usually remain subordinate to the dialogue or text.

There are two distinct possibilities; music and song may interrupt the dialogue at certain strategic moments in the course of the play to underline, elaborate on, or decorate some aspect of the action, and/or the whole production may be geared to a musical rhythm which moves in conjunction with the emotional tempo of the action and helps to express it. On the other hand, when such devices or techniques of production become the main vehicle of expression and dominate the text, no matter how complete and complex it is, instead of merely assisting to express its central idea or theme, the result is no longer literary drama, but rather mime, dance drama, ballet, musical comedy or opera.

Characterisation

Characterisation in drama, like the structuring of action, is very similar to that of narrative fiction with but a few exceptions. Since normally there is no narrator to intervene and enter into the consciousness of characters, it is often necessary to manage situations so that the audience is sure that the figure is speaking his or her innermost thoughts. The soliloquy is perhaps the most common convention and leaves characters on stage alone to speak out their minds as an interior monologue. The device is certainly artificial, as people don't carry on quite such lengthy and detailed conversations with themselves, and usually not out loud, but it is perfectly acceptable as a theatrical convention. With the development of sound–recording and electronic repro- duction, the speeches can even be pre–recorded and played back as though one were hearing the unspoken thoughts in the character's mind as he or she moves about the stage.

The 'aside' is another method of distinguishing between what a character really thinks and what he or she chooses to say or do in public. The device is far more artificial than the soliloquy and requires the actor to 'step outside' the stage action and address the audience directly while the other characters pretend not to hear what is being said. The convention arises out of the desire to warn the audience that the character's real intentions and reactions are not what they appear to be, but that circumstances alone require outward falsification. The device is only useful in a work which does not depend on an illusion of reality.

The favoured and most natural method of showing a character's inner consciousness and motive is to provide a foil, a friend or confidant whose presence has no real bearing on the plot, but merely serves to engage the main figure in conversation and invite the revelation of character. Foils also reflect or emphasise particular qualities of their counterparts through parallels and contrasts of character, and although they do occur in novels, especially those in which the point of view is limited as in the case of a first–person, subjective narration, they are, properly speaking, a dramatic conception. The reason for this, of course, is the central importance of character in drama and the extreme limitations resulting from the presentation of character without the mediation of a narrative point of view. The play-wright is always the narrator in one sense, but in most cases he or she remains hidden from sight and the audience is left to deduce the nature of the characters from the direct evidence of speeches and actions.

Patterns of parallels and contrasts become even more effective in drama than in narrative fiction and repeated verbal images as well as the physical setting can also assume the stature of actual characters; that is, they may assume the force and effect of a character. It is not at all uncommon to find such lines as: This house, (ship, etc.) is driving us on, destroying us. The subway car in which the action of LeRoi Jones's *Dutchman* (1964) takes place is more than just a train compartment or a modern version of 'the Flying Dutchman's' ship. It assumes the proportions of the confining, isolating and emasculating white culture in America in which Lulu seduces and destroys the helpless black youth. Characterisation through dialogue, action and imagery is only part of the story, however; one must also consider the definition of character through acting technique, which involves both the choice of actor for physical characteristics as well as a choice of acting styles.

1. *Actors and roles.* The art of acting is to make the audience believe in the character represented or impersonated by actors, to accept that character as a theatrical fact and to respond to his or her nature and conduct, but not necessarily to believe that the fictional character is actually real apart from his or her presence on the stage. The physical type of the person to be chosen for a part is largely determined by the qualities of the play, but a certain amount of freedom exists, and the producer's choice has a marked effect on the interpretation presented. In the first place, the actor must look the part of the character to be played. Juliet, for example, must be young, innocent and physically attractive for the action of the piece to be believable, but she need not be blond, small, lively, or even European for that matter.

The problem of choosing live actors to play particular roles is actually the same as imagining the theatrical characters when reading a play. How old, for example, should the King of France be in *King Lear?* If he is a man in the prime of life, then there will be more than a hint of sexual attraction in his admiration for Cordelia. If he is a white–haired, wise old man, then his interest in her is more likely to appear a product of his love of justice and esteem for her moral worth. Both interpretations of the relationship are perfectly possible and the one actually chosen must be consistent with all other elements of the producer's (director's) interpretation and visualisation of the play.

The point is that the nature and impact of a characterisation can be even further revealed and developed by the selection of actors who play lesser characters or foils, just as flatness of character can be suggested physically and visibly by choosing actors with peculiar looks or encouraging them to peculiar gestures and mannerisms. In dialogue flatness or caricature can also be achieved by giving characters a particular formula of words which is repeated often enough to become identified with them and to indicate their significance or representational value in the text, but the immediate visual effect is of primary concern in drama. It is the physical appearance and gestures of the actors which lead (or do not lead) to the acceptability and meaningfulness of the characters being represented. We actually see the figures on stage from the outside just as we see people in real life, deducing their motives, feelings and interrelationships from their exterior looks, speeches and actions.

Certain characters in all cultures are easily stereotyped by their looks and people will normally recognise and respond to certain physical types and modes of behaviour as being broadly representative of recognisable character types. A character actor is one whose peculiar looks recommend him or her for one sort of role, perhaps that of villain, temptress, village elder, rich businessman, etc. Such roles occur in many plots and the same actor can be cast for any number of such individualised stereotypes. Flattened characterisations exploit such peculiarities and direct attention away from personality and towards some representational value or significant relationship which contributes directly to the theme. The degree to which a character is developed as a realistic figure depends on the extent or depth of self–revelation involved, the responses of the individual to a number of experiences. When reading drama, one needs to visualise characters, their looks and gestures, as well as their movements, and in as much detail as possible. The reader should thus attempt to work out an interpretation in the same way that one makes use of the direct description provided in narrative fiction.

2. *Acting techniques.* Movement and gesture are even more effective on stage than mere looks and we understand a great deal more about a person's nature and inner consciousness by the way he or she carries himself, both habitually and in particular situations. To see someone stomp into a room, slamming the door and banging a book on the table is to understand his or her emotional state. No amount of frowning or screwing up the face will give the same effect. The mistake that most amateur actors make is to translate all feeling into exaggerated facial contortions or shouting rather than suggesting states of being by characteristic bodily movements. Social discomfort and uncertainty, for example, can be implied by hesitating and stiff movement or by some slight nervous agitation such as tapping a foot or fingering a familiar object (a button, ring or ear, for example) much more accurately and completely than by altering the voice.

In fact, a very strong effect is achieved by coupling a calm and reassuring manner of speaking with some 'unconscious' manifestation of a different inner state. In a novel one might have to be told of the discrepancy between outward manner and inner state, both the deduction and its relevance might be pointed out, while in drama, both the observation and the deduction must be made directly by the audience. To overlook the discrepancy is to miss a basic element of the composition and therefore to reduce the possibility of making a valid analysis and interpretation.

Because the human figure, seen full length, is the focal point of drama, movement and gesture are at least as expressive as dialogue in projecting character and character relationships. Only those physical actions necessary to the plot are written in the stage directions, however, and in studying a play rather than seeing it performed, the reader must be his own producer/director and elaborate the characterisation beyond the outlines given in the dialogue. Through imagination, he should try to see the characters acting out their roles in physical detail.

Stylisation and abstraction is as central to acting techniques as it is to all other aspects of drama production. On the one hand there are those devices which create an illusion of reality, a simulation of the way people in real life act and react; on the other, there are those that destroy illusionism, a recognition of unnatural or depersonalised conduct which distances the audience from direct involvement with character or action. By their very nature, mime, dance, music and song all have a distancing effect because they are not very common to human intercourse in everyday life, but there are also ways of speaking and moving when acting out human situations which have the effect of stylising character as well as action.

For example, if the voice exaggerates the normal inflections of speech, on the one hand, or ignores its rules altogether by remaining on one note and allowing an equal amount of time for saying each syllable, very different effects are created. In the first case the character will seem frenzied and, if the device is exaggerated enough, an embodiment of intense emotion rather than a person. In the second, the character will appear to be totally without passion or feeling: a statue, a supernatural figure, or an embodiment of some abstract quality. Of course, the exact impact depends on the actual situation and dialogue as well as the accompanying style of physical movement, but subtle changes in the delivery of speeches do have a marked effect on characterisation and hence on the work as a whole. The same range of possibilities exists for physical movement on stage. A stiff, erect carriage, measured movements and sweeping or self–conscious gestures along with statuesque posing give the sense of an extremely heroic and superhuman personage, while casual, unstudied and random movement reminds us of everyday life. Illusionistic acting depends on the re–creation of life–like speeches and movement, of finding an exact counterpart in inflection and gesture for the idea or feeling to be expressed, and of playing together with other actors in a convincing approximation of normal intercourse. Anti–illusionistic acting frankly recognises the artificiality of stage convention and requires the actor to play directly to the audience, declaiming lines even at the edge of the stage: ranting and raving, sometimes chanting and even singing in order to achieve a heightened and exaggerated effect.

Between these two extremes there is a kind of middle ground where any combination of technique might occur. For example, actors might faithfully reproduce normal, human events but slightly stylise the dialogue, movement and gesture, thus suggesting that the audience comment on the action rather than allow themselves to be carried away by it. Instead of being caught up sympathetically in character and situation, the audience is constantly reminded that the action is being re–created for a purpose and is challenged to think about that purpose, to exercise its faculties of criticism. Another possibility is to combine slight stylisation of acting technique with strange or unnatural actions, as in Wole Soyinka's *Dance of the Forests* (1960) where ghosts and figures of myth or folklore are introduced together with contemporary characters in order to raise issues concerning ethnic identity and traditional culture. Characters who are little more than personifications of ideas are very useful when presenting and investigating ideas and they normally require stylised acting techniques in order to be distinguished from 'real' characters.

Setting

In addition to casting and acting techniques there are many other aspects of stage presentation which affect drama. Setting is the physical location or psychological climate for action, and the way in which an expressive setting is achieved in the theatre is as important as the literary style in which direct descriptions of a novel's setting are written. Costume, stage properties, playing area, scenery and lighting are all essential parts of the play's composition, of realising or interpreting the relationship between its subject matter and theme.

1. *Costume and stage properties.* A good many effects can be created with costuming in addition to the accurate documentation of an historical period. Theatrical costumes are usually exaggerated in any case, and styles, colours and textures are chosen for their suitability to the desired effect of the production. They may be sumptuous and opulent or bleak and dreary. They can either be harmonised or contrasted in colour and texture with relation to the background in order to concentrate on a particular response through conventions of association. If cruelty in a given fictional world is to be emphasised, for example, costumes might use a great deal of leather, metal chains and unyielding, dark-coloured fabrics in boots, belts, accessories and clothing. If a mood of gaiety is required, ribbons of many bright colours, soft flowing garments and garlands of flowers might be worn.

Because of the expressive possibilities in costuming, it follows that clothes need not be faithful period re-creations nor even consistent throughout a performance. Shakespeare produced plays set in ancient Roman times using contemporary dress, and Renaissance artists painted pictures of biblical personages in the clothes of their own time rather than holding to historical accuracy. There is no external reason why plays cannot be costumed in a period other than the one indicated by the author, especially if it is a question of bringing a play up-to-date and emphasising the contemporary relevance of action and theme. Nor is there any reason why period costumes cannot be mixed in a single performance, especially if a comic and anti-illusionistic effect is desired.

There are also many ways in which dramatic characters can be depersonalised or dehumanised through costumes. Buskins (platform shoes) and masks were used on the classical Greek stage, for example, to alter the normal stature and appearance of actors playing gods and make them imposing or larger than life. In modern expressionist drama, costumes often conceal and even alter the very shape of characters, turning them into objects and sometimes into even representational symbols. Many critics have held that John Pepper Clark's *Ozidi* (1966) is unstageable because it calls for several grotesque monsters with more than the normal number of heads and arms, not to mention one which belches out fire and smoke. The supposedly unsophisticated villagers who actually perform the saga in the open air have no such difficulty and manage quite well with elaborate masks and fire pots. No play is unstageable. It is only a question of finding a suitable stage convention.

The role of the unborn child in Derek Walcott's *Ti–Jean and His Brothers* (1970) is perhaps off–putting to the unimaginative, but at least in one production I have seen a perfect solution, borrowed from the masquerade convention of traditional Yoruba theatre. The child was played by a young girl sewn into a large, formless sack in which she hopped, crawled and danced, suggesting the vital and protean aspect of her nature. When she was 'born', she merely emerged demurely from the sack. It was a tremendously moving piece of theatre.

In the same way stage properties need not be realistic; a gangster, for example, might well carry a toy pistol or even a two–dimensional cardboard revolver. Such representation may also be distorted, enlarged or diminished in order to qualify its relationship to the action and therefore a judgement on it. In fact the character in a determinedly anti–illusionistic production need not even carry a visible object at all, but might mime the aiming of a gun, the answering of a telephone, or drinking from a non–existent glass. The art of acting only requires that stage action convince and communicate. The presence of a real gun, telephone or glass is no substitute for the movements and gestures of an actor. What does matter is the degree of illusionism or stylisation desired in that particular production.

Stage properties, as well as the verbal images and elements of physical settings, such as a house, ship or forest in which the action takes place, can and do take on the stature of an independent character or personage. Desdemona's handkerchief in *Othello* (1622), for example, assumes tremendous weight as a symbol of her innocence and as an agent of evil or injustice. The husband's gift reported to have been in Cassio's possession convinces him utterly of his wife's guilt, and in that handkerchief we see her very innocence turned against her as Othello's credulity and passion is turned against himself.

Similarly Miss Prism's handbag in Oscar Wilde's *The*

Importance of Being Earnest (1895) has great comic force when it is produced on stage to unravel the mystery of Ernest's birth. He was found in the handbag as an infant at the left–luggage office of a London train station, having been deposited there by mistake by a scatterbrained and romantic young nursemaid who thought she was leaving the manuscript of a novel she had written. By coincidence, Ernest is trying to explain his lack of family to the mother of the woman he wishes to marry when Miss Prism appears, and Lady Bracknell, who is actually Ernest's aunt, questions her closely about the past. Ernest runs out to get the bag for identification and the riddle of his birth is happily resolved. The bag itself is by this time far more significant than any mere carry–all.

2. *Playing area.* However effective stage properties and costumes are, it is the human figure which is the consistent focus of interest in drama, and for this reason the architectural area in which the actor exists is of central concern to the conception and execution of a play. The dramatic character exists and moves in space. He or she is seen in relation to the playing area, and that space also has a specific relationship to the audience, a relationship which affects both the degree of illusionism created and that of distancing from realism. Basically, there are four distinct stage designs in European drama: the amphitheatre, the apron stage, the proscenium or Baroque stage, and the arena. The distinguishing feature of each is the relation of the audience to the playing area.

(a) *Classical amphitheatre.* The amphitheatre was developed by the ancient Greeks and later imitated by the Romans. It was a vast semicircular affair cut into a hillside in steps or tiers, with a flat playing area at the bottom in which an altar originally stood, and a narrow, raised stage behind with some architectural ornamentation such as pillars, etc. Most of the action took place on the semicircular forestage where the chorus danced and chanted between the episodes, but the ceremonial raised platform was also used for special effects such as the descent of gods, etc. The amphitheatre was exposed to the elements and performances relegated to daylight hours. The great benefit of the arrangement, however, was that large numbers of people could sit down together, with no one being too far from the playing area, and everyone could see perfectly well as each row of people looked over the heads of those in front and below them. The steeply rising stone tiers were engineered so as to reflect sound and one could hear very well, even from the last row, when the actors were speaking in a more or less normal tone of voice. Because of the physical features of the amphitheatre with its audience ranged halfway around the playing area and looking down on the action, a great deal of intimacy between audience and action was fostered. The actors moved and spoke in the midst of the audience, as it were, and imaginative participation was encouraged. On the other hand a certain amount of distance and overtones of awe were exploited when the action was removed to the raised stage at the farthest extreme from the audience. The empty forestage now divided audience from actor and the distance was further exaggerated by having to look up at the action, or at least to change one's angle of vision.

A smaller and more rectangular version of the amphitheatre was also developed in which the deep forestage disappeared as a playing area and all action took place on a long raised platform before the rear wall facing the audience. The odeon was roofed against the elements, but presented the problem of lighting the darkened room as well as emphasising the artificiality of theatrical performance. Actors and audience were brought together more closely in a physical sense, being enclosed in a small covered space, but the fictional world of the play was in marked contrast to that of the audience and the distancing between them was emphasised by the disappearance of the forestage which had separated the tiered seating from the elevated stage.

(b) *Elizabethan apron stage.* The popular theatre of Elizabethan times shared some characteristics of the classical forms, but it actually developed from a purely local design. The earliest companies of actors moved about from place to place, playing in castle halls or, more often, the courtyards of country inns which were generally rectangular, surrounded by buildings with balconies and open to the sky. When the first theatre buildings were constructed, they were small enclosures, balconied and partly open to the sky, with a raised platform stage which projected out into the central pit of the building. There were doors in the wall at the rear of the stage leading to the changing rooms behind and these were used for stage entrances and exits. There was also a recessed alcove underneath a balcony which could be curtained off when not needed as an inner room if the action demanded a transfer from the stage proper. In the same way the balcony might also be used as a playing area; an upper room, a terrace or battlement, for example.

The audience sat on the tiered but covered balconies surrounding the stage and the poorer spectators stood in the pit around the projecting or apron stage. Stools were sometimes placed at the sides and front of the stage itself and members of the audience sat there too, which increased the intimacy of the spectator's engagement in the action as all barriers between audience and action were broken down. There was no question as to the artificiality of the stage presentation. The Elizabethan theatre was small without being dark or confining, and the audience nearly surrounded the action which progressed naturally either near the centre of the enclosed space or in the familiar and everyday setting of an inner room or balcony not far removed.

Towards the end of Shakespeare's life, however, a more artificial and aristocratic theatrical design was developing from the tradition of performance in palace halls as well as from classical precedents. Drama was carried back indoors and permanent theatres were built in rectangular shape with raised platforms at the narrow end of the room. A number of limitations resulted, such as a reduction of visibility from seating arrangements on a level floor and the greater distance of the rear seats from the stage because of the shape of the auditorium. Lighting was another problem, but gains in the direction of realism far outweighed the disadvantages of the new theatres.

(c) *Baroque proscenium stage.* The drama of the period was undergoing a great change. Heroic and imaginative subject matter was giving way to more bourgeois concerns and the illusion of reality was beginning to be in great demand. Instead of imitating the platform stage of later classical times which stood before the rear wall of the room, the proscenium or Baroque stage was recessed into the wall of the auditorium, behind the pillars and arch which gave it its name. With the separation of audience from action, the ultimate distancing was achieved. Whatever takes place on such a stage appears to be happening in a different world from that of the audience which follows separate rules and conventions.

The illusion that dramatic action is actually taking place rather than being artificially re-created in a theatre is as complete on the proscenium stage as is possible in drama. In the first place it is possible to use elaborate machinery and equipment to create illusions and yet hide the means of achieving them from sight. The view of stage action is restricted to what happens within the picture frame of the proscenium arch, while stage props, built-up sets, lighting, etc. can be moved into place or operated from adjacent areas that remain hidden from view. The visible playing area can be completely enclosed to simulate a real room by building a box-set, and all manner of complicated machinery can be used such as was impractical on a platform or apron stage. Scenery might be highly stylised, looking like nothing on earth, or, on the other hand, highly realistic and the playing area can either remain flat and open, or be broken up into various levels and smaller areas of action depending on the play and the imagination of the producer or designer.

Towards the end of the nineteenth century when illusionism had reached its peak, the theatre exulted in what is known as 'fourth-wall' realism where interior scenes were so perfectly reproduced that the audience was led to think that it was looking through a transparent fourth wall of a real room. To foster this idea actors might sometimes turn their backs on the audience when speaking to other characters, and empty picture frames or a stylised fireplace might be placed in the empty space of the proscenium arch with the actors actually looking at the non-existent pictures or warming their hands at the imaginary fire.

One of the greatest factors in creating such a high degree of illusionism was the technical ability to control lighting and so darken the auditorium while illuminating the stage. Not until gas lights were perfected was there any practical means for changing the intensity of lighting, either on stage or in the auditorium, and until the 1870s the house lights (candles) burned brightly throughout performances, emphasising the surroundings of the audience and making them conscious of themselves as theatre-goers in a social situation. Darkening the auditorium reduces that self-consciousness, shuts out the everyday world of the spectator and further encourages the acceptance of dramatic action as being real.

(d) *Modern arena stage.* Having come full circle, contemporary drama exploits all possible forms of stage construction, and theatres are often built with large open spaces that can be rearranged and organised in order to gain the effects of an amphitheatre, apron stage or proscenium production. The distinctive form of staging that has developed since the turn of the present century, however, is the area (arena) stage or theatre–in–the–round. The form evolves from the circus of classical times which was normally the scene of athletic contests and is also closely related to the modern entertainment of the same name which presents displays of trained animals, jugglers, acrobats, etc. The area stage is completely encircled by an audience, exactly as happens in the traditional ritual drama of Africa, for example, and this places limitations on the use of sets and properties as well as forcing actors to face the audience in segments by turns as there is no rear wall or principal direction of focus. On the other hand actors must also enter and exit through the audience, thereby breaking down conventional barriers and encouraging anti–illusionism, while many more spectators can sit or stand close to the playing area.

In an arena theatre the stage may be of any shape or at any level in relation to that of the audience. Lighting equipment and other apparatus is exposed, and this emphasises the theatrical or artificial aspects of the performance, but the house lights are usually lowered for more intimate participation through imagination and sympathetic feeling. Even plays such as those of Henrik Ibsen and George Bernard Shaw, which benefit from a high degree of realistic representation and accurate reproduction of everyday scenes, are perfectly at home on an arena stage. On the other hand, the audience is less readily carried along by the action alone because this kind of production is more distanced and anti–illusionistic than that of a box–set or a proscenium stage. As a consequence, the significance of the play as well as its inner construction come under closer scrutiny.

To a very large extent the construction or choice of playing area has a far–reaching effect on the qualities to be emphasised in any given play, and, indeed, an impact on the very conception of a play as individual authors write for a particular stage design or convention. Characters and action should be visualised on a stage and dialogue imagined as it would be heard by the audience, whether by playwrights, producer/directors or readers. The relation of audience to actor, of actor to playing area, and of stage to auditorium is a significant factor in the total effect of drama as well as an element of dramatic expression.

3. *Scenery.* Given a particular playing area, much can be done by way of decoration to evoke a suitable setting and influence the expressive quality of any production. The space can be left open and bare, for example, while the action is played out before formal and permanent architecture as in the case of the classical amphitheatre or Elizabethan apron stage. In such cases the setting is evoked through the speeches of the characters and the eye is not distracted by superfluous sets and hangings. Even a proscenium stage can be left unadorned as an anti–illusionistic device, with its wings and backstage areas exposed to full view, the stage hands standing about and actors waiting for their next entrances. The area stage alone begs for some physical object or decorative motive because there is no rear wall and hence no natural focus of interest, nothing in fact to look at, except the faces of the audience who sit opposite. On other stages the actors move against a solid, physical background, but on the area stage, no matter where one sits, they are seen against the audience, and a solid, central pivot or focus of interest for them to move about or through is welcome. Because of its nature, properties must be kept to a minimum on an area stage and they should be both unobstructive and three–dimensional.

On the proscenium stage, however, the background can be infinitely varied in shape, colour and texture with each new combination having a different impact on the production. For example, the playing area can be draped and hung round with material, or screened with a stretched backcloth on which any kind of picture or design can be painted. Early stage painting was elaborately formal and architectural in three–dimensional perspective on flat screens, while later designs attempted to suggest more intimate scenes, even interiors with furniture, curtains and pictures painted on flat canvas. Still later came built–up sets with seemingly solid walls, doors, windows and even ceilings which blocked out backstage areas and gave the illusion of real rooms and interiors. The box–set, however, is not the only possibility of free–standing scene construction. Open scaffolding, ramps, stairs and platforms have also been effective in modernist and contemporary theatre, with the added impact of very sophisticated lighting which provides a further focus of attention and mood.

4. *Lighting.* In terms of altering the spectator's perception of the playing areas, the cyclorama is the most spectacular of lighting devices. A curved wall of white plaster or canvas stretching into the wings on either side of the stage can be so lit that an illusion of infinite, open space is created. A small built–up set in front of a cyclorama provides a point of visual interest and emphasises by contrast the actors who loom larger than life in such a scene, especially if raised above the level of the stage on steps or platforms. Pools of light may define particular areas of the stage or pick out (spotlight) individual characters or action which might otherwise be lost to the audience in the multiplicity of elements which make up the visible scene. (Limelight, by the way, is an old–fashioned kind of spotlight using lime heated in an oxyhydrogen flame which was common in Victorian times.)

Lighting is also capable of many effects beyond the realistic services of reproducing the gradually fading light of evening or the effect on a room when a lamp is lit or adjusted. Lighting admits of control in colour as well as in focus and intensity, and, through the conventional associations of colours with particular emotional states, it can be used to create an atmosphere suitable to a given action and so emphasise its impact on the audience. For the last fifty years, at least, the lighting of a play has been worked out scene by scene so that complex sequences of lighting changes keep pace with the progress of stage action. Lighting, like all other paraliterary devices, is an effective technique of production in so far as it helps to present or express subject matter and theme.

Implicit/Explicit Point of View

Although drama does rely on various techniques of theatre production rather than on a narrator to indicate an attitude towards the subject matter and an interpretation of the relation-ship between composition and theme, it is not altogether true that narrative point of view is totally absent from the literary text.

Minor characters and even foils, for example, may comment on the action and establish a standard of normal conduct for that particular fictional world against which the audience will measure the conduct of the main figures. The outcome of action is itself a commentary as we have already seen in narrative fiction, and a point of view becomes even more explicit when a chorus is used.

Instead of indirect methods, classical drama relied upon a group of characters whose major functions were to represent a relevant segment of society, to reveal past action and to comment on the present course of happenings. Choruses tend to reflect a rational view of dramatic action and emphasise by their very presence the relationship of that action to a larger social context. The Renaissance theatre preferred more indirect methods of indicating points of view, and Shakespeare, for example, often uses the older convention of a court jester or fool whose jokes and jibes amount to an absolute value judgement and comment on the action. The primary function of a chorus has, in this case, been invested in a single realistic character. As Elizabethan drama developed towards an heroic and Neo–Classical mould, the use of prologue and epilogue as a choral device shifted commentary from within the play to a more artificial spokesman who was exterior to the action. The judgement and commentary so offered were invested with something of the character and authority of the author who was sometimes assumed to speak directly to the audience in this way.

In modernist drama the prologue and choral figure combine to produce a true narrator who need not be actually involved in the action but often appears on stage and talks directly to the audience, mediating between the action and the spectator's view of it. Such a narrator sometimes acts as a guide and arranges the action, as it were. At other times he or she provides background information, speculates on outcome or morality and even offers considered value judgements on both character and action. In Thornton Wilder's *Our Town* (1938), for example, the Stage Manager appears as a personage in his own right and is used as a distancing device. He directs the action, arranges stage properties, takes on minor roles in several scenes and freely comments on all aspects of the play. In Robert Bolt's *A Man for All Seasons* (1960), the Common Man takes on very similar functions and establishes a much more specific relationship between the audience and the action because of the nature of his own relationship to the characters of the play. Whether addressing the audience directly as a representative or archetypal figure or assuming the part of Sir Thomas Moore's steward, boatman and finally jailer, the Common Man prompts the audience to exercise critical detachment and judgement, to evaluate the action not only as it affects the hero and his family but also all Englishmen from that time onward. Certainly, narrative methods can be as effective in drama as any other technique of production that creates or destroys the illusion of reality on which drama depends.

Spoken Language — Realistic Dialects

Because characterisation is achieved more through the style of language employed than by means of direct description, the question of register or dialect as the basis of written dialogue must be examined, first as the reproduction of natural speech common to a region or class of language users, and then as a means of creating or distancing illusion.

Realistic dialogue in narrative fiction is, of course, capable of identical effects, as we can easily see in the work of Joseph Conrad, for example. In real life people rarely speak elegantly, or even coherently, for that matter. The following passage is taken from *Typhoon* (1902), where at least there is a reason for incoherence.

> The voices of the lost group reached him after the manner of men's voices in a gale, in shreds and fragments of forlorn shouting snatched past the ear. All at once Jukes appeared at his side, yelling, with his head down.
> 'Watch—put in—wheelhouse shutters—glass—afraid—blow in.'
> Jukes heard his commander upbraiding.
> 'This—come—anything—warning—call me.'
> He tried to explain, with the uproar pressing on his lips.
> 'Light air—remained—bridge—sudden—north–east—could turn—thought—you—sure—hear.'
> They had gained the shelter of the weather–cloth, and could converse with raised voices, as people quarrel.

'I got the hands along to cover up all the ventilators. Good job I had remained on deck. I didn't think you would be asleep, and so . . . What did you say, sir? What?'

(Conrad, pp. 37–8)

The problem, however, is more obvious and all–pervasive in drama. Spoken language is not always grammatical; incomplete phrases and expressions are understood in context, and the density of colloquial figures or dialect usages depends on the age, class, situation, regional background and historical period of the speaker. Whenever the question of realistic presentation arises, the audience or reader must compare the style of a fictional or dramatic character with examples drawn from real–life speakers of a similar dialect. On stage the actors must reproduce the kind of pronunciation and intonation of the dialect, while at home the reader imagines the movement of the speeches, the natural tones of native speakers as different words and rhythms join together with their meanings to produce a dramatic effect. The words and their meanings are, first of all, an indication of objective facts or information from which we come to deduce or interpret the situation, the emotional condition or state of being of the character and the progress of the action. The question is not so much how true to life the character is, but rather how effective the language is in suggesting an inner state or feeling. In order to achieve this, the speeches must be heard as if spoken aloud and with much feeling, but they do not have to be consistent. For example, in the following speeches from Derek Walcott's *Dream on Monkey Mountain* (1967) both characters normally speak the same West Indian dialect, but in Makak's speech we find that the localising accents disappear in favour of a more lyrical or poetic quality which transcends time and place.

Moustique
You remember one morning I come up and from the time I break the bush, I see you by the side of the hut, trembling and talking, your eyes like you crazy, and was I had to gather bush, light a fire and make you sweat out that madness? Which white lady? You is nothing. You black, ugly, poor, so you worse than nothing. You like me. Small, ugly, with a foot like a 'S'. Man together two of us is minus one.

(Walcott, p. 237)

Makak

Rise. Take off your boots. Doesn't the floor of the forest feel cool under your foot? Don't you hear your own voice in the gibberish of the leaves? Look how the trees have opened their arms. And in the hoarseness of the rivers, don't you hear the advice of all our ancestors? When the moon is hidden, look how you sink, forgotten, into the night. The forest claims us all, my son. No one needs gloves in his grave.

(pp.300–1)

1. *Stylisation.* The creation of natural and realistic dialogue is not the only possibility for dramatic speech, and stylisation, in varying degrees, often proves as effective in expressing thought or feelings behind the words themselves. Contrast is the basis of stylisation; that is, the substitution of a register which is different from the natural dialect of the speaker, or the surprising presence of a style at variance with the expected emotion of a given situation. Compare, for example, the natural and realistic dialogue of Arthur Miller's *Death of a Salesman* (1949) or J. M. Synge's *Riders to the Sea* (1905) with the more formal and stylised speeches in Eric Bentley's translation of *The Good Woman of Setzuan* by Bertolt Brecht (1947) or Gilbert Murray's translation of *The Bacchae* by Euripides (1904).

In the first excerpt Willy Loman, a failure in life, has just committed suicide. His sons, Happy and Biff, are at the grave-side with their mother.

Happy: I'm not licked that easily. I'm staying right in this city, and I', gonna beat this racket! *[He looks at Biff, his chin set.]* The Loman Brothers!

Biff: I know who I am, kid.

Happy: All right, boy. I'm gonna show you and everybody else that Willy Loman did not die in vain. He had a good dream. It's the only dream you can have – to come out number–one man. He fought it out here, and this is where I'm gonna win it for him.

Biff:[With a hopeless glance at Happy, bends toward his mother.] Let's go, Mom.

Linda: I'll be with you in a minute. Go on, Charley.*[He hesitates.]* I want to, just for a minute. I never had a chance to say good–by.

[. . . *The flute begins, not far away playing behind her speech.]*

Linda: Forgive me, dear. I can't cry. I don't know what it is, but I can't cry. I don't understand it. Why did you ever do that? Help me, Willy, I can't cry. It seems to me that you're just on another trip. I keep expecting you. Willy, dear, I can't cry. Why did you do it? I search and search and I search, and I can't understand it, Willy. I made the last payment on the home today. Today dear. And there'll be nobody home. *[A sob rises in here throat.]* We're free and clear. *[Sobbing more fully, released.]* We're free. *[Biff comes slowly toward her.]* We're free . . . We're free . . .

(Miller, pp. 138–9)

Maurya in *Riders to the Sea* is an old Irish woman living on the Aran Islands whose youngest and only suriving son has just been drowned.

Maurya: They're all together this time, and the end is come. May the Almighty God have mercy on Bartley's soul, and on Michael's soul, and on the souls of Shemus and Patch, and Stephen and Shawn *[bending her head];* and may he have mercy on my soul, Nora, and on the soul of everyone is left living in the world.

She pauses, and the keen rises a little more loudly from the women, then sinks away.

Continuing: Michael has a clean burial in the far north, by the grace of the Almighty God. Bartley will have a fine coffin out of the white boards, and a deep grave surely. What more can we want than that? No man at all can be living for ever, and we must be satisfied.

(Synge, p. 106)

Shen Te in *The Good Woman of Setzuan* has been so beset by the evils of human nature and the socio–economic system under which she lives that, in order to survive, she has been forced to hide behind a mask and act as a representative of that evil, even though it is against her real nature. She is speaking to the gods who have been searching vainly for an example of goodness on earth.

> Your injunction
> To be good and yet to live
> Was a thunderbolt:
> It has torn me in two
> I can't tell how it was
> But to be good to others
> And myself at the same time
> I could not do it
> Your world is not an easy one, illustrious ones!
> When we extend our hand to a beggar, he tears it off for us
> When we help the lost, we are lost ourselves
> And so
> Since not to eat is to die
> Who can long refuse to be bad?
>
> (Brecht, p. 104)

In *The Bacchae* Cadmus, once King of Thebes and now sentenced to exile, laments the death of his grandson whose impiety towards the god Dionysus has brought about his own downfall. The scene is particularly harrowing as Pentheus' mother, who is a worshipper of Dionysus, has just learned of her own part in her son's death while possessed by the god.

> And now I fare
> Forth in Dishonour, outcast, I, the great
> Cadmus, who sowed the seed–rows of this state
> Of Thebes, and reaped the harvest wonderful.
> O my belovéd, though my heart is dull
> In death, O still belovéd, and alway
> Belovéd! Never more, then, shalt thou lay
> Thine hand to this white beard, and speak to me
> Thy 'Mother's Father'; ask 'Who wrongeth thee?
> Who stints thine honour, or with malice stirs
> Thine heart? Speak, and I smite injurers!'
> But now — woe, to me and thee also,
> Woe to thy mother and her sisters, woe

Alway! Oh, whoso walketh not in dread
Of Gods, let him but look on this man dead!
                              (Euripides, p. 75)

2. *Lyrical prose and poetry.* Formality and measured emphasis
can have still another use in dramatic speech besides contrast by
understatement as in Shen Te's speech, or elevating, as in that of
Cadmus. As required, both natural and artificial dialogue can be
raised to the level of verse and even beyond to the condition of
poetry. The methods of poetry and techniques of musical devices
are discussed in detail in the next chapter, but for the moment it
is enough to think of poetry as formally structured language
having a rhythmic movement and internal patterns of sound,
whose music either evokes an emotion or mood directly, or, more
probably, emphasises and helps to express the specific meaning
of the words that have been so arranged. Music, after all, is
capable of affecting our emotions quite arbitrarily and lends itself
readily to other forms of art as a means of intensifying and
directing effects. Through a musical composition of words, a
further level of aesthetic appreciation and significance is added,
which helps to express and emphasise meaning.

Poetical speech is held to elevate both characters and actions,
not so much because it isn't a natural way of talking, but rather
because its musical basis and organisation render it more forcefully expressive and moving. It is just as possible to write verse
dialogue in a natural and realistic dialect as it is to write more
formal and highly artificial speeches, and in both cases poetry is
eminently suitable for drama because of its brief intensity. Poetry
need not be used consistently throughout a play; in fact, it can
even be varied in form from scene to scene, or from character to
character, as well as being mixed with prose at times in order to
encourage contrasts and comparisons.

Elizabethan drama was highly poetic and verse was held to be
necessary to it as a mode of expression, but it was not until the
Romantic period that the conception of verse drama as distinct
from dramatic poetry was developed. Instead of the logical
progression of a plot in which actions convince us of their truthfulness by their resemblance to real or everyday life, the plays of
Lord Byron and Percy Bysshe Shelley, for example, depended on
the inner structuring or unifying design of ideas, images, figures

of speech and stylistic devices. They convince by the unity and expressiveness of their design.

Verse drama was again revived in the twentieth century by W. B. Yeats and T. S. Eliot, while contemporary drama in the work of Harold Pinter or Samuel Beckett gives us examples of plays constructed according to the principles of poetic composition, but not actually written in verse. In the same way contemporary novels are becoming more and more dependent on poetic techniques of composition and presentation. After all, any fiction, whether narrative or dramatic, can also be so constructed as to incorporate a rhythm of action which may quicken its pace, pause and slacken, much as a piece of music moves in time.

In verse drama the pace of language as well as the intensity of action determines the rhythmic structure, and it is not at all unusual for a whole dramatic production to be performed according to a musical or lyric pattern which underscores its composition and reflects its significance. Rhythms of bodily movement and of speech can be directly related to the mood or theme of a scene and changed contrastively from episode to episode, as in a modern or imagistic plot construction, just as they may progress in a continuous modulation of intensities as in a classical structure of rising and falling action or a well–made plot. A production can be said to be poetic when its rhythm and movement echo its structure and overall theme, just as the language can be said to be poetic in its continuous use of rhythm and sound pattern to heighten the emotional effect of the dialogue and the action.

Ruins of the classical amphitheatre at Epidaurus, Greece.

PERFORMANCE OF A DRAMATIC MYSTERY AT COVENTRY.

A reconstruction of the float or waggon stage of mediaeval Miracle Plays.
The Mansell Collection

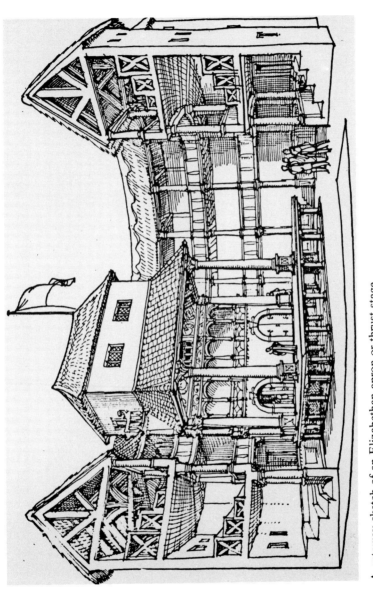

A cutaway sketch of an Elizabethan apron or thrust stage.

The covered amphitheatre of the Olympian Academy at Vincenza, Italy (sixteenth century).
The Mansell Collection (Alinari)

Seventeenth century proscenium stage with architectural scene. Interior of
Teatro Regio, Turin: *c*. 1740. Painting in oil by D. Olivero.

Museo Civico, Turin

Nineteenth century proscenium stage with realistic outdoor scene.

The Mansell Collection

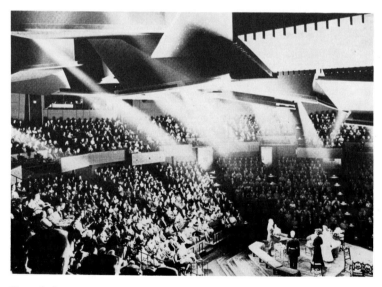

Twentieth century area stage (theatre in the round) with realistic production.

Minnesota Theatre

Contemporary mixture of realism and anti-illusionism with split level playing
area and musicians on stage.

Peter Stöckli

Dehumanisation of characters for anti-illusionistic effect.

Bert Andrews

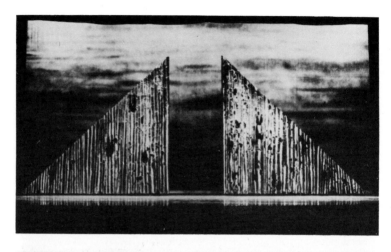

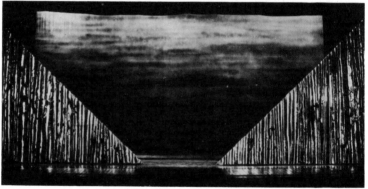

Stylised stage setting in which a single change of positions suggests situations such as siege and suffocation.

Mula Haramaty

4 *Poetry and the Music of Speech*

Poetry as a Pattern of Sounds

While narrative fiction as a literary form is distinguished by point of view and drama by production method, poetry is characterised by musical patterns of sounds which are based on the natural qualities of spoken language. Poetry is normally written and published, as are plays, but its proper medium is the human voice. Poetry is also a performing art and relies on the musical interpretation of phrases and lines in order to realise its full value. Whether one listens to a recitation of poetry or re–creates the music of the language in the imagination as one reads privately, the rhythms and sound patterns of the poem figure largely in an interpretation and understanding of the work.

Playing with the musical possibilities of a language is a very natural and normal human activity. Children, for example, have a spontaneous and immediate love of musical speech and the repetition or patterning of sounds. Poetry, in the form of rhymes, riddles, verses and songs, gives much simple pleasure, and peoples living close to the land, before education and urbanisation, also delighted in poetry and musical speech as a means of capturing and formulating their experience of life. Poetry is certainly one of the oldest forms of literature and celebrates man's ability to observe and apprehend experience as well as to manipulate language expressively.

The evocation of feelings and states of being is of primary importance in poetry, and plot or story element is normally held to a minimum. Narrative, dramatic and descriptive poetry are common enough, but the tendency in our time is to concentrate on poetry as the communication of abstract feeling, the direct presentation of individual experience as well as of commentary, observation or emotion which derives from a poet's perception of life. Structure and style are the principal devices of poetry and its language is far more condensed and intensified than even that of drama. The attraction of poetry is wholly one of aesthetic delight in language play, the re–creation of intense feeling through structures of words which express the self or inner nature of both poet and listener.

The Form and Spirit of Poetry

In general, poetry has no fixed form other than that of its basic structural units — the line (verse), stanza, canto or book — and these are almost infinitely variable. A line of poetry in English is usually from eight to twelve syllables in length and stanzas are normally from two to perhaps twelve lines long. Lines, stanzas and the larger structural forms are unified by the repetition of rhythm patterns as well as of other technical devices. A complete poem may consist of only two lines, as in the case of the epigram, while narrative poems may extend over thousands of lines depending on the subject. There are accepted patterns for both lines and stanzas — that is, fixed and formal structures which have identifying names and specified characteristics, such as blank verse, terza rima, rhyme royal, etc.* — but a poet may create a distinctive and individual line or stanza pattern to suit his or her material and verbal style. Certain conventional forms such as the ballad or sonnet, for example, actually specify a fixed line length, rhythmic pattern, stanza form and rhyme scheme which is used throughout the poem (see below), while organic poetry allows original invention and variation in all these matters as the need of the material dictates. Even more than in the novel or drama, fixed poetical forms become rigid moulds into which the subject matter is to be fitted. The opposite extreme is the organic poem which grows naturally and eccentrically out of the subject matter.

Not all arrangements of ideas and words based on a musical structure of lines and stanzas can be considered poetic, however. A critical distinction must be made between poetry and mere

---

*See any handbook or dictionary of literature (literary terms) for definitions and examples.

verse. Poetry subordinates musical structures of language to the direct expression or communication of experience, but it is also possible to arrange words into musical patterns for other purposes, such as for the communication of information in a form which is easily remembered.

> Thirty days hath September,
> April, June and November.
> All the rest have thirty–one,
> Save February alone,
> To which twenty–eight we do assign
> Till leap–year gives it twenty–nine.

Because there is no expression or communication of human experience, such verses can hardly be called a poem in any serious discussion of literature, but, of course, there is a middle ground between the extremes of expressive poetry and mere versification in which distinctions are blurred and definitions become a question of critical judgement.

Primary Modes of Poetic Expression

The major kinds of poetry are narrative, dramatic, satiric and lyric, but only in the case of the last mentioned do we find a large number of fixed forms and clear subdivisions. Narrative, dramatic and satiric poetry are generalised concepts which involve the substitution of verse for prose in the telling of a story, the presentation of dramatic dialogue, or the formulation of moral commentary.

Narrative Poetry

Narrative poetry merely tells a tale in verse, usually, but not always, from an omniscient point of view, and the plot is action–packed more often than not because it is difficult to sustain interest and intensity over longer works. In the folk literature of many peoples verse narratives commemorating real events as well as fictional ones have been passed on through oral tradition, especially in the form of songs. The epic is one of the few fixed

forms of narrative poetry and it developed from the oral tradition
of a pre–literate society. Such works as *The Iliad* and *The
Odyssey*, sometimes attributed to the Greek bard, Homer, grew
up in folk tradition and later came to be fixed as they were written
down. Epics do include dramatic and lyric passages for the sake
of variety and aesthetic interest, but essentially they are
concerned with telling a story. The form has been discussed in
some detail above (p. 42) and need not be repeated here, but
something of the historical development of the epic as it has
come down to us should be noted.

In Roman times the natural epic of the Greeks was synthesised
and formalised as a literary form while its subject matter was
often adapted to the social and political conditions of the period,
as in Virgil's *Aeneid* (22–19 BC). During the early Renaissance
the form came back into popularity with Dante's *Divine Comedy*
(1313–21) and in the later English tradition we have John Milton's
Paradise Lost (1674). The genre had great appeal in sixteenth and
even seventeenth century England, not only because of classical
precedent but also because of the contemporary belief in an
ordered universe which was reflected in the authoritative form
itself. In the Neo–Classical period translations and imitations of
Greek and Roman originals were common, as were mock or
comic epics such as *The Rape of the Lock* (1714) by Alexander
Pope, and this sub–genre remained a popular form well into the
Romantic period with its major expression in Lord Byron's *Don
Juan* (1819–24). The idea of the epic as a cultural focus or touchstone came back into vogue with the long poem in the twentieth
century when writers were seeking a coherent and unified world
view in a disintegrated society. Many modern long poems share a
number of features or qualities with the epic form, but perhaps
none is so closely associated with that genre as *The Cantos*
(1930–69) by Ezra Pound .

Dramatic Poetry

Dramatic poetry has also been discussed above as an alternative
mode for writing dialogue (p. 141). Verse was generally the rule
for the heroic drama of the Elizabethan and early Neo–Classical
periods, and especially so for tragedy, but it soon gave way to
prose in the bourgeois comedies of the Restoration and was not

revived until the early Romantic period when it was used by poets such as Percy Bysshe Shelley and George Gordon Lord Byron for their imaginative closet dramas. In the twentieth century there has been a revival of interest in verse drama, that is, conventional plays written in verse, and even in more experimental drama in verse or prose which convince or move an audience by the unity and expressiveness of their poetic design or structure. This more contemporary form of poetic drama aims at the presentation of states of mind and being rather than logical or sequential action.

It is also possible to write a short poem in dramatic form, presenting a dramatic situation or character through direct speech in either monologue or even dialogue form, as is the case in 'At the Draper's' by Thomas Hardy (1840–1928).

> 'I stood at the back of the shop, my dear,
>   But you did not perceive me.
> Well, when they deliver what you were shown
>   *I* shall know nothing of it, believe me!'
>
> And he coughed and coughed as she paled and said,
>   'O, I didn't see you come in there —
> Why couldn't you speak?' — 'Well, I didn't. I left
>   That you should not notice I'd been there.
>
> 'You were viewing some lovely things. *"Soon required*
>   *For a widow, of latest fashion"*;
> And I knew 'twould upset you to meet the man
>   Who had to be cold and ashen
>
> 'And screwed in a box before they could dress you
>   *"In the last new note in mourning"*,
> As they defined it. So, not to distress you,
>   I left you to your adorning.'

(Hardy, pp. 396–7)

The dramatic lyric is a modern development which was popularised by Robert Browning in the Victorian period and has been taken up by a number of poets since that time.

Satirical Poetry

Satirical poems are variable in length and the form originally derives from classical models which set out to comment on human experience and especially to expose the folly or vice of men. All that has been said above about prose satire is equally true for satirical poetry, and in order to criticise actual life in a coherent poetic structure of any length, some sort of plot motif such as a journey, adventure or comparable narrative is often used to serve as an organising principle. The tone of a piece may range from bitterness to hilarity, depending on the poet's faith in human nature, and the value of satirical poetry depends on its originality, wit and elegance. Language play, rather than plot, characterisation or musical intensity is its main preoccupation and the form appealed to the Neo–Classical age more than to any other.

The following example is taken from John Dryden's 'Absalom and Achitophel' (1681) in which he satirises the political and especially the religious confrontations of his day. The tensions existing in Restoration England between Catholics and Protestants is the point of the analogy.

> Th'inhabitants of old *Jerusalem*
> Were *Jebusites*: the Town so call'd from them;
> And their's the Native right —
> But when the chosen people grew more strong,
> The rightfull cause at length became the wrong:
> And every loss the men of *Jebus* bore,
> They still were thought God's enemies the more.
> Thus, worn and weaken'd, well or ill content,
> Submit they must to *David's* Government:
> Impoverisht, and depriv'd of all Command,
> Their Taxes doubled as they lost their Land,
> And, what was harder yet to flesh and blood,
> Their Gods disgrac'd, and burnt like common wood.
> This set the Heathen Priesthood in a flame;
> For Priests of all Religions are the same:
> Of whatsoe'r descent their Godhead be,
> Stock, Stone, or other homely pedigree,
> In his defence his Servants are as bold
> As if he had been born of beaten gold.

(Dryden, p. 192)

Lyric Poetry

Lyric poetry, on the other hand, is a relatively fixed form which has appealed to almost every age, particularly to the Renaissance and the Romantic or Modern periods. During the Renaissance the lyric was especially prized for its musical quality and as a vehicle for the expression of individual passion, usually idealised love. For the modern world the lyric has been seen more as a vehicle for romantic imagination and it has accommodated subjective feelings more akin to the general disillusionment of our times. The following passage from Ezra Pound's 'Hugh Selwyn Mauberley' (1920) expresses the reaction of intellectuals to the wholesale death which characterised the First World War.

> There died a myriad,
> And of the best, among them,
> For an old bitch gone in the teeth,
> For a botched civilization,
> Charm, smiling at the good mouth,
> Quick eyes gone under earth's lid,
>
> For two gross of broken statues,
> For a few thousand battered books.

> (Pound, p. 191)

Lyrics are normally short poems, rarely exceeding one hundred lines, and as the name implies, they are characterised by a heightened musical quality which helps to express an intense and personal statement of emotion or attitude. The lyric represents an ideal relationship between subject matter and technique, something akin to that between a dancer and the dance. Emotions and states of mind are more fully communicated by exploiting the musical resources of language but the intensification of musical speech cannot be effectively extended over long periods. Longer poems usually consist of heightened lyrical moments interspersed with narrative, dramatic and/or satirical passages.

1. *The ballad.* Of the fixed lyric forms the ballad is one of the oldest and it originates from the oral tradition of pre–literate peoples. Ballads are generally meant to be sung rather than recited and they usually express basic human emotions such as love or hate on the one hand, or fear of and wonder at both the

physical and supernatural worlds on the other. Ballads lend themselves readily to simple melodies and a four–line stanza of iambic verse with interlocking rhyme and a refrain (a repeated line) is the basis of the form in English. There is often a slight narrative element in the ballad which sustains interest, and the following song which was popular at the time of the American Revolution (1776–83) is a good example of the form. 'Johnny Has Gone for a Soldier' was collected by John Allison.

> There I sat on Buttermilk Hill,
> Who could blame me cry my fill;
> And every tear would turn a mill;
> Johnny has gone for a soldier.
>
> Me oh my, I loved him so,
> Broke my heart to see him go,
> And only time will heal my woe;
> Johnny has gone for a soldier.
>
> I'll sell my flax, I'll sell my wheel,
> Buy my love a sword of steel
> So it in battle he may wield;
> Johnny has gone for a soldier.
>
> (Allison, p. 15)

2. *The pastoral.* Pastoral poetry is another identifiable kind of lyric and one which was originally developed in classical times. Unlike the ballad its distinguishing feature is its subject matter rather than a combination of subject matter and form. It has no fixed stanza structure or length, but its very looseness of construction lends itself to lengthy development. Its characteristic techniques are elaborately stylised language devices and a measured or decorous rhythm, a gentle and consistent movement of sounds and ideas. The traditional subject of pastoral poetry is an idealised world of nature peopled by highly romanticised rustic figures, often shepherds and shepherdesses. The theme is invariably a celebration of fertility in nature, the cycle of birth, maturity and death, but purged of all its ugliness and pain. The human condition and all the ills it is heir to undergo regeneration by association with the pastoral world and become reconciled with death.

The elegy, as a separate lyric form, is really part of the pastoral tradition and the combination of natural setting, elaborate stylisation and a poetic lamentation or speculation on death is known as a pastoral elegy. 'Lycidas' by John Milton (1608–74) and 'Adonais' by Matthew Arnold (1822–88) are important examples of the genre.

Both the pastoral and the pastoral elegy were in fashion during the Renaissance and returned to favour again at the end of the eighteenth century as part of a popular reaction against the urban and artificial culture of the Neo–Classical period. The opening passages of 'An Elegy Written in a Country Churchyard' by Thomas Gray (1716–71) offers an excellent example of the genre.

> The Curfeu tolls the Knell of parting Day,
> The lowing Herd winds slowly o'er the Lea,
> The Plow–man homeward plods his weary Way,
> And leaves the World to Darkness, and to me.
>   Now fades the glimmering Landscape on the Sight,
> And all the Air a solemn Stillness holds;
> Save where the Beetle wheels his droning Flight,
> And drowsy Tinklings lull the distant Folds.
>   Save that from yonder Ivy–mantled Tow'r
> The mopeing Owl does to the Moon complain
> Of such as, wand'ring near her secret Bow'r,
> Molest her ancient solitary Reign.
>   Beneath whose rugged Elms, that Yew–Tree's Shade,
> Where heaves the Turf in many a mould'ring Heap,
> Each in his narrow Cell for ever laid,
> The rude Forefathers of the Hamlet sleep.
>   The breezy Call of Incense–breathing Morn,
> The Swallow twitt'ring from the Straw–built Shed,
> The Cock's shrill Clarion, or the ecchoing Horn,
> No more shall rouse them from their lowly Bed.
>   For them no more the blazing Hearth shall burn,
> Or busy Houswife ply her Evening Care:
> No children run to lisp their Sire's Return,
> Or climb his Knees the envied Kiss to share.

(Gray in Hayward, p. 225)

3. *The ode.* The ode is another classical form, and it is also a longish poem, but usually of less than one hundred lines. It has no fixed stanza form or verse pattern and generally celebrates an abstract concept by presenting a developed image or scene through which that concept is expressed accompanied by speculation or commentary as to its exact nature or character. The form had particular appeal for the poets of the early Romantic period because of their interest in ideal and imagined experience. 'To Autumn' by John Keats (1795–1821) is something more than just a description of the transitional season which comes between summer and winter in temperate climates.

> Season of mists and mellow fruitfulness,
>   Close bosom–friend of the maturing sun:
> Conspiring with him how to load and bless
>   With fruit the vines that round the thatch–eaves run;
> To bend with apples the mossed cottage–trees,
>   And fill all fruit with ripeness to the core;
>   To swell the gourd, and plump the hazel shells
> With a sweet kernel; to set budding more,
>   And still more, later flowers for the bees,
>   Until they think warm days will never cease,
>   For Summer has o'er–brimmed their clammy cells.
>
> Who hath not seen thee oft amid thy store?
>   Sometimes whoever seeks abroad may find
> Thee sitting careless on a granary floor,
>   Thy hair soft–lifted by the winnowing wind;
> Or on a half–reaped furrow sound asleep,
>   Drowsed with the fume of poppies, while thy hook
>   Spares the next swath and all its twinèd flowers:
> And sometimes like a gleaner thou doth keep
>   Steady thy laden head across a brook;
>   Or by a cider–press, with patient look,
>   Thou watchest the last oozings hours by hours.
>
> Where are the songs of Spring? Ay, where are they?
>   Think not of them, thou hast thy music too, —
> While barred clouds bloom the soft–dying day,
>   And touch the stubble–plains with rosy hue;
> Then in a wailful choir the small gnats mourn

Among the river sallows, borne aloft
 Or sinking as the light wind lives or dies;
And full–grown lambs loud bleat from hilly bourn:
 Hedge–crickets sing; and now with treble soft
 The red–breast whistles from a garden–croft;
 And gathering swallows twitter in the skies.

(Keats in Perrine, pp. 46–7)

4. *The sonnet.* The sonnet is the most formal of the more common lyric poems and, like the ballad, has remained in poetic fashion since its creation. The form was developed by Petrarch (1304–74) and the Italian or Petrarchan version is readily distinguished from the English or Shakespearean. Both sonnet forms consist of fourteen lines with fixed stanza forms, verse patterns and rhyme schemes, while the characteristic subject matter is idealised love or commentary on the human condition.

The Petrarchan sonnet is divided into two distinct stanzas, an octave (made up of two quatrains) which states the subject of the poem, and a sestet (made up of two tercets) which offers a development of that subject, a reflection on it, or an application. The rhyme scheme acts as a structural device, marking the subdivisions of the poem as well as providing an additional sound pattern. Petrarchan sonnets in English are often modified to some extent. Sometimes the stanza–breaks are ignored and the lines printed one after the other without a division, as is always the case with Shakespearean sonnets. The unity of thought and of language patterning within each subdivision remains intact, however, even though the divisions are not obvious to the eye. Another common modification is to substitute a variant rhyme scheme in the sestet. 'Leda and the Swan' by William Butler Yeats (1865–1939) follows the classical pattern – ABBA/ABBA/CDE/CDE. This poem celebrates the Greek myth of Leda, a mortal woman, who was possessed by the god Zeus in the form of a swan. One of the children of that union was Helen of Troy, whose beauty caused the Trojan War, the destruction of that city and the death of King Agamemnon among thousands of others. The poem suggests that the physical act of making love is closely akin to that of making war.

A sudden blow: the great wings beating still
Above the staggering girl, her thighs caressed
By the dark webs, her nape caught in his bill,
He holds her helpless breast upon his breast.

How can those terrified vague fingers push
The feathered glory from her loosening thighs?
And how can body, laid in that white rush,
But feel the strange heart beating where it lies?

A shudder in the loins engenders there
The broken wall, the burning roof and tower
And Agamemnon dead.
                                Being so caught up,
So mastered by the brute blood of the air,
Did she put on his knowledge with his power
Before the indifferent beak could let her drop?
                                            (Yeats, p. 441)

The Shakespearean sonnet is not divided into distinct stanzas, but rather allows for the continuous development of an idea throughout three related quatrains, each built around a significant image with the conclusion, deduction or application expressed in a final couplet. Again, the rhyme acts as a structural device, but the Elizabethan form gains in strength and flexibility because of its cumulative or serial development towards a definite climax. Number 73 of the sonnet sequence by William Shakespeare (1564–1616) develops the idea of transiency and mortality through the images of autumn leaves, the fading light of evening and the dying embers of a fire.

That time of year thou mayst in me behold
When yellow leaves, or none, or few, do hang
Upon those boughs which shake against the cold,
Bare ruin'd choirs where late the sweet birds sang.
In me thou seest the twilight of such day
As after sunset fadeth in the west,
Which by and by black night doth take away,
Death's second self, that seals up all in rest.
In me thou seest the glowing of such fire
That on the ashes of his youth doth lie,

As the death–bed whereon it must expire,
Consum'd with that which it was nourish'd by.
    This thou perceiv'st which makes thy love more strong,
    To love that well which thou must leave ere long.
                                        (Shakespeare, p. 1320)

The sonnet is an amazingly flexible poetic form, capable of infinite variety as well as great intensity within the confines of a formal or fixed outline which challenges the poet's ingenuity and invention. The whole idea of fixed forms and formal construction is intriguing, especially in poetry where stylistic structuring rather than plot narration is called into play.

The Structuring of Poetry

Both narrative and dramatic poetry rely upon plot incidents and characters. Satire on the other hand may or may not employ a narrative base. When it does not, it joins with lyric poetry in relying on a progression of ideas or attitudes which function as a plot and are reinforced by the repetition and patterning of stylistic elements such as line length, stanza form, rhetorical devices, figures of speech, rhythm and repetition of sounds. Note, for example, the change in tone of the ballad above (p. 158) from distressed lamentation to determined action. However lonely and heart–broken the girl may be, she also responds courageously and patriotically: 'I'll sell my flax . . .' Rather than a single emotion being expressed, there is a dynamic shift or change within the piece which reflects the complexity and multiplicity of human experience as well as evoking a corresponding sequence of responses in the reader.

When analysing the structure of a poem, the best method to follow is to deduce and state the idea or attitude being expressed by each component part. An understanding of the relationship of parts to each other discloses the structure of the work, while the progression of ideas or responses which intensify them points directly to the theme.

Action (events), characterisation and setting are generally less important in satirical and lyrical poetry then in narrative or dramatic verse because ideas and states of being are the centre of interest, but they must be taken into consideration whenever they are brought into play. Point of view, on the other hand, is as effective a technique in lyric poetry as in the other sub–genres, and a good reader will be just as careful to identify the speaker's precise attitude and tone in a poem as well as the degree to which his or her character is developed and the effect that this has on the subject matter and theme.

The speaker of a lyric, that is, the voice which is speaking or the consciousness overheard, is not always to be identified as the poet in his or her own person. The use of a persona is not uncommon. The speaker in 'The Love Song of J. Alfred Prufrock', for example, is not T. S. Eliot (1888–1964), but rather a fictional character with a social background, personality, ideas and attitudes which Eliot has chosen as an aid in expressing a particular idea or theme. The speaker of a lyric poem need not be so completely developed and easily identifiable, however. More often than not the point of view or attitude towards the subject matter is suggested by the style of the poem and must be inferred from word choice and speech rhythm, much as one does in the case of dramatic characters.

Patterns of Language

Above all other considerations, it is style (the patterning of language) that provides the basis of poetic composition. The elaboration of language shapes and intensifies meaning. It is style alone that indicates the nature of a poet's sensibility and the analysis of style (the combination of syntactical, semantic and musical devices) confirms the reader's emotional response to tone and point of view and leads to a complete understanding or interpretation of the poem. Because of the extreme concentration of language in poetry, the slightest variation in syntax has noticeable effects. To take only one example, the patterning of verb forms can be a powerful device. A static quality and emphasis on imagery is achieved by omitting verbs altogether or reducing their number to a minimum, while the greatest action, immediacy and force is achieved by the repeated use of present participles. All sorts of other emphasis can be achieved by restricting verbs to a particular tense, aspect, condition, voice or mode, according to the effect desired. The patterning of any grammatical feature, for that matter, along with the use of rhetorical devices and word associations from identifiable registers are bound to create more startling effects in poetry than in prose because the selection and combination of these features constitute both the structure and the meaning of a poem.

Word choice and the connotative values involved, as well as the direct evocation of sensory experience (images), are also of greater significance in poetry, and grammatical ambiguities are highly prized as a means of multiplying meaning by encouraging the presence of more than one interpretation. The closing lines of 'The Love Song of J. Alfred Prufrock', for example, offer at least two different readings.

> We have lingered in the chambers of the sea
> By sea–girls wreathed with seaweed red and brown
> Till human voices wake us and we drown.
> (Eliot, *Complete Poems*, p. 7)

A paraphrase of the two readings gives us the following: We have lingered in the chambers near or with sea–girls who are wreathed; or: We have lingered in chambers which have been wreathed by sea–girls. The very imprecision and presence of multiple meaning help to suggest the dream–like quality of the image and are part of the achievement of the poem.

Figures of Speech

In order to complete the discussion of style in chapter 2, the question of figures of speech must be taken up in some detail. Figurative language surprises the reader because the statement or idea expressed does not make sense on the surface level, and, since literal meaning is denied, an act of imagination is required before the intended meaning becomes clear. The sense must be inferred from some naturally relevant association, comparison, substitution, contrast or inversion of image and idea. The point most often being emphasised by a figure of speech is the common factor or relationship which exists between the images involved, that quality or attribute which they have or do not have in common.

In technical discussions of figurative language the first image or idea (that which arises from the subject matter) is called the tenor, the relationship is the ground, and the second image (that which is brought in for the sake of comparison) is the vehicle. For example:

O, my luve is like a red, red rose.
(Burns in Perrine, p. 87)

person or emotion	[Beauty or passion]	red rose
(tenor)	(ground)	(vehicle)

The red rose in European tradition is associated with passion as well as with beauty and perfect natural form; these are the qualities that the beloved and the rose have in common. The qualities of the woman and/or the love felt for the woman are being praised and celebrated although they are never explicitly stated. The missing ground must be identified in order to understand the point that the author is making. Merely defining the figure of speech by name is of no use at all; one must understand the precise idea being emphasised and the purpose for which the figure is being used within the poem.

More often than not, the tenor is also missing and the vehicle alone presented.

Their path lay upward, over the bald skull, half grass, half stubble.

[hill]	[shape or texture]	skull
(tenor)	(ground)	(vehicle)

The context of the statement makes it impossible to give the word 'skull' its literal meaning. No real skull is so big that a path could pass over it and people walk there. They can only be walking up a hill or over an outcropping of rock. The substitution of the word 'skull' for hill forces the reader to seek a common ground of association between the two images and the only conceivable similarity within the context is in terms of shape and texture. The writer implies that the hill is steep–sided, rounded on top, smooth and hard–surfaced by superimposing the image of a skull upon that of a hill. As one reads the sentence, the scene of people walking up a hill is replaced by the vision of a skull. The two images then fuse together with the hill taking on the shape and texture of a skull. The sudden imposition of the skull image is startling and forces upon the idea of a hill qualities and connotations that it does not naturally have. If someone should die or come close to death on the climb, we would not be surprised since such an association has already been made. An understanding of figurative language relies almost entirely on the normal and natural associations or connotations of words and ideas, and one must recognise the exact denotation and connotation of the vehicle in order to deduce the ground which is, after all, the point of emphasis.

There are a large number of accepted and recognised figures of speech as well as of different ways of categorising them. The following scheme is based on a consideration of the relationship between vehicle and tenor, but includes only the most basic figures, those in common usage.

Comparison and substitution
    simile, metaphor
    allusion, metonymy
    analogy, allegory
Representation by substitution
    synecdoche
    personification
    symbol
Contrast by discrepancy and inversion
    overstatement, understatement
    paradox (oxymoron)
    irony: verbal, situational, dramatic

1. *Comparison and substitution.* As we have seen above, figures of speech which are based on comparisons of vehicle and tenor may be either direct and overtly stated, or, on the other hand, they may be indirect and achieved by substituting a vehicle in place of the tenor.

        And the men
        Do not leave their chins
        To grow bushy

> Like the lion's neck,
> Like the chin
> of a billy goat.
>   (p'Bitek, p. 54)

Both tenor and vehicle are stated and a straightforward contrast between men and animals is set up which emphasises the sophistication and superiority of men who beautify themselves by shaving. Such figures are known as similes and are so recognised because a stated comparison is being made using the words 'like' or 'as'.

A very different and equally common figure of speech is characterised by the direct substitution of vehicle for tenor and this is known as a simple metaphor. In the following example the tenor of each metaphor is unstated, as is the ground, but there are clues enough to lead us to the meaning.

> 'Las Palmas'
>
> The Canaries,
>   bald brood
> of primordial beasts,
>   basking contorted
> and burdened
>   in a bath
> spilling forgotten in the sun.
>   (Clark, p. 26)

Canaries are birds, not beasts, and normally they are not bald. The statement of the text cannot be taken as literal and we must find some other meaning. These Canaries are islands as we can see from both the capital letter and the title of the poem; Las Palmas is, after all, the capital city of the Canary Islands. And islands are not prehistoric beasts, but they might appear so, as might the Atlantic Ocean seem the size of a bath, from an aeroplane. The words 'brood of beasts' have been substituted for the unstated phrase 'group of islands' and 'bath' for 'ocean' because of similarities in shape and appearance which are emphasised by these particular comparisons.

A very special kind of metaphor occurs when the substituted word creates an unusual and jarring combination with those around it. The collocation of words in every language is governed by convention, and fixed collocations normally cannot be altered. In the line, 'The hand that signed the paper felled a city' (Thomas, p. 66), the word 'felled' stands out, not because it fails to make literal sense but because it violates a basic convention of word choice and combination. The verb 'to fell' is only used with trees and the conventional collocation leaps to mind as soon as it is used. Instead of 'tree' in the present example, the object of the action is 'a city'. It is not possible to chop down a city, but from the context of the poem we understand that the signing of a document resulted in the destruction of a city. The word 'felled' has been substituted for related words such as 'destroyed' or 'razed' in order to lay emphasis on the suddenness and completeness of the action. The result of superimposing the image of a tree being cut down and falling to the ground on a city being destroyed or razed to the ground is to intensify and particularise the action, to increase the concentration of detail. In the example above there is also a secondary contrast set up between 'signed' and 'felled': a hand that signs a declaration of war and a hand that fells trees are rather different in character and usually attached to different kinds of people. A hidden or disguised quality of the statesman (the rude force and determination of a woodsman) is also being exposed through the comparison which results from forcing an unconventional collocation between 'felled' and 'city'.

Another kind of comparison altogether is achieved by bringing into play some image or idea which recalls to the reader's mind an outside, but known and universally recognisable image, personage or happening. Vehicles of this type are drawn from contemporary life, history or prior literature and are called allusions. The figure is actually a special kind of simile or metaphor in which the vehicle has an already accepted quality and authority invested in it by cultural tradition. For example:

> The blues were composed in the middle passage
> of autumn, in the frail tossing ship.
> (Haynes, p. 407 in Jones)

'The blues' refers to a kind of music written and performed by black Americans and is meant literally, but 'the middle passage' is really a substitution for the literal idea of slavery. 'The middle passage' is a term which refers to the mid–Atlantic sea route between Africa and the Caribbean, and by association to the transporting of African slaves to the New World. Although the phrase refers objectively to the slave trade, its connotations of inhuman conditions and extreme suffering are the ideas which are being emphasised. Blues were not actually composed during the Atlantic crossing, but developed much later as a response to the savage and degrading conditions of the slaves and their descendants which began with that journey.

Another possible relationship between vehicle and tenor is based on a logical and fixed association of activity or idea which conventionally links the two images. As soon as the vehicle is mentioned in the given context, the unstated tenor jumps to mind ·because of a natural relationship, such as we find in the following description of a man standing on a New York city street.

> On the corner — 116th and Lenox
> all in brown down to his kickers.
> (Bethune, p. 382 in Jones)

The word 'kickers' makes little sense on the literal level since one expects an item of dress. The obvious relation between clothes and kicking is a shoe, something worn on the foot which is capable of kicking. The figure is known as a metonymy, a straight substitution of vehicle for tenor because of an inherent relation of function or action. Metonymy is a very common figure of speech, especially in colloquial language and slang. No real comparison is involved, but emphasis is achieved through recognition of the ground which associates vehicle with tenor. In every form of comparison and substitution it is the ground which is significant and determines the point of emphasis or function of the device.

Neither similes nor metaphors need be restricted to a single vehicle or image, however, and the device can be extended to some considerable length. In a work about a famous poet the author writes of a man whose creative efforts have left him wrecked.

> And monstrously, so,
> As a Stegosaurus, a lumbering obsolete
> Arsenal of gigantic horn and plate

From a time when half the world still burned, set
To blink behind bars at the zoo.

(Hughes, p. 13)

Every detail of the extended simile applies to the famous poet. The way people stare at him and set him apart from normal society makes him feel like a prehistoric beast, grotesque and obsolete, imprisoned and on show.

Substitutions (metaphors) are also compounded and extended as a matter of course, sometimes to great length, indeed. Extensions of this sort are generally descriptions of a process or progressions of events whose inner relationships are both fixed and familiar. Allusions may also be introduced as vehicles for both extended similes and metaphors, just as they can be for simple comparisons and substitutions. If an extended comparison is used as the basis of argument, however, it is usually referred to as an analogy.

When X, an unknown process, is explained by showing that it functions in the same way as the known process Y, an analogy is at hand, and also when X is assumed to result in such and such an outcome or effect because its progression is similar to that of Y, and Y ends in just such a way. Analogies of both types are found in the following poem although the last stanza offers us a negative comparison (contrast) which emphasises dissimilarities.

Death is the twin of Sleep, they say:
    For I shall rise renewed,
Free from the cramps of yesterday,
    Clear–eyed and supple–thewed.
But though this bland analogy
    Helps other people to face
Decrepitude, senility,
    Madness, disease, disgrace,
I do not like Death's greedy looks:
    Give me his twin instead —
Sleep never auctions off my books,
    My boots, my shirts, my bed.

(Graves, p. 196)

Analogy is sometimes thought of as a rhetorical device because of its use in logic and argumentation, but even there, it is founded in a vehicle–ground–tenor relationship and follows the rules of extended comparisons.

Allegory is yet another figure of speech which has developed from the extension of simile and metaphor. In allegory the process or fixed interrelationship of elements is organised as a plot whose agents and actions follow one another in a coherent sequence of logical developments. Each element or image on the surface level (vehicle) presupposes an unstated tenor on a secondary level which has meaning in the context of the same narrative (ground).

> There was a Prince of old
> At Salem dwelt, who lived with good increase
> Of flock and fold.
>
> He sweetly lived; yet sweetness did not save
> His life from foes.
> But after death out of his grave
> There sprang twelve stalks of wheat;
> Which many wond'ring at, got some of those
> To plant and set.
>
> It prospered strangely, and did soon disperse
> Through all the earth:
> For they that taste it do rehearse,
> That virtue lies therein,
> A secret virtue, bringing peace and mirth
> By flight of sin.
>
> Take of this grain, which in my garden grows,
> And grows for you;
> Make bread of it: and that repose
> And peace which ev'rywhere
> With so much earnestness you do pursue,
> Is only there.
>
> (Herbert in Perrine, pp. 72–3)

From the specific details of the story and the relationship of the images (vehicles) to one another we quickly come to recognise the

Prince, twelve stalks of wheat and grain (vehicles) as Christ, the twelve apostles and the word of God (unstated tenors). The ground is the narration itself which binds the two levels together and helps us to discover the underlying meaning. As it does in all figures of speech based on comparison and substitution, the ground is the most important feature, but in allegory it functions differently in that it is directly stated. In the case of allegory it is the reconstruction of the secondary level (tenor) which leads to the recognition and emphasis of the original narration (ground). Note, too, that in allegory the tenor rather than the vehicle may introduce the authority and wider association of allusions. Allegory is not restricted to religious teaching, however, although it has certainly been exploited for this purpose, especially in the form of parables which are special forms of allegory whose intention is the teaching of moral and ethical precepts.

The unsettling aspect of allegory is that its narrative basis makes it a valid literary form as well as a figure of speech to be employed in other kinds of writing. Allegories such as *The Faerie Queene* or *Pilgrim's Progress* are independent sub–genres, while a novel such as *Moby Dick* has allegorical levels of interpretation but the device is not so dominant that the whole work can be considered an allegory. In that particular case not enough of the elements which make up the surface level (vehicle) have exact equivalents on the secondary level (tenor).

2. *Representation by substitution.* A second category of figurative language also depends on the substitution of vehicle for tenor but not so much emphasis is placed on the nature of the ground. In representational figures it is more often the recognition of tenor which bears significance and the vehicle merely serves to point towards that meaning. In the case of synecdoche, for example, the image that acts as vehicle is always a subordinate part or aspect of a larger image or idea. Synecdoche is very commonly used in English, even in everyday speech. One does not think twice about so ordinary a phrase as farm or factory hand. The word 'hand' is substituted for the complete human being because that is the operative part of the man or woman in so far as manual work is concerned. The part is merely substituted for the whole and the ground recognised in the obvious relationship. Synecdoche, however, is not restricted to physical

relationship and in the line, 'Give us this day our daily bread', the word 'bread' represents the whole class of foodstuffs which sustain and nourish mankind. The common use of the word 'metaphor' or 'metaphorical language' to refer to all figures of speech, whether characterised by substitution or inversion, is also an example of just such an extension of meaning in everyday usage.

Another kind of representational figure is found in the use of a vehicle to represent a tenor which is difficult to present directly as an image. Literature in general, and especially poetry, depends on imagery and the evocation of direct sensory responses to the ideas presented. Abstractions and large philosophical concepts are very difficult to incorporate in literature, especially if they must be repeated from time to time in a given work. The best solution is to find some concrete and objective image, character or action to represent them. The image chosen as vehicle acts as a kind of counter or short–hand form of reference to the larger and more complex idea behind it.

For example, 'justice' has a very well–defined meaning but the word does not evoke an immediate sensory response. It cannot be visibly portrayed without a concrete form and so it is often pictured as a rather heroic and handsome woman who is blind-folded and carries a pair of balance scales. Such an image is a vehicle for the unstated tenor, the ideal of justice, and achieves its aim by representing a number of inherent qualities or charac-teristics belonging to that abstraction. Justice is an ideal and hence the idealisation or heroic form of the woman; justice is objective and impartial, therefore the woman is blindfolded in order to avoid being prejudiced by anything but the facts; justice is based upon the judgement of evidence presented, hence the scales. It is not enough to represent justice as a woman — that is, to lend the abstract concept a complete human body and independence of action. The woman must be seen to suggest or engage in acts of justice which are images of the idea itself.

In literature we find examples such as the figure of the woman who represents the season in John Keats's ode 'To Autumn':

> whoever seeks abroad may find
> Thee sitting careless on a granary floor,
>   Thy hair soft–lifted by the winnowing wind;
> Or on a half–reaped furrow sound asleep.

The woman is nothing more than a figure of speech, but one which is much elaborated and defined. At one and the same time she is compared to a real woman of the fields such as was common in rural England at the time, and becomes an embodiment of every quality or attribute associated with autumn. The vehicle acts out what the tenor stands for and therefore can be substituted for it, while the tenor is identified by the qualities and attributes of the vehicle. Such a figure of speech is called personification, but only when a whole and complete human being represents an abstract or incorporeal concept.

Inanimate objects, on the other hand, are also compared to parts, actions or attributes of human beings, but this is usually a case of simple metaphor. Using human qualities or characteristics as vehicles does not necessarily turn the figure into personification. In the line, 'The screaming shells burst overhead', it would be absurd to think of the artillery shells as complete human beings, flying through the air and exploding. The sound the shells make as they fly overhead is being compared to the sound of a person screaming (metaphor) and so introduces connotations of danger and human fear. In the following example from 'Sailing to Byzantium', however, the soul is personified as a complete human figure:

> An aged man is but a paltry thing,
> A tattered coat upon a stick, unless
> Soul clap its hands and sing, and louder sing
> For every tatter in its mortal dress.
>
> (Yeats, p. 407)

The point of the personification is to express the abstract idea of the soul's spontaneous and vital joy, without which an old man is little more than a scarecrow. In this case the poet represents that idea by substituting an image in which we can easily recognise those qualities.

The most complex representation of tenor by vehicle is through symbols, where some difficulty presents itself because the word is so often used loosely; even when handled with precision, it is understood to refer to more than one kind of relationship. In everyday language the word 'symbol' means to represent or to stand for (stand in place of), and international traffic symbols, for example, include ⊖, meaning No Entry, and ⊘, meaning No Left Turn. Each symbol of this type has one and only one accepted meaning or significance. One also calls x a mathematical symbol because it can represent or stand for any number one wishes to assign to it. Literary symbols function in both these ways, but they also include other subdivisions or distinctions according to the kind of meaning and the way in which it is assigned.

In the first instance there are images which have a definite and conventional meaning, such as the acceptance of the lily as a symbol of purity, the bald eagle as the symbol of the United States government, or the cross as the symbol of Christianity. An objective image (vehicle) is chosen to represent an abstraction (tenor) because of an implied association of qualities or characteristics between the two (ground). Such symbols are widely accepted within a given cultural context. In the case of the lily, the ground is discovered in its white colour and unmarred texture, while the strength of the bald eagle and its natural habitat make it an appropriate symbol for the American government. For historical (allusive) reasons, the cross is the central image of Christianity, but it is very difficult to state in a word what that symbol really represents, other than the general concept of Christianity which embraces a very wide–ranging and complex system of thought as well as particular actions and associations. The point is that some fixed symbols have an almost one–to–one relationship of vehicle and tenor — the worm or serpent symbolising evil and destructive forces, for example. Other symbols are more open–ended and meanings radiate from a single vehicle which represents a cluster of ideas and associations that cannot be stated simply or concisely. The same principle is at work in this latter case as in personification, but instead of a human being as vehicle, an inanimate object or image is chosen to represent the abstract tenor.

Fixed symbols do depend on their wide acceptance within a given culture, and it is always possible to create new symbols to add to the stock of existing fixed relationships. Instead of taking an established system of symbols and exploiting them for their own ends, such writers as William Blake and Percy Bysshe Shelley introduced new schemes of images, characters and actions which had no conventional correspondences or accepted tenors, yet the images they used were obviously vehicles which represented or symbolised some other meaning. Those meanings had to be patiently worked out over a period of time by readers and critics using both evidence from the texts themselves and outside sources. The creation of new symbols with fixed meanings may not be immediately understood, but, when such creations are well–conceived and exploited, they soon become familiar and pass into normal usage.

Another kind of symbol, that which acquires meaning through the context of a particular work, is perhaps a more interesting device, but also a more demanding one. On the simplest level the representation is based on a metaphorical relationship. For example, we have the symbolism of the stone in Yeats's 'Easter 1916', which celebrates the permanent achievement of a handful of Irish heroes who rose above the everyday concerns of life, took up arms against British rule and were executed. The stone comes to stand for their hearts' purpose which forever altered the course of national life as the unchanging stone in the living stream alters its flow.

> Hearts with one purpose alone
> Through summer and winter seem
> Enchanted to a stone
> To trouble the living stream.
> The horse that comes from the road,
> The rider, the birds that range
> From cloud to tumbling cloud,
> Minute by minute they change;
> A shadow of cloud on the stream
> Changes minute by minute;
> A horse–hoof slides on the brim,
> And a horse plashes within it;
> The long–legged moor–hens dive,
> And hens to moor–cocks call;
> Minute by minute they live:
> The stone's in the midst of all.
>
> Too long a sacrifice
> Can make a stone of the heart.
> O when may it suffice?

> That is Heaven's part, our part
> To murmur name upon name . . .

> (Yeats, pp. 393–4)

A third kind of symbol is one which allows a wider possibility of interpretation, usually by setting up a larger structure of images in much the same way as an analogy or allegory, but without a defined or specific meaning. In this case a whole poem may be seen as a symbol, just as an allegory may become a sub-genre rather than a mere technical device. In 'My Star' by Robert Browning (1812–89) there is no way of knowing what the star represents but we can deduce that it is something personal and not particularly conspicuous. The unstated tenor might be a person, a place, a thing, or even an action.

> All that I know
>   Of a certain star
> Is, it can throw
>   (like the angled spar)
> Now a dart of red,
>   Now a dart of blue;
> Till my friends have said
>   They would fain see, too,
> My star that dartles the red and the blue!
> Then it stops like a bird; like a flower, hangs furled:
>   They must solace themselves with the Saturn above it.
> What matter to me if their star is a world?
>   Mine has opened its soul to me; therefore I love it.

> (Browning, 1, pp. 280–1)

In fact, the unstated tenor need not be identified, and we can be certain of this fact because the poet has offered no clue. In this kind of symbol it is the ground that assumes primary importance, the relationship between the poet and the idea being symbolised. What we recognise and respond to is the implied parallelism between the poet's feelings towards his star and the reader's relationship to his or her own.

Symbols of this kind can also be based on a narrative, but usually one which comes to no conclusion and describes a common or universal action. There is, of course, always a hint that the action is more significant than it appears and should not be taken at its mere face value. In 'The Road Not Taken' by Robert Frost (1874–1963) the decision to follow one forest path instead of another is the pivot of the poem and symbolises any such decision in the reader's experience which could make a distinctive difference in his or her life.

> Two roads diverged in a yellow wood,
> And sorry I could not travel both
> And be one traveller, long I stood
> And looked down one as far as I could
> To where it bent in the undergrowth;
>
> Then took the other, as just as fair,
> And having perhaps the better claim,
> Because it was grassy and wanted wear;
> Though as for that the passing there
> Had worn them really about the same,
>
> And both that morning equally lay
> In leaves no step had trodden black.
> Oh, I kept the first for another day!
> Yet knowing how way leads on to way,
> I doubted if I should ever come back.
>
> I shall be telling this with a sigh
> Somewhere ages and ages hence:
> Two roads diverged in a wood, and I —
> I took the one less travelled by,
> And that has made all the difference.

(Frost, p. 131)

3. *Contrast by discrepancy and inversion.* Figures of speech based on contrasts are equally as expressive and as widely used as those which suggest comparisons and representations. The degree and kind of difference between tenor and vehicle is as central in contrastive figures as the identification of a common ground is in metaphorical language. The method common to all comparative and representational figures is to compare seemingly dissimilar images, while in contrastive devices it is normal to set up an opposition of meaning, either between tenor and vehicle or

between the vehicle and the context of reality in which it exists. In one of the most common types of contrastive figures both vehicle and tenor share the same general meaning or significance but differ greatly in degree of strength or emphasis.

In the case of overstatement and understatement a discrepancy or contrast is introduced between what is said and what is meant. It is not uncommon to hear such figurative statements as 'I could have killed him for saying that' or 'What an uncomfortable house, I nearly froze to death.' The first merely expresses the speaker's anger and desire to hurt the other person, the second, that the speaker was cold. The emphasis that has been made in each case is measured by the degree and kind of contrast which exists between vehicle and tenor. Overstatement is also known as hyperbole and exaggerates the quality of the tenor, sometimes to a fantastic degree, in order to emphasise it the more. The exaggeration is always obvious and such statements can not be taken as literal truth. In the following example from *A Esssay on Man* by Alexander Pope (1688–1744) the nature of pride is exposed and derided by encouraging the proud to even greater acts of pride.

Weigh thy opinion against Providence . . .
Snatch from His hand the balance of the rod,
Rejudge His justice, be the God of God.
(Pope in Barnet, p. 353)

It is also possible to exaggerate below the level of the literal meaning, and understatement is just as common as overstatement. In understatement something less than the full truth is stated. The vehicle offers a diminution by negative contrast of the intended meaning which underlies its qualities. Rosalind's remark in *As You Like It* (1600) is a classical example: 'Men have died from time to time.' The fact that they die every minute and in very great numbers is strongly emphasised by the unexpected understatement. Another example is found in 'To His Coy Mistress' by Andrew Marvell (1621–78) who is proposing that they make love now and not wait too long.

The grave's a fine and private place,
But none, I think, do there embrace.
(Marvell in Perrine, p. 58)

Paradox is another of the figures of speech that rely on contrasts but its characteristic discrepancy is created by a seeming illogicality in the surface meaning. Whereas a paradox in everyday language is defined as an illogical or self–contradictory statement, a literary (figurative) paradox is a statement in which this only seems to be the case. 'The empty room is full of people' is an example of a non–literary paradox. The statement does not make sense because a room cannot be empty and full at one and the same time. 'The pen is mightier than the sword', however, is an example of a figurative paradox. The statement only seems to be contradictory to fact. As weapons which share similar shapes but have different sizes, the pen is certainly not mightier than the sword. The statement may be interpreted figuratively, however, and on that level it does make sense. If pens are not being compared to swords, but rather writing (pen as tool) to fighting (swords), the statement reads: Argument is more effective than violence. In this case metonymy must be recognised in each of the images and the tenors discovered before the figure delivers up its meaning. A simpler example is seen in the line, 'The child is father of the man.' Biologically the reverse is true, but there is a sense in which the seeming paradox can be resolved. The word 'father' may be understood as a figure of speech implying that certain physical and psychological characteristics are being passed on or reproduced in another. Read in this way the statement makes excellent sense; the man's nature is formed or determined by that of the child, he assimilates qualities and characteristics from his former self. In a literary paradox the logic of a statement is always reasserted when one or more elements in it are recognised as a figure of speech and interpreted on a non–literal level.

There is also a special form of paradox known as oxymoron, in which contrasting images are reduced to single words and placed close together, sometimes side by side, for even greater contrast.

> I crave the stain
> Of tears, the aftermark
> Of almost too much love,
> The sweet of bitter bark
> And burning clove.
> (Frost, 'To Earthward', p. 279)

As qualities, sweet, bitter and burning are applicable, but surprise and delight us by their sharp and obvious contrasts one to the other. Oxymoron depends more on the denotative and connotative values of words than figurative usage and it is very nearly as effective as paradox.

Irony is the last figure of speech to be discussed, and like paradox it is recognised by illogicality of statement, but in one of several ways: a contrast between what is said and the fact of the situation (verbal irony), the actual situation and what ought or ought not to be (irony of situation), and what is said or understood by a fictional character as opposed to what the far more omniscient reader or audience knows and understands (dramatic irony). In every case there is a contradiction, not only between various elements of the statement, but also between the statement and an expectation derived directly from the context.

As in the case of overstatement, judgement is needed in determining whether a statement or situation is to be taken at face value or whether it suggests its opposite by contrast. For example, if one reads a letter to the editor of a newspaper saying that the people of another country are politically dangerous and should be attacked or destroyed before they develop enough military strength to make them a threat, there may be some difficulty in deciding whether the writer is serious or not. If a reader approves of aggressive violence for the protection of a narrow nationalism, he or she will assume that the letter is meant literally. Bombing and killing are within the limits of conceivable action for that person. If the reader is a non–violent and open–minded internationalist, there is a dilemma. The published letter may be seen as the work of an extremist who meant every word of it, but it could also be seen as being ironical because the ideas it contains are so extreme, so immoral and unacceptable. In the case of such a public letter one would have to know more of the writer in order to decide how to interpret it, but in literature there are usually sufficient clues in the context by which to make a judgement. Irony is a very subtle device and there is always the possibility that it might go unrecognised by some readers.

Verbal irony involves stating the exact opposite of what is meant or intended, and an author relies on the context as well as the reader's personal values to discover the figurative (intended) meaning. The unstated tenor (meaning) is usually an exact inversion of the vehicle. When, for example, Mark Antony opens the funeral oration in *Julius Caesar* (1600) with the words:

> For Brutus is an honourable man;
> So are they all, all honourable men,
> (Shakespeare, p. 986)

we take the statement at its face value. But as the speech progresses, the context changes. Brutus and his supporters appear less and less honourable while each repetition of the adjective becomes more and more ironical.

A similar and more direct inversion is seen in the following anonymous poem of the sixteenth century which alludes to the former religious practice of abstaining from meat on Fridays in commemoration of Christ's crucifixion. To abstain from eggs as well, since they are the embryos of future chickens is a rather fine point of piety. To some people it would certainly seem an extreme.

> No egg on Friday Alph will eat,
> But drunken he will be
> On Friday still. Oh, what a pure
> Religious man is he!
> (Anonymous in Perrine, p. 90)

Irony occurs on all levels of language usage and like other figures that depend on contrast it may involve a discrepancy between vehicle and context as well as one between vehicle and tenor. The opening stanza of a song by John Donne (1573–1631) provides a good example.

> Go and catch a falling star,
> Get with child a mandrake root,
> Tell me where all past years are,
> Or who cleft the Devil's foot.
> (Donne, p. 5)

Each command is meant literally and there is no figurative level or unstated and contrasted tenor to be found. The irony lies in the fact that each command constitutes an impossibility. No one can catch a falling star, etc.

Another feature of irony and its use is its close relationship with sarcasm. A sarcastic tone or manner is adopted when attempting to belittle, deride or ridicule a person or situation and show them to be inferior. Verbal irony, as in the case of Mark Antony or Alph above, lends itself to the purpose, but irony is also possible without sarcasm as in the case of 'Go and catch a falling star'. Similarly, one can express sarcasm alone and without any hint of irony. The opening of 'September 1913' by W. B. Yeats (1864–1939) is meant to be both bitter and wounding (sarcastic) but he means exactly what he says about the materialism and pettiness of his countrymen.

> What need you, being come to sense,
> But fumble in a greasy till
> And add the halfpence to the pence
> And prayer to shivering prayer, until
> You have dried the marrow from the bone?
>   (Yeats, p. 289)

Irony of situation, on the other hand, is merely a verbal irony translated into action. Instead of something being said that contrasts with the context or generally understood truths, something happens that contrasts with normal expectations. There is an inversion of action or situation and the contrast provokes a deeper or wider understanding of the subject matter. A good example is seen in the poem by Thomas Hardy above (p. 155). It is one thing to satirise a woman's vanity and lack of feeling by showing her in the act of looking over material for a mourning costume when her sick husband is still alive. It is far stronger to have the tubercular husband observe her doing it, and the emphasis is derived from the discrepancy and inversion of the situation. Laughter is often provoked by ironies of situation, but the effect can also be serious and intellectually stimulating, depending on subject matter and style.

Irony of situation is more common in lyric poetry than one might think, but it is more obviously suited to narrative and dramatic literature, whether in poetry or prose. Irony of situation is the pivot of such a poem as 'Ozymandias' by Percy Bysshe Shelley (1792–1822) which describes the broken remains of an ancient Egyptian pharaoh's statue lying half buried in the desert.

And on the pedestal these words appear:
'My name is Ozymandias, king of kings:
Look on my works, ye Mighty, and despair!'
Nothing beside remains. Round the decay
Of that colossal wreck, boundless and bare,
The lone and level sands stretch far away.
                              (Shelley, 2, p. 62)

Here, pride is being exposed and satirised, not through overstatement as in the quotation from Alexander Pope above, but
through the incongruousness of the situation.

Another example is seen in 'The Golf Links' by Sarah N.
Cleghorn (1876–1959).

> The golf links lie so near the mill
>   That almost every day
> The laboring children can look out
>   And see the men at play.
>   (Cleghorn in Barnet, p. 353)

Situating the factory and golf course side by side is itself ironical
and gives rise to the fact that the poor workers watch the idle rich
enjoying themselves. That the workers are children gives another
turn to the screw since it adds the contrast between working
children and playing adults (paradox). A further irony is present
in this example, the contrast between the moral indignation or
anger which the reader experiences through recognition of the
discrepancies and inversion, and the objective, unemotional
language of the poem (understatement). Compare the tone of this
poem, in relation to its other elements and theme, with that of the
Yeats quotation above.

Dramatic irony is perhaps least common of all contrastive
figures in lyric poetry, but it is a very useful device and especially
so in poems having a definite persona or speaker. Rather than a
contrast of images and ideas, dramatic irony arises from differing
degrees of awareness. What the speaker knows or understands of
a particular situation, usually his own, is contrasted with the
wider knowledge of the reader and audience. The conventional
example is the hero of the play *Oedipus Rex* by Sophocles
(495–405 BC), who publicly announces that he will pursue and

punish the man who killed the former King of Thebes and so purify the land. Although he is not aware of the full meaning of his words, the audience knows that Oedipus himself is the culprit.

In lyric poetry, however, dramatic irony is often used to draw attention to the values which the persona advances and to the kind of character he or she is. As in the classical example of Oedipus, a contrast or inversion exists between the understanding of the character and that of the audience. The little boy of 'The Chimney Sweeper' may be able to conclude that 'if all do their duty they need not fear harm', but William Blake (1757–1827) wishes us to conclude something quite different about the miserable lives of innocent children, sometimes no more than four or five years old, who in his day were often badly treated by their masters and suffered disease and physical deformity as a result of climbing up through endless chimneys to clean them, collecting the soot in bags.

When my mother died I was very young,
And my father sold me while yet my tongue
Could scarcely cry 'weep!' 'weep!' 'weep!'
So your chimneys I sweep, and in soot I sleep.

There's little Tom Dacre, who cried when his head,
That curled like a lamb's back, was shaved; so I said,
'Hush, Tom! never mind it, for, when your head's bare,
You know that the soot cannot spoil your white hair.'

And so he was quiet, and that very night,
As Tom was asleeping, he had such a sight!
That thousands of sweepers, Dick, Joe, Ned, and Jack,
Were all of them locked up in coffins of black.

And by came an Angel who had a bright key,
And he opened the coffins and set them all free;
Then down a green plain leaping, laughing, they run,
And wash in a river, and shine in the sun.

Then naked and white, all their bags left behind,
They rise upon clouds and sport in the wind;
And the Angel told Tom, if he'd be a good boy,
He'd have God for his father, and never want joy.

And so Tom awoke, and we rose in the dark,
And got with our bags and our brushes to work.
Though the morning was cold, Tom was happy and warm;
So if all do their duty they need not fear harm.

(Blake in Perrine, p.91)

From the long discussion of figurative language in its many aspects it should be obvious that they constitute one of the most effective stylistic devices of literature, and especially so in poetry, where the condensation of language and intensification of multiple meaning is vital. In any given poem, play or novel the kinds of figures that appear, their density and interrelationship may range from one or two decorative examples scattered about the text to a structural core which carries the burden of meaning and expresses the theme directly. In addition to identifying images and figures and evaluating their effectiveness within a line or short passage, one must also recognise patterns of imagery and figurative language which extend through the entire work and give it shape as well as significance. Space will not allow a full discussion of examples, but the use of such an image pattern, for instance, is central to *The Beautyful Ones Are Not Yet Born* (1968) by Ayi Kwei Armah. Throughout that work there is an opposition of gleaming, shining metal and images of excremental filth and rottenness which is vital to the exposure of moral corruption in contemporary Ghana. The attraction and repulsiveness of materialism comes alive in that pattern of images.

The Rhythmic Resources of English

Musical devices are even more important to poetry than are figures of speech, but questions of rhythm, metre and sound patterning are more complex and require an accurate description of spoken language, of its phonology and intonation. Poetry is, after all, merely heightened or stylised speech in which its musical characteristics are patterned for beauty, emphasis and independent meaning. Many African languages, for example, are monosyllabic and the tone or pitch (high, middle or low) on which the syllable is pronounced directly influences its meaning. In these languages all syllables receive nearly equal stress and an equal duration of time is given to each. As in all languages,

African poetry is naturally based on the stronger variable element
— in this case, the tonal nature of the language. Within the
conventions for normal phrasing and grammar, words are chosen
in such a way as to make a repeating pattern of tones which
supplies a musical basis for words and meaning. The pattern of
tones may even become so dominant that an individual word
may have a false tone forced upon it.

English, on the other hand, is neither wholly monosyllabic nor
polysyllabic, but a mixture of the two because of its historical
development. It also varies in both pitch and stress, but has no
fixed system of tones which are linked directly to meaning. The
musicality of poetry in English comes from the manipulation of
pitch and stress into rhythmic patterns.

1. *Pitch*. Pitch is an indication of sound quality and functions
something like tone in that syllables are pronounced on one of
several levels or notes: low (1), middle (2), high (3) and very high
(4), but the choice has nothing to do with the meaning of the word
on which the change of pitch occurs. In English, pitch variation
marks off the grammatical units of a statement and indicates a
change in the relative quality of sound, giving a rising and falling
movement within a sentence. Stress, on the other hand, is an
indication of sound quantity and concerns the force with which
syllables are pronounced. It is a question of the loudness or
softness of the sound. Stressed syllables can be marked (−) and
unstressed ones (ˇ). Intonation refers to the patterns of pitch and
stress in actual sentences of different grammatical structures as
they are spoken. For example, a simple declarative sentence uses
the three common pitch levels.

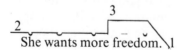

Middle pitch (2) is the norm in English and variation to a level
above (3) or below (1) is used in every spoken sentence. The
highest pitch (4) only comes into use in moments of emotional
intensity and can be recognised in written language from the
context. One must imagine how the sentence would be spoken in
that situation. In the example above, the change of pitch

coincides with the strong stress of the intonation pattern, before falling away to the lowest pitch as an indication that the sentence is a completed assertion of fact. Each polysyllabic word has a fixed strong stress on one of its syllables; standard English requires one to say cŏmmitteē not cŏmmittee, for example, and the intonational stress of an utterance will always fall on the stressed syllable of a word in a stressed position in the sentence. The doubling of sound quantity is the same for a mono syllable in a stressed position.

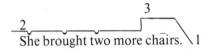

2. *Stress.* All syllables are not given equal stress in English, nor even equal duration of time in speaking, and this important characteristic is the feature which makes musical effects in English poetry possible. A syllable occurring in a stressed position is said more loudly and held for a longer duration of time than are unstressed syllables, which are softer in volume and shorter in length. Intonational stress tends to fall on nouns, verbs, adjectives and adverbs rather than on parts of speech which link words and ideas together and indicate structural relationship. Stress is very closely related to grammar and when sentences become more complex, breath pauses are used to interrupt the continuous flow of sound and to mark off the smaller units of sense. Each sense unit will have a stronger stress toward the end, and the pitch will vary at the same time to further emphasise the coherence and unity of the phrase. For example:

² Shĕ wănts mŏre freĕdŏm. 1

² Whăt shĕ wants|² ıs mŏre freĕdŏm. 1

Instead of a single stress unit, two of them occur in the second example; the subject is itself a complex unit — 'What she wants'. A slight break or hesitation comes into being between the two phrases that make up the sentence. The second example is also characterised by a definite rhythm; there is now a repeated pattern of unstressed and stressed syllables.

The time it actually takes to say each unit out loud tends to equalise even though the word 'freedom' gives the second phrase an extra unstressed syllable. As a general rule, unstressed syllables are compressed in time more drastically than stressed syllables are lengthened. For example:

$$2 \ \text{Thĭs ĭs thĕ hōuse} \mid^2 \text{thăt Jāck būilt.} \quad 1$$

Although the ideal is never actually achieved, there is an equalising process at work in English which tends to alter the duration of stress units and make them approximate to one another in length. In the example above the two stress units are of unequal syllable count, but in speaking, compression and elongation overcome the differences. The most natural reading is with a single break between 'house' and 'that', but the sentence can be read as having three stress units with a longer and artificial break for emphasis between 'Jack' and 'built'. Silent pauses are often counted into the duration of time it takes to say a whole stress unit, sometimes even equalling the duration of an unstressed syllable.

Prose rhythms are created by revising English sentences into smaller sense units so that a roughly repeating pattern of stress comes into being. Prose rhythm is heard in the recurrence of intonational stress which normally occurs towards the end of each sense unit. A more regular distribution of stress and roughly equal numbers of unstressed syllables between them produces verse rhythm which in turn is the basis of poetry.

3. *Effect of syntax on intonation.* English grammar (syntax) is a very flexible and plastic instrument allowing the writer much freedom with and control over stress distribution. There is great flexibility in the placing of modifiers, phrases and clauses within a sentence and a very wide vocabulary which allows limitless possibilities for rhythmic composition. The formal rigidity of both Germanic and Romance languages has been lost through historical assimilation and development which allows for great subtlety and almost infinite variation of rhythmic effect.

A number of other features also contribute to the creation of rhythm. For example, extra stress occurs in a sentence whenever there is a contrastive situation:

This house, not that one.

The red chair, not the gold one.

In fact, both objects of comparison need not be stated as contrastive stress is obvious from the context alone.

This, not that, is the house that Jack built.
This is the house, not the garage, that Jack built.
This is the house that Jack, not Olu, built.

Another feature of English that helps to intensify stress patterns is the syntactical concept of a noun group which is made up of a head–word and all its qualifiers. A noun group functions as a single noun, either subject or object, and the head–word is the main noun which is qualified by all other words in the group. There are two types:

The sixth form teacher is . . .

The most experienced teacher of sixth–form English is . . .

In the first example the word 'teacher' is the one that all other words modify. It is the head–word and so receives stress to mark it as the main or central word of the unit. It also happens to be the last word of that noun group and would in any case receive intonational stress to mark off the unit from the rest of the sentence. In the second, the head–word is still 'teacher', but qualifiers come both before and after it. As head–word, the tendency is to mark 'teacher' with a stronger stress, while the word 'English' receives intonational stress as well because of its position.

Both position and type of qualifier affect the distribution of stress, and stress, in turn, acts as rhetorical emphasis, calling attention to key–words, as well as providing a rhythmic pattern when equally distributed throughout speech. English is particularly flexible in allowing both pre– and post–modification, as well as encouraging alternative phrasing in order to express the same idea with different emphases and rhythm.

ă măd ōld wōmăn
ă wōmăn, whŏ iš măd ănd ōld
ă wōmăn, măd ănd ōld

One of the reasons for such remarkable flexibility of expression and stress distribution is the open choice between the Latinate possessive, 'the cover of the book', and the Saxon genitive, 'the book's cover'. Rhythmically, the difference between the two lies in syllable count, concentration of stress and coincidence of head–word with intonational stress. Choosing one over the other does not alter the meaning, but it does affect rhetorical emphasis. In 'the book's cover' the intervening unstressed syllables are omitted and the significant words are brought together with reinforced stress. Adjectives coming before the head–word take on strong stress and they are particularly effective if monosyllabic as in 'the mad old woman'.

The use of nouns in English to modify other nouns also figures in the emphasis of stress to be gained by pre–modification.

thĕ rāilwăy stātiŏn māster's house
thĕ house ŏf thĕ stātiŏn māster ŏf thĕ rāilwăy
thĕ house ŏf thĕ māster ŏf thĕ stātiŏn ŏf thĕ rāilwăy

The second and third examples would be, perhaps, a little ridiculous in English conversation, but a good deal of freedom with conventional phrasing is allowed in poetry. They are included here only as a demonstration of the possibilities for stress patterning in English.

By manipulating the modification of complex verb and noun groups, the number and density of stressed and unstressed syllables can be altered within the limits of intended meaning. Writing effective prose rhythms and especially verse requires such patterned distribution.

Shĕ wănts mŏre freedŏm.
Thĕ ōld wōmăn | wănts mŏre freedŏm.

Shĕ hăd bĕen gīvĕn | ă sēcond–hănd car.
Thē mād old woman | hăd bĕen gīvĕn | ă sēcond–hānd car.

Shē hăd bĕen shōt.
Shē hăd bĕen shŏt | iň frŏnt ŏf hĕr hoūse | bў ă cōwařd.
Sĕekiňg freēdom, | shĕ hăd bĕen shŏt | iň frŏnt ŏf hĕr house | bў ă
cōwařd.

The tendency in longer sentences is to stress all head–words regardless of coincidence with intonational stress as a way of marking off the separate sense units, whether or not the units are formally punctuated. Whenever there is an interruption of the basic sequence, or closely related parts of a sentence are distanced by an intervening qualification, the sense units themselves are distinguished by pauses.

The man facing us | looked scornful.
An old man whom we knew | brought us some oranges.
Alexander, | whom we had known for a long time, | came to
visit us.

The longer and more complex the interruption, the greater the need for signposts to guide us through the sentence, and formal punctuation is required. The sentences above are very similar in construction and the first two are short enough to be spoken as two stressed units because of the interruptions (The man ... looked/An old man ... brought). The third statement is more complex, and the qualifying clause must be said as a separate sense unit that is subordinated to the main idea (Alexander ... came). The flexibility of grammatical construction in English lends itself to multiple variations of stress.

My brother denied everything when he was arrested by the
police.
When arrested by the police, my brother denied everything.
Arrested by the police, my brother denied everything.
My brother, when arrested by the police, denied everything.

The normal grammar of English allows much scope for the revision of sentences in order to create a desired emphasis, stress pattern and syllable count.

4. *Rearrangement of syntax.* Beyond the natural and grammatical rearrangment of sentence elements, a convention of inversion is also in use as a rhetorical device. Words and phrases can be displaced from their normal order without loss of meaning and several examples should suffice as demonstration. It was common enough in older poetry to delay the verb until the end of the sentence, in order to baffle both understanding and expectation while creating a sudden illumination at the last moment when all the pieces fit together. Modern poets also take advantage of the device.

Slowly the poison the whole blood stream fills.

(Empson, p. 60)

Another common poetical device is to disrupt the natural sequence of head–word and modifier.

She was dark and beautiful.
Dark she was | and beautiful.

He spoke of evil and eternal damnation.
He spoke of evil | and damnation eternal.
Of evil and damnation eternal, | he spoke.

The very last sentence has become so artificial and heightened that the verb 'to speak' is no longer perfectly suitable, something rather grander is needed in its place: he preached or mused, perhaps. In any case, conscious inversion provides suspense and tension through the displacement of normal grammar and, like the other methods of intensifying stress patterns, creates extra force or stress in each new sense unit that comes into being.

5. *The line as a rhythmic unit.* The effect of breaking up a connected sequence of words is to introduce a strong intonational stress on the final word before the break, and the device is carried to its logical conclusion in poetry where sentences are broken into artificial line lengths and, consequently, extra stress is also placed on the first word or words of the new unit. Of course, it is possible to confine the sentence to the line and so end each line or every other line with a full stop or question mark, but this might become monotonous and unsuitable for certain subjects or

themes. In fact, the sentence is run over into another line more often than not in order to encourage a sense of continuity and flow.

There are only two alternatives: either ending the line with a completed sense unit and conventional punctuation (end-stopped), or a run–on line in which the normal sense unit is broken off at the end of one line and continued at the beginning of the next. In end–stopped verse the sense is complete in each line, subjects and verbs are never separated from one another, but an object or qualifying phrase may be added in a subsequent line. A clear example of end–stopped lines is seen in the opening stanza of an untitled lyric by Lord Byron (1788–1824).

> The isles of Greece, the isles of Greece!
> Where burning Sappho loved and sung,
> Where grew the arts of war and peace,
> Where Delos rose, and Phoebus sprung!
> Eternal summer gilds them yet,
> But all, except their sun, is set.
> (Byron in Hayward, p. 281)

A much less formal kind of verse is found in the opening lines of 'Kubla Khan' by Samuel Taylor Coleridge (1772–1834), a contemporary of Byron.

> In Xanadu did Kubla Khan
> A stately pleasure dome decree:
> Where *Alph*, the sacred river, ran
> Through caverns measureless to man
> Down to a sunless sea.
> (Coleridge, p. 94)

The first line contains only a subject and verb, and raises the question: What did Kubla Khan do? The next line finishes the thought and gives us the object of the verb, while the succeeding lines qualify that action further in terms of location and secondary action. The lines are really run–on (enjambed) — although each unit is relatively complete. Notice also the different ways in which the syntax has been manipulated to give a more intense and varied rhythm. A paraphrase of the first two lines might read: Kubla Khan decreed [built] a beautiful palace at Xanadu.

The effect of more radical enjambment however, is to influence the occurrence of stress at both the end of the line and the beginning of the next.

> And the sliding of the water
> Seems the stroking of a dear
> Hand upon her.
> (Lowell, p. 5)

The first line break separates subject and verb, and the word 'Seems' receives more stress than normal, both because of that break and its unexpected position in the line. Tension and expectation are raised and heightened by the pause at the end of the line which separates subject and predicate. The word 'Hand' is even more heavily stressed because the line break interrupts the indivisible sense unit, 'of a dear hand'. At first the second line is understood to mean that a dear (deer or dear person?) could stroke her or be stroked since 'dear' appears to be the object of the preposition. Reading on, one finds that 'dear' is an adjective modifying the word 'Hand', and one gives extra stress to both 'dear' and 'Hand' while groping across the gap of the line break to resolve the ambiguity and complete the sense of the statement. The varieties of enjambment differ only in degree; both depend upon the build up or force of expectation and its resolution. The device is rather like a spark–gap or flash of lightning in that an electric charge accumulates in the impasse of meaning and jumps forcefully across the pause to complete its intensified potential. Enjambment certainly adds force and extra stress to the line as well as providing the narrative thrust and continuity of the run–on line.

On the other hand, the heroic couplet which was developed in the late seventeenth and eighteenth centuries gains its force and emphasis by exploiting the potential of end–stopped lines which tend to isolate complete thoughts in self–contained and detachable units. The 'Epitaph. Intended for Sir Isaac Newton' by Alexander Pope is a case in point.

> Nature and Nature's Laws lay hid in Night.
> God said, *Let Newton be!* and All was *Light*.
> (Pope, VI, p. 317)

Rhythm as a Structural Element

Whereas enjambment exploits tension between incomplete or cut–up phrases and normal syntax at the beginning and end of individual lines, lineation is a much more basic and structural element in poetry. The line length isolates and therefore emphasises a repeated rhythm or stress pattern within a statement or sequence of statements and provides a unifying device for the entire poem. Moreover, rhythm is expressive in that the movement of the phrase, line, stanza or whole poem can echo a subjective pattern and dynamics of thought or the objective progress of an action described by imitating its pattern or flow of movement.

The music of the poetry, its modulation of stress, duration and pitch is itself moving and pleasurable, as well as contributing directly to the expression of theme and meaning. In order to respond to the musical basis of the poem it is necessary to read the work line by line, balancing the intonation of the actual sentences with the arbitrary division into rhythmic line lengths. One can neither ignore the line endings nor the continuation of meaning within the sentences, and every pause, whether punctuated or not, figures in the time scheme of the rhythm. Even stressable words in unstressed positions receive greater force in reading verse according to the repeated pattern that has been set up.

Perhaps the best way to approach the problem of strict or metrical verse and its relationship to line length is to begin with simple prose rhythms and their transformation into a loose poetic form known as accentual verse. Prose rhythm is the hardest of all to define, but the following is a valiant attempt.

> A sentence or passage is rhythmical if, when said aloud, it falls naturally into groups of words each well fitted by its length and intonation for its place in the whole and its relation to its neighbours.
>
> (Fowler, p. 526)

Prose rhythm is a question of setting up a varied pattern of stress units in which key words, phrases and ideas are emphasised by their placement and the flow of sense units 'is like waves of the sea, moving onward with alternating rise and fall'. The following example is from *To The Lighthouse* (1927) by Virginia Woolf.

The house was left; the house was deserted. It was left like a shell on a sandhill to fill with dry salt grains now that life had left it. The long night seemed to have set in; the trifling airs, nibbling, the clammy breaths, fumbling, seemed to have triumphed. The saucepan had rusted and the mat decayed. Toads had nosed their way in. Idly, aimlessly, the swaying shawl swung to and fro. A thistle thrust itself between the tiles in the larder. The swallows nested in the drawing–room; the floor was strewn with straw; the plaster fell in shovelfuls; rafters were laid bare; rats carried off this and that to gnaw behind the wainscots. Tortoise–shell butterflies burst from the chrysalis and pattered their life out on the window–pane. Poppies sowed themselves among the dahlias; the lawn waved with long grass; giant artichokes towered among roses; a fringed carnation flowered among the cabbages; while the gentle tapping of a weed at the window had become, on winters' nights, a drumming from sturdy trees and thorned briars which made the whole room green in summer.

(Woolf, pp. 206–7)

Composition according to the musical phrase (accentual verse) depends on striking a balance between varying lengths and numbers of rhythmic units. The repetition of a conventional or even a recognisable stress pattern is avoided, and thought units are composed for sonority, often according to the number of strong stresses in a line, regardless of intervening unstressed syllables. It is not the nature and composition of stress units that counts, but merely the number of beats or accents in each line. Line lengths are often staggered and may change drastically from passage to passage according to the desired sense and mood as in 'The Garden' by Ezra Pound (1885–1972).

Like a skein of loose silk blown against a wall
   She walks by the railing of a path in Kensington Gardens,
  And she is dying piece–meal
     of a sort of emotional anæmia.

And round about there is a rabble
Of the filthy, sturdy, unkillable infants of the very poor.
They shall inherit the earth.

In her is the end of breeding.
Her boredom is exquisite and excessive.
She would like some one to speak to her,
And is almost afraid that I will commit that indiscretion.

(Pound, p. 83)

Metre and Rhythmic Variation

Metrical verse, on the other hand, involves fixed sequences of stressed and unstressed syllables which are divided into basic units called feet, each of which has a specific Greek name. Poetic forms are identified by the name of the characteristic foot together with the average number of units in each line — iambic pentameter, for example.

iamb(ic)	ˇ —		dimeter	2 units
trochee(aic)	— ˇ		trimeter	3 units
spondee(aic)	— —		tetrameter	4 units
dactyl(ic)	ˇ ˇ —		pentameter	5 units
anapest(ic)	— ˇ ˇ		hexameter	6 units

For many years both teachers and pupils have spent a great deal of time scanning verse — that is, analysing its rhythmic patterns, identifying the kind of basic unit involved and calculating the average number of them in each line. Scansion of this old–fashioned sort implies that the importance of poetry lies in its closeness to an arbitrary and mechanical pattern, to a regularity of stress and duration such as can be simulated by a metronome or the ticking of a clock. In fact, the measurement of rhythm is quite unrelated to themes or human experience, and the questions to ask are: What kind of experience is the poem trying to communicate? What part does the rhythm play in that communication? To answer by saying that the poem is written in trochaic tetrameter is not at all helpful. It is like asking someone what kind of person his or her new friend is and being told: My friend is five feet ten inches tall and weighs one hundred and seventy pounds.

Metronomic or perfectly regular rhythm is rarely achieved in poetry and when it is, the effect is monotonous and mechanical.

> Listen, my children, and you shall hear
> Of the midnight ride of Paul Revere.
> 'Twas the eighteenth of April, in Seventy–five;
> Hardly a man is now alive
> Who remembers that famous day and year.
>   (Longfellow, p. 207)

A regular arrangement of stressed and unstressed syllables does not have to give such a monotonous effect, however. In 'The Passionate Sheepheard to His Love', Christopher Marlowe (1564–93) introduced enough variation and suggestiveness to overcome any mechanical or monotonous effect.

> Come live with mee, and be my love,
> And we will all the pleasures prove,
> That Vallies, groves, hills and fieldes,
> Woods, or steepie mountaine yeeldes.
>
> And wee will sit upon the Rocks,
> Seeing the sheepheards feede theyr flocks,
> By shallow Rivers, to whose falls,
> Melodious byrds sing Madrigalls.
>   (Marlowe in Hayward, p. 31)

In the first example, the dynamics and music of a normal speaking voice, of natural intonation, is completely cancelled out by an exaggerated regularity of syntax, syllable count and stress. Natural rhythm has been reduced to a contrived metre instead of allowing a certain amount of contrast between the two, as in the second. In good poetry the metre or basic stress pattern is merely an imaginary ideal and only a basis from which the actual speech rhythm departs and returns. Metrical regularity is suggested by the rhythm of the poem, but should not be imposed on it. Variation in stress and timing brings about a subtle play of dynamics which acts as an expressive device and makes the poem lively and individual. In addition to the basic language rhythms created by the poet, more subtle variations of stress and speed are supplied by the reader as a response to the context or meaning of the work. Every reading of a poem, like every production of drama, implies an interpretation.

Broadly speaking, there is only one distinction to be made when identifying the basic metre of a poem. Stress units are made up of either two or three syllables. Dupal metre (units of two syllables) is closer to natural speech in English while triple metre is more obviously artificial. Dupal metre derives from rhythm that has a steady marching movement and is suitable for serious and reflective themes, while triple metre has a swinging, dancing movement which is suited to lighter subjects and certain kinds of action. The choice between the two depends on the effect desired and any criticism of poetry should point out the relationship between rhythm and theme.

The opening lines of 'Ulysses' by Alfred Lord Tennyson (1809–92) gives us a good example of dupal metre, in this case iambic. It is suitably formal and elevated for the subject matter: the lament of a world–wandering and adventurous hero who feels frustration and desire for his former life.

It little profits that an idle king,
By this still hearth, among these barren crags,
Matched with an aged wife, I mete and dole
Unequal laws unto a savage race,
That hoard, and sleep, and feed, and know not me.

(Tennyson, pp. 561–2)

Triple metre, on the other hand, is used to express a faster, more swinging flow of action as in 'The Destruction of Sennacherib' by Lord Byron (1788–1824).

The Assyrian came down like the wolf on the fold,
And his cohorts were gleaming in purple and gold.

(Byron, 1, p. 139)

Triple metre is also used for humorous effect, as in this anonymous limerick.

Ĭ săt nĕxt thĕ Dūchĕss ăt tēa. _
Ĭt wăs jŭst ăs Ĭ fĕared ĭt wŏuld bĕ:
  Hĕr rŭmblĭngs ĭntĕrnăl
  Wĕre sīmplў ĭnfĕrnăl,
Ănd ēverȳonĕ thōught ĭt wăs mē.
(Anonymous in Perrine, p. 189)

In poetry each departure from an established metre is a feature to be observed and studied in order to appreciate poetic methods and effects. Variations of line length, for example, and those of syllable count or stress pattern within a line are likely to have an ornamental effect as well as an emphatic or demonstrative purpose. Lyric beauty and intensity is a direct result of such musical variation, but cannot exist independent of words and meaning. It is possible that attention is also being focussed on images or ideas, as in the following line.

(ideal)   ˘   ¯ ˘   ¯   ˘   ¯ ˘   ¯   ˘ ¯
(actual)   ¯   ¯ ˘   ¯   ˘   ¯ ˘   ¯   ¯   ¯
        Bare ruined choirs where late the sweet birds sang.

The inversion of normal word order here gives us a metrical scheme, but pre–modification (2 examples) and the placing of the word 'birds' in a normally unstressed position within that scheme cause a significant distortion; the extra stress emphasises the nature of the choirs and the singing of the birds. The phrase 'Bare ruined choirs' is also emphasised because it is an elaborate metaphor for the bare branches of trees in winter on which the birds sing, and also carries the connotations of religious services (choir stalls in a church) as well as the dissolution of the monasteries in the time of Henry VIII when many Catholic churches fell into ruin.

Variation from the implied metre can also be used to emphasise an action by directly imitating its motion.

(ideal)   ˘   ¯   ˘   ˘   ¯ ˘   ¯
(actual)   ˘   ¯   ¯   ¯   ˘   ¯ ˘ ˘ ¯
        She brought palm wine that carelessly slips

(ideal)   ᵕ   ⁻ ᵕ   ⁻   ᵕ   ⁻ ᵕ ⁻
(actual)   ᵕ ᵕ   ⁻ ᵕ   ⁻   ⁻   ⁻ ᵕ ⁻
          From the sleeping palm tree's honeyed lips.

(Laluah in Hughes, p. 177)

Of course, the precise effect achieved here is not due to rhythmic variation alone. The extra stress of the two pre–modifications, 'palm wine' and 'palm tree' — in contrast with the two triple metre units, 'carelessly slips' and 'From the sleeping', which fall between — produces a slight swinging movement between points of rhythmic regularity which conveys the sense of the palm's sap welling up and flowing over at the top of the tree. There is no significance or meaning in the rhythm pattern itself, but in conjunction with the context the movement suggests and augments the meaning.

Spectacular effects can be achieved in this way.

(ideal) ᵕ –   ᵕ   ⁻ ᵕ   ⁻ ᵕ   ⁻ ᵕ   ⁻
(actual) ᵕ –   ᵕ   ⁻ ᵕ   ⁻ ᵕ   ⁻ ᵕ   ⁻
       I caught this morning morning's minion, King–

(ideal)   ᵕ ⁻ ᵕ   ⁻ ᵕ   ⁻ ᵕ   ⁻   ᵕ
(actual)   ᵕ ᵕ ⁻ ᵕ   ⁻ ᵕ   ⁻ ᵕ   ⁻   ⁻
      dom of daylight's dauphin, dapple–dawn–drawn

(ideal)   ⁻ ᵕ ⁻ ᵕ ⁻
(actual)   ⁻ ᵕ ᵕ ᵕ ⁻ ᵕ
       Falcon, in his riding

(ideal)   ᵕ   ⁻ ᵕ   ⁻ ᵕ   ⁻ ᵕ   ⁻   ᵕ   ⁻ ᵕ ⁻
(actual)   ᵕ ᵕ   ⁻ ᵕ   ⁻ ᵕ ᵕ   ᵕ   ᵕ   ⁻ ᵕ ⁻
       of the rolling, level, underneath him steady air.

(Hopkins, p. 69)

In describing a bird seen on the wing, the wonder of its beauty and the mystery of its flight is then celebrated as a manifestation of the divine presence in creation. In order to provide a rhythm which echoes or imitates the movement of the bird as it flaps its wings, changes direction, swoops and glides, exaggerated syntactical arrangements have been brought into being, especially heavy pre–modification.

Kingdŏm ŏf Dāylĭğht's daŭphĭn
dapplĕ–dāwn–drawn Fălcŏn
rŏllĭnğ, lĕvĕl, ŭndĕrnĕath hĭm stĕadў aĭr

The metre is dupal with several triple units to emphasise the actual movement of the flight. The unmarked pauses — such as that between the words 'morning' and 'morning's', and those which indicate that 'underneath him steady air' is a single sense unit — along with the short burst of triple metre, punctuate the basic rhythm pattern in exactly the same way that the bird flaps its wings suddenly and then continues to coast on the wind. One imagines the flight of the bird in exact detail through the suggestive power of the rhythm.

Sound Patterning

From the example above it should be obvious that rhythmic effects are closely linked to sound patterning. In fact, the quality or texture of the sounds employed, as well as their repetition, affects the movement of the line. In conjunction with pitch variation patterns of harmonised sounds produce melody as well. Sound patterning can be used to speed up or slow down the rhythm, to produce rich harmonies of sound, to ornament and emphasise ideas or images by calling attention to them, and to imitate or suggest the meaning of the context. When discussing sound patterns or chiming, however, care must be taken to think in terms of the values of natural speech and not the way the words are spelled. The written language only approximates to the actual qualities and textures of sound in any case, and a knowledge of phonetic transciption is very helpful.

Speech sounds are classified by the place in the mouth or throat where they are made or by the method of making them. Vowels, for example, are distinguished one from another as being formed in either an open or closed mouth cavity and in the front, middle or back of that cavity. In addition vowels may be

short
  (as in hid, head, had, hud, hod, hood and sitter),
long and pure (non–gliding)
  (as in heed, fool, hard, hoard and heard), or

long and gliding (diphthongal, composite)
  (as in fail, foal, hide, fowl, foil, beard, bared and poor).

A gliding vowel begins in one location in the mouth and moves to another. For example, the vowel sound in the word 'fowl' begins in the centre of the mouth cavity when it is held slightly closed and moves to the back in a fully closed cavity. Very subtle patterns can be made by choosing words with sounds which harmonise together or sharply contrast.

Consonants, on the other hand, are formed in a variety of different ways using the position of lips, tongue, teeth and palate, as well as the vibration of vocal chords to affect the column of air forced out by the lungs. Consonants are distinguished by the manner of articulation and the kind of sound made. For example, the initial consonant in the words 'pin' and 'bin' are technically described as a voiceless /p/ and voiced /b/ pair of plosive bilabials. The sounds are made by causing an explosion of air between closed lips. There are two other pairs of voiced plosives, /t, d/ and /k, g/, which are formed farther and farther back in the mouth. Together they form close relationships and can be played off against one another in harmonies as well as contrasted with patterns of consonants which are formed by air friction (/f,v/ or /s,z/, for example) or nasalisation (/m,n, or ŋ/, the last being the sound of the letters 'ng' in the word 'sing'). An understanding of families of sounds is a great help towards appreciating the way in which they are matched and contrasted in expressive patterns.

The most commonly employed devices of sound patterning are assonance and consonance. Assonance is the repetition of similar vowel sounds in two or more words that are relatively close together, and the sounds usually occur in a medial position in each word. The vowels need not be identical to be effective, but only of similar formation and duration. The result of three long and open vowels in a line of verse, for example, would greatly affect timing or rhythm, even if they were not identical. Such a pattern would also affect total sound quality as well as duration of time. For example, the opening lines of 'An Elegy Written in a Country Churchyard', quoted at length above, offers an excellent example of many prominent vowels clustered together to underscore the long, slow evening sounds and motions which express the mournful, elegiac theme.

> The Curfeu tolls the Knell of parting Day,
> The lowing Herd winds slowly o'er the Lea,
> The Plow–man homeward plods his weary Way,
> And leaves the World to Darkness, and to me.

Consonance, on the other hand, is the repetition of the same or closely related consonant, and can occur in the initial, medial or final position in any word. A sound that is repeated or chimed in three different words need not appear in the same position each time, however, but a variant of consonance, known as alliteration, requires the repetition of initial sounds in succeeding words. In Keats's ode 'To Autumn', also quoted above, there are examples of both general consonance and alliteration.

> Season of mists and mellow fruitfulness,
> Close bosom–friend of the maturing sun.

The sibilant /s/ occurs three times in the first line and thrice in the second but never close together in initial positions. The nasal /m/, however, first occurs as an alliteration in the first line and then echoes as consonance twice more in line two. Notice that the kindred nasal /n/ also occurs four times in the two lines and adds to the general effect of fullness and beauty which characterises the season. Consonance has little effect on duration of syllable, but the quality or characteristic of the sound produced often has associations of meaning which can reinforce content and become a strongly expressive element, while other sound patterns are merely ornamental and used only to focus attention.

1. *Sound and meaning.* The relationship of sound to meaning is very imperfectly understood, but it can be assumed to depend on conventions of association. For example, the combination of the sibilant /s/ and the semi–vowel /l/ can be accepted as a sound image which suggests or supports the actual meaning of such words as solitude, lassitude, listless and leisure. The sharp breaking sound /kr/ in crash, crack, crush, crunch and crumble has the same relationship to the meanings of the words, and the combination /fl/, which is found in words denoting suddenness or hurried movement such as fly, flee, flash, flick, flit and fling. The effect is most common in consonant clusters, and the doubled

consonant in a medial position, for example, lends itself to the idea of intermittence as in glimmer, shimmer, glitter, twitter and flutter, or /sl/ in words that describe something wet, smooth and vaguely unpleasant such as slime, slippery, slush, slick, slurp and slither. Of course, that combination also exists in words such as 'sleep' and 'slave' where no association of the sound with meaning is conceivable, but sounds contained in words often do help to intensify their meaning. Patterns of such words and sounds are very useful stylistic devices.

Onomatopoeia is a special case of phonetic intensification in which the meaning or referent of a word is nothing more than a sound or an action characterised by the sound — for example: bow–wow, splash, buzz or wheeze. The word itself is an image for the action or sound associated with the action, and one must recognise that the sound image is often quite arbitrary and a question of mere convention. Onomatopoeic words change greatly from one language to another, even for the same act or sound. In French, for example, the barking of a dog is *ouah ouah* and roosters (cocks) cry *cocorico*. The English versions occur in the following song from *The Tempest* (1611).

> Hark, hark!
>   Bow–wow.
> The watch–dogs bark!
>   Bow–wow.
> Hark, hark! I hear
>   The strain of strutting chanticleer
> Cry, 'Cock–a–doodle–doo!'
>   (Shakespeare in Perrine, p. 168)

The exploitation of sound patterning, like that of rhythm, is both decorative (aesthetically pleasing in its own right) and structurally unifying. More to the point, chiming of sounds can also be used to create emphasis on particular images and ideas being expressed, and it can also help to characterise them, as in the quotation from Shelley's 'Ozymandias' discussed earlier.

> And on the pedestal these words appear:
> 'My name is Ozymandias, king of kings:
> Look on my works, ye Mighty, and despair!'

> Nothing beside remains. Round the decay
> Of that colossal wreck, boundless and bare
> The lone and level sands stretch far away.

The proud words of Pharaoh are followed ironically by a vivid description of desolation. The desert scene with its few fragments of ancient statuary is called to mind by the words, but the rhythms and sound patterns play a larger role in characterising the scene. The last three lines begin with a short, emphatic statement of the basic irony: the works of the great king have passed away. Then follows a longish description in which patterns of hard–edged sounds — /d/, /k/ and /b/ — are succeeded by softer combinations of /l/, /s/ and long open vowels. The harsh, aggressive sounds are associated with the statue as an image of Pharaoh's pride, and contrast with the vision of enduring nature which is characterised by the softer, quieter pattern.

A cumulative effect of assonance and consonance is always possible whether or not the tensions of contrast are also introduced. In 'The Lotos Eaters' by Alfred Lord Tennyson (1809–92), the sense of restful tranquillity is expressed by the interplay of images and the sounds /z/, /s/, /l/, /t/ and /d/. Notice that the plosive sounds are used in an alliterative sequence to emphasise the image on which the comparison rests.

> Music that gentler on the spirit lies
> Than tir'd eyelids upon tir'd eyes.
> (Tennyson, p. 431)

In another context, plosives and harsh consonant clusters with closed or half–closed vowels can help to suggest the rising fury of inner tensions, as in the last three lines of Hamlet's denunciation of his mother's husband, the usurper of his father's throne and marriage bed.

> A murderer and a villain!
> A slave that is not twentieth part the tithe
> Of your precedent lord; a vice of kings;
> A cutpurse of the empire and the rule,
> That from a shelf the precious diadem stole
> And put it in his pocket.
> (Shakespeare, p. 1055)

2. *Chiming and meaning.* Rhyme is perhaps the most complex of the chiming devices and has to do with the repetition of combined sounds, or even whole syllables. For example, the combination of vowel and final consonant in the last syllable of one word may be paired with the same or similar sounds similarly positioned in another word. Rhyme is really a combination of assonance and consonance that is limited to the final position of a word. There is no obligation to use rhyme in verse and many poems avoid it altogether. Rhyme comes in and out of literary fashion periodically, as do most other styles and devices.

In normal usage, one of the rhyming words comes at the end of the line and a chime may be struck with another word in the middle of the same unit (internal rhyme) or at the end of lines nearby (end–stopped rhyme). Standard English (known as Received Pronunciation in Britain) is a difficult language for rhyming because of the extensive range of vowel sounds. There are over twenty distinguishable vowels which are all modified to one degree or another by the consonant that follows them, particularly by /r/. In other dialects of English, vowels are less variable and fewer in number, which makes rhyming a little easier, but flattens the subtle melodies achievable in Standard English poetry by the contrast of approximate rhymes.

Perfect rhymes do exist in English — mat and sat, keys and please, for example — but many different kinds of approximate rhymes have also come into use. Both perfect and approximate rhymes occur in masculine and feminine forms: that is, either a single syllable in a word chiming with one in another, or two (or more) syllables in a polysyllabic word (sometimes even succeeding monosyllables) rhyming with two or more others. Decks and sex, support and retort are perfect masculine rhymes. Straying and displaying, spitefully and delightfully are perfect feminine rhymes. Sap and soap, rip and rap, sing and tong are approximate masculine rhymes and each pair is based on a different contrast of vowel sounds. Feminine rhymes are rarely approximate since the last syllables will chime perfectly. Lightly and frightful, however, can be considered approximate because the final syllables do not rhyme. Eye rhyme is also a possibility, but depends on chiming of the spelling, the way the words look, rather than their sounds: wind (an east wind is blowing) and mind, cough and bough, for example.

Unlike rhythmic variation and other forms of sound patterning, rhyme is not used so much to draw attention to or emphasise
images and ideas within the text, but rather to enrich the musical
quality of the work. Rhyme imposes severe limits on the poet and
a good deal of ingenuity and imagination must be exercised to
reconcile the artificially imposed sound pattern with natural
speech and heightened meaning. Rhyme is thought to be elevating because of its artificiality, and the reassuring sense of a
controlled and stable world is held to be present whenever it is
used. Certainly, there is a good deal of technical accomplishment
and aesthetic pleasure to be found in the complex interrelationship of syntax, rhyme and rhythm.

Rhyme gives us the strongest and most obvious sound pattern
possible in poetry, and the repetition of sound gives more weight
to the words on which it falls. When only a few rhymes are introduced into a stanza or poem, the contrast causes them to stand
out even more than when a complete rhyme scheme is used. The
main functions of rhyme, however, are to mark off the line
endings in the most audible kind of way and also to suggest the
length of larger units of thought. In the first instance, rhyme helps
to isolate and identify the repeating rhythmic units of the line,
while in the second, it helps to isolate and mark off larger ideas in
groups of lines.

There are only two possible kinds of rhyme schemes but only
one of them permits a number of variations. The first is called
couplet rhyme (a, a, b, b . . .) in which a line of verse chimes with
the one directly succeeding it. A complete grammatical unit
containing a complete thought is often framed in each couplet,
but subsequent couplets may continue the larger idea and flow of
meaning. The formation of stanzas in couplet rhyme depends on
the length of the idea to be expressed, but a fixed number of lines
may be decided upon and stanzas of equal or alternating length
created. Not much is gained in this last case since the couplet
form always repeats itself in any case, whether there is a stanza
break or not.

The second scheme or pattern is called interlocking rhyme,
(a, b, a, b . . .) and tends to alternate rhymes, making much larger
and more complex units possible. For example, a set of five–line
stanzas might be given.

```
a, b, a, b, a          c, d, c, d, c
a, b, c, b, a          c, d, e, d, c
a, b, b, a, b          c, d, d, c, d
```

The point of an interlocking rhyme scheme is that it repeats itself as a recognisably larger group of lines, each of which contains a complete thought. The unit of thought may or may not form a separate stanza but the repeating rhyme scheme does emphasise the unity of the thought and its relation to other units.

The following poem is far too rhetorical and lacking in concrete imagery to be a particularly good one, but it does offer an interesting combination of interlocking and couplet rhyme schemes which mark off the subdivisions of the structure. Notice that all three rhyming sounds in the first six lines are related to one another as approximate rhymes, setting that unit off from the following ten lines in which each couplet has a different rhyming sound. The two questions expressed in the first unit are further distinguished, one from the other, by a repeated pattern which shares the interlocking rhyme (b).

Breathes there the man, with soul so dead,	a
Who never to himself hath said,	a
This is my own, my native land!	b
Whose heart hath ne'er within him burned,	c
As home his footsteps he hath turned,	c
From wandering on a foreign strand?	b
If such there breathe, go, mark him well;	d
For him no minstrel raptures swell;	d
High though his titles, proud his name,	e
Boundless his wealth as wish can claim—	e
Despite those titles, power, and pelf,	f
The wretch, concentered all in self,	f
Living, shall forfeit fair renown,	g
And, doubly dying, shall go down	g
To the vile dust from whence he sprung,	h
Unwept, unhonoured, and unsung.	h

(Scott in Perrine, p. 211)

Demonstration Analysis

No single poem utilises all the techniques and devices available, but once one is familiar with the various possibilities of word choice, rhetorical devices, figures of speech, rhythm and sound patterning, it is possible to recognise both their presence and the effects created in expressing the subject matter and theme. Hunting through a poem for metaphors, etc. is not very edifying, nor is it conducive to sharing in the experience of the poem which depends upon a combined response to its form and content.

The sense of a poem should be established first, a paraphrase of what it says on the surface level, and then a careful examination of the techniques and devices that have been used to intensify the subject matter and suggest the theme.

'Meeting at Night' by Robert Browning (1812–1889) gives us a fairly short, straightforward poem which serves well as subject for an introductory analysis.

> The grey sea and the long black land;
> And the yellow half–moon large and low;
> And the startled little waves that leap
> In fiery ringlets from their sleep,
> As I gain the cove with pushing prow,
> And quench its speed i' the slushy sand.
>
> Then a mile of warm sea–scented beach;
> Three fields to cross till a farm appears;
> A tap at the pane, the quick sharp scratch
> And blue spurt of a lighted match,
> And a voice less loud, through its joys and fears,
> Than the two hearts beating each to each!

> (Browning, 1, p. 259)

On the surface level the poem is nothing more than a description of someone travelling through the night by boat and then on foot to a prearranged meeting with a lover. Although there is nothing concrete in the text on which to base the idea, it is probably a young man going to see his sweetheart. The poet was a Victorian Englishman and in those bad old days men were conventionally the pursuers and women the pursued. The poem is about love, or more specifically it is about the attitudes and feelings we have when we are in love. The poet, however, does not attempt to tell us anything about love, or even about the lovers; he merely presents us with a situation, realistic images of the scene, rhythm and sound patterns which combine to express those unspoken attitudes and feelings.

The first stanza is made up of a series of natural images (sea, land, moon, waves, cove, boat, sand) which at first seem disconnected, but which in fact suggest the stages of the journey. The initial confusion arises because the main verb of the sentence is missing. On reading through the stanza, the relations between the images become clear. At the end we realise that the subject and predicate of the sentence are understood: I see. The lack of a verb (action) is further emphasised by the perfect, and therefore static, balancing of the phrasing in the first two lines. There is the sea *and* the land; *and* the moon [which is] large *and* low. The heavy pre–modification of the three major images helps to underline the parallelism and also to emphasise them, while the concentration of long, open vowels and repetition of the liquid /l/ sound characterises the sweep of the scene and quiet softness of the night.

The dupal rhythm is deliberate and regular but the pattern is enlivened in line three by the short, sharp movement of the phrase 'startled little waves'. The line itself is shorter than the previous two, having only four stresses rather than five, and contains words of action and motion as opposed to static description. In addition to the phonetic intensive sounds of 'startled' and 'little', the line is run–on with a verb (action word) in a position of extra stress. The word 'leap' continues the consonant patterning of /l/ and one notices that, instead of rhyming, the first three lines end in words that alliterate. Lines three and four do rhyme and the rhyming sound, being a plosive, is very strong. Line four continues to suggest the presence and the very movement of the action which began in the line above, and the couplet rhyme emphasises the centrality of those lines and their importance in the stanza.

The last two lines continue to develop the feeling of mounting action. The prow of the boat pushes the water as it enters the cove and also pushes the sand as it lands on the beach. The rhythm returns to the pattern of lines one and two but a new note of mounting tension is struck by the harsher sounds which are also present. The subtle alliteration of closely related sounds in 'gain', 'cove' and 'quench', for example, contrasts with the softness of

/l/, while the very sound of the water moving against the boat and the landing of the boat upon the sand is heard in the words 'pushing', 'quench', 'speed', 'slushy' and 'sand'.

As the stanza progresses, static images and rhythmic elements give way to devices that suggest movement and sound, and the whole is delivered in a completely objective, unemotional way. The greatest indication of movement is found in the central couplet, and the rhyme scheme (a, b, c, c, b, a) echoes the movement of both rhythm and feeling through that climax to a heightened resolution in the man's arrival on shore. The stanza progresses from the vision of a placid seascape on a soft moon–lit night through the agitation of the water reflecting the light to the noises of the landing, and the description parallels the man's feelings of anticipation, impatience and excitement as he journeys to meet his sweetheart. The reader shares the man's experience, responding sensually to every sight and sound, but more especially to the inner feelings which are natural to the situation and strongly characterised by the musical elements of the poem.

Figures of speech are not given much prominence in the first stanza; only one example occurs, and that was probably selected because of its sound value rather than for any other purpose. The second stanza makes more use of figurative language and places it in a position of some structural importance. The sound of heartbeats cannot be louder than the whisperings of the lovers. In other respects the techniques and devices of the second stanza are fairly similar to those of the first and the original pattern is repeated, but with enough variation to avoid monotony. Rather than work out the detailed analysis, it is better to leave the reader to his or her own appreciation, not only of this poem but also of others. Subject matter and technical complexity vary greatly in poetry, but all poems communicate their pleasures and meaning in much the same way.

It may be, for example, that another lyric will concentrate more heavily on figurative language and a highly charged emotional vocabulary. Instead of a realistic description another poem may use a pattern of interrelated images and ideas to express its theme. No matter what techniques and devices are included, the method of analysis is the same. First make sure of the surface level meaning, identify the devices and evaluate their effects on the surface meaning, preferably in the order of their appearance. A consistent pattern of implications, attitudes and values will soon emerge and suggest the poem's theme.

References

An asterisk by an author's name indicates that this is an alternative source for works cited in anthologies.

Chinua Achebe, 'Girls at War' in *Girls at War and Other Stories* (London: Heinemann, 1971).

A. Adedeji (ed.), *Nigerian Administration and Its Political Setting* (London: Hutchinson, 1968).

John Allison, *Around the U.S.A in Song* (Morristown: Burdett, 1965).

Anonymous, 'I sat next the Duchess at tea' in Laurence Perrine, *Sound and Sense, An Introduction to Poetry* (New York: Harcourt Brace Jovanovich, Inc., 1956).

Anonymous, 'No egg on Friday Alph will eat' in Laurence Perrine, *Sound and Sense, An Introduction to Poetry* (New York: Harcourt Brace Jovanovich, Inc., 1956).

James Baldwin, *Go Tell It on the Mountain* (London: Corgi, 1976).

Sylvan Barnet *et al.* (ed.), *An Introduction to Literature* (Boston: Little Brown, 1961).

Samuel Beckett, *Watt* (London: Calder, 1963).

Lebert Bethune, 'Harlem Freeze Frame' in LeRoi Jones and Larry Neal (eds.), *Black Fire, An Anthology of Afro–American Writing* (New York: Morrow, 1968).

Bhabani Bhattacharya, *So Many Hungers!* (Bombay: Jaico, 1964).

*William Blake, 'The Chimney Sweeper' in *The Complete Writings of William Blake,* ed. Geoffrey Keynes (London: Oxford University Press, 1966).

Bertolt Brecht, *Parables for the Theatre,* trans. E. Bentley (Harmondsworth: Penguin, 1966).

Robert Browning, 'Meeting at Night' in *The Poetical Works of Robert Browning,* ed. Augustine Birrell (London: Smith, Elder, 1905).

——, 'My Star' in *Poetical Works.*

*Robert Burns, 'A red, red Rose' in *The Poems and Songs of Robert Burns,* ed. James Kinsley (Oxford: Clarendon, 1968).

George Gordon Lord Byron, 'The Destruction of Sennacherib' in *Byron's Poems,* ed. V. de Sola Pinta (London: Dent, 1963).

*——, 'The Isles of Greece, the Isles of Greece' in *Byron's Poems.*

Stokely Carmichael, 'Towards Black Liberation' in LeRoi Jones and Larry Neal (eds.), *Black Fire, An Anthology of Afro–American Writing* (New York: Morrow, 1968).

John Pepper Clark, 'Las Palmas' in *A Reed in the Tide* (London: Longman, 1965).

Sarah N. Cleghorn, 'The Golf Links' in Sylvan Barnet *et al.* (ed.), *An Introduction to Literature* (Boston: Little, Brown, 1961).

Samuel Taylor Coleridge, 'Kubla Khan' in *The Poetical Works of Samuel Taylor Coleridge,* ed. James Dykes Campbell (London: Macmillan, 1905).

Joseph Conrad, 'The Lagoon' in *Almayer's Folly and Tales of Unrest, The Collected Edition of the Works of Joseph Conrad* (London: Dent, 1950).

——, *Typhoon* in *The Nigger of the 'Narcissus', Typhoon . . . , Collected Edition.*

James Fenimore Cooper, *The Prairie* (New York: New American Library, 1964).

John Donne, 'Song' in *The Songs and Sonnets of John Donne,* ed. Theodore Redpath (London: Methuen, 1956).

John Dryden, 'Absalom and Achitophel' in *The Poems and Fables of John Dryden* (London: Oxford University Press, 1961).

Thomas Sterns Eliot, *Notes towards the Definition of Culture* (London: Faber & Faber, 1948).

——, 'The Love Song of J. Alfred Prufrock' in *The Complete Poems and Plays. 1909–1950* (New York: Harcourt Brace Jovanovich, Inc., 1962).

William Empson, 'Missing Dates' in *Complete Poems* (London: Chatto & Windus, 1955).

Euripides, *The Bacchae,* trans. G. Murray (London: Allen & Unwin, 1904).

William Faulkner, *As I Lay Dying* (Harmondsworth: Penguin, 1963).

E. M. Forster, *A Passage to India* (Harmondsworth: Penguin, 1936).

H. W. Fowler, *A Dictionary of Modern English Usage* (Oxford: Clarendon, 1965).

Robert Frost, 'The Road Not Taken' in *Complete Poems of Robert Frost* (New York: Holt, Rinehart & Winston, 1949).

——, 'To Earthward' in *Complete Poems.*

William Godwin, *The Adventures of Caleb Williams; or, Things As They Are* (New York: Holt, Rinehart & Winston, 1960).

Robert Graves, 'The Twin of Sleep' in *Collected Poems 1975* (London: Cassell, 1975).

*Thomas Gray, 'Elegy Written in a Country Churchyard' in *The Complete Poems of Thomas Gray,* ed. H. W. Stars and J. B. Hendrickson (Oxford: Clarendon, 1966).

Thomas Hardy, 'At the Draper's in *The Collected Poems of Thomas Hardy* (London: Macmillan, 1962).

Albert E. Haynes, 'Eclipse' in LeRoi Jones and Larry Neal (eds.), *Black Fire, An Anthology of Afro–American Writing* (New York: Morrow 1968).

John Hayward (ed.), *The Penguin Book of English Verse* (Harmondsworth: Penguin, 1956).

Ernest Hemingway, *For Whom The Bell Tolls* (Harmondsworth: Penguin, 1955).

*George Herbert, 'Peace' in *The Works of George Herbert,* ed. F. E. Hutchinson (Oxford: Clarendon, 1953).

Calvan C. Hernton, 'Dynamite Growing out of Their Sculls' in LeRoi Jones and Larry Neal (eds.), *Black Fire, An Anthology of Afro–American Writing* (New York: Morrow, 1968).

Gerard Manley Hopkins, 'The Windhover' in *The Poems of Gerard Manley Hopkins* (London: Oxford University Press, 1967).

Ted Hughes, *Selected Poems 1957–1967* (London: Faber & Faber, 1972).

*John Keats, 'To Autumn' in *The Poetical Works of John Keats,* ed. H. W. Garrod (Oxford: Clarendon, 1958).

Frank Kermode *et al.* (ed.), *The Oxford Anthology of English Literature,* 2 vols. (New York: Oxford University Press, 1973).

Aquah Laluah, 'The Serving Girl' in Langston Hughes (ed.), *An African Treasury* (New York: Pyramid, 1960).

George Lamming, *In the Castle of My Skin* (New York: Macmillan, 1970).

Henry Wadsworth Longfellow, 'Paul Revere's Ride' in *The Complete Poetical Works of Longfellow* (Boston: Houghton Mifflin, 1922).

Amy Lowell, 'Patterns' in *Men, Women and Ghosts* (New York: Macmillan, 1917).

*Christopher Marlowe, 'The Passionate Shepherd to His Love' in *Poems,* ed. L. C. Martin, *The Works and Life of Christopher Marlowe* (London: Methuen, 1931).

*Andrew Marvell, 'To His Coy Mistress' in *The Poems and Letters of Andrew Marvell,* ed. H. M. Margoliouth (Oxford: Clarendon, 1952).

John Stuart Mill, *Autobiography,* ed. Harold J. Laski (London: Oxford University Press, 1963).

Arthur Miller, *Death of a Salesman* (New York: Viking, 1952).

George Moore, *Esther Waters* (London: Heinemann, 1952).

Yambo Ouologuem, *Bound to Violence,* trans. R. Manheim (London: Heinemann, 1971).

Okot p'Bitek, *Song of Lawino* (Nairobi: East African, 1966).

Laurence Perrine, *Sound and Sense, An Introduction to Poetry* (New York: Harcourt Brace Jovanovich, Inc., 1956).

Alexander Pope, 'Epitaph. Intended for Sir Isaac Newton' in *Minor Poems, The Poems of Alexander Pope,* ed. Norman Ault (London: Methuen, 1954).

*———, *An Essay on Man* in *The Poems of Alexander Pope,* ed. Maynard Mack (London: Methuen, 1950).

Ezra Pound, 'The Garden' in *Personae, The Collected Shorter Poems of Ezra Pound* (New York: New Directions, 1926).

———, 'Hugh Selwyn Mauberley' in *Personae.*

*Sir Walter Scott, *The Poetical Works of Sir Walter Scott,* ed. Francis Turner Palgrave (London: Macmillan, 1906).

William Shakespeare, *Hamlet* in *The Complete Works* (London: Collins, 1951).

——, *Julius Caesar* in *Complete Works.*

——, 'Sonnet 73' in *Complete Works.*

*——, *The Tempest* in *Complete Works.*

Percy Bysshe Shelley, 'Ozymandias' in *The Complete Works of Percy Bysshe Shelley,* ed. Roger Ingpen and Walter E. Peck (London: Bern, 1965).

Wole Soyinka, *The Interpreters* (London: Deutsch, 1965).

Richard Steele, *The Spectator,* ed. Donald F. Bond (Oxford: Clarendon, 1965).

John Millington Synge, *The Plays and Poems of J. M. Synge* (London: Methuen, 1963).

Alfred Lord Tennyson, 'The Lotos Eaters' in *The Poems of Tennyson,* ed. Christopher Ricks (London: Longmans, 1969).

——, 'Ulysses' in *Poems.*

Dylan Thomas, *Dylan Thomas, The Poems* (London: Dent, 1974).

John Updike, 'Flight' in *Pigeon Feathers and Other Stories* (New York: Fawcett, 1963).

Derek Walcott, *Dream on Monkey Mountain and Other Plays* (New York: Farrar, Straus & Giroux, 1970).

Virginia Woolf, *Mrs. Dalloway* (Harmondsworth: Penguin, 1964).

——, *To the Lighthouse* (New York: Harcourt Brace Jovanovich, Inc., 1955).

Malcolm X, *The Autobiography of Malcolm X* (Harmondsworth: Penguin, 1968).

William Butler Yeats, 'Easter 1916' in *The Variorum Edition of the Poems of W. B. Yeats,* ed. Peter Allt and Russell K. Alspach (New York: Macmillan, 1957).

——, 'Leda and the Swan' in *Variorum Edition.*

——, 'Sailing to Byzantium' in *Variorum Edition.*

——, 'September 1913' in *Variorum Edition.*

Index

point of view *contd*
   implicit/explicit, 134–6
   see also narration, narrator
Pope, Alexander, 45, 90, 154, 180,
   185, 196
*Portrait of the Artist as a Young
   Man, A,* 63, 77
Pound, Ezra, 38, 154, 157, 198–9
Prairie, The, 85
Prism, Miss, 127–8
problem play, *see under* drama
production, theatrical, *see*
   performance, stage
Prometheus Unbound, 105
pronouns, relative, 83
properties, *see under* stage
proscenium stage, *see under* stage
prose, 40, 45, 46, 48, 99, 141–2,
   155, 156, 184
   poetic, 137, 141–2
Protestantism, 26, 28

Raju, 52
Ramayana, 43
Rape of the Lock, The, 90, 154
realism
   'fourth wall', 131–2
   stylistic technique, a, 32–3, 34
   world-view, 62
   see also reality
reality
   distortion of, 8–9, 10, 46, 50,
     62, 69, 103–4, 105, 110, 118,
     122–5, 126, 127, 128, 129,
     130, 131–42, *see also*
     stylisation
   illusion of, 9, 10, 11, 46, 62, 69,
     103–4, 105–6, 117, 122–5,
     127, 128, 129, 130, 131–42
   reflected in literature, 1–9,
     12–13, 14, 42, 44, 45, 46,
     47–8, 50, 51, 56–7, 59, 62–3,
     67, 86–7, 100, 101, 103, 105,
     108, 109, 112, 122, 151, 153,
     157–8, 163–4
   see also realism
Received Pronunciation, *see under*
   English (standard)

refrain, 158
Regan, 118
Reginald, 88
register (language), 8, 86–7, 88,
   89, 92, 136–42, 137, 165
   see also style
Remus, Uncle, 42
Renaissance literature, *see
   under* literature, English
Restoration literature, 21, 25–8,
   69, 105, 117, 154, 156
   see also literature, English
   (Neo-Classical)
Revere, Paul, 200
Revolution, Industrial, 32, 34
rhetorical devices, 8, 83, 89, 91,
   95–9, 100, 163, 165, 172,
   191, 192, 211, 214
   co-ordination, 95, 96–7
   inversion, 95, 96, 194
   parallelism, 95, 97–9, 213
   series, extended, 95–6
   subordination, 95, 96–7
   see also style
rhyme, 99, 152
   approximate, 209
   couplet, 162–3, 196, 210–11
   end-stopped, 209
   eye, 209
   feminine, 209
   interlocking, 158, 161, 210–11,
     213–14
   internal, 209
   masculine, 209
   perfect, 209
   scheme, 161, 162, 210–11, 214
   see also style
rhythm, 90, 99, 100, 120, 141,
   136–42, 151, 152, 158, 163,
   164, 187–204, 205, 207, 210,
   213–14
   intonation, 99, 136–42, 151,
     187–204
   prose, 190, 197–8
   see also line/lineation, metre,
     style
Richardson, Samuel, 47
Riders to the Sea, 108, 138, 139

West Indian (dialect), 137
West Indies, *see* Caribbean
Whitbread, Hugh, 36
Wilde, Oscar, 127–8
Wilder, Thornton, 135
Winter's Tale, The, 111
Women's literature, *see under*
    literatures, other
Woolf, Virginia, 35–6, 63, 198
word choice, *see* vocabulary
Wordsworth, William, 29
World War
    First, 47, 157
    Second, 113
Wuthering Heights, 64, 78

Wycherley, William, 69, 115

X, Malcolm, 88
Xanadu, 195

Yama, 31
Yeats, William Butler, 142, 161,
    175, 177–8, 184, 185
Yoruba, 109, 127

Zeus, 161

NATIONAL UNIVERSITY
LIBRARY SACRAMENTO